STUDIES IN NAVAL HISTORY

General Editor
N. A. M. RODGER

THE ROYAL NAVY IN
AMERICAN WATERS
1775-1783

This book is dedicated to my cousin,
Lt Michael M. Joslin, USNR
lost at sea, 31 January 1969

THE ROYAL NAVY IN AMERICAN WATERS 1775–1783

David Syrett

Scolar Press

© David Syrett 1989

All rights reserved. No part of this publication may be reproduced, stored in a retrieval system, or transmitted in any form or by any means, electronic, mechanical, photocopying, recording, or otherwise without the prior permission of Gower Publishing Company Limited.

Published by
Scolar Press
Gower Publishing Company Limited
Gower House
Croft Road
Aldershot
Hants GU11 3HR
England

Gower Publishing Company
Old Post Road
Brookfield
Vermont 05036
USA

British Library Cataloguing in Publication Data

Syrett, David
  The Royal Navy in American waters 1775-1783
  1. War of American Independence. Role of
  Great Britain. Royal Navy
  I. Title
  973.3'5

Library of Congress Cataloging-in-Publication Data

Syrett, David.
    The Royal Navy in American waters, 1775-1783/David Syrett.
      p. cm.
    Bibliography: p.
    Includes index.
      1. United States—History—Revolution, 1775-1783—Naval operations, British. 2. Great Britain. Royal Navy—History-Revolution, 1775-1783. I. Title.
    E271.S96 1989
    973.3'5—dc19

ISBN 0 85967 806 7

CONTENTS

Preface	vi
Acknowledgements	vii
Standard abbreviations used in the notes	viii
1 American coastal waters, 1775–76	1
2 One decisive campaign, 1776	28
3 The failure of the British effort in America, 1777	61
4 On the defensive in America, 1778	92
5 American coastal waters: Towards Yorktown, 1779–80	117
6 Yorktown and beyond, 1781–83	177
Bibliography	227
Index	237

PREFACE

For many years, I have been interested in the Royal Navy's role in the American Revolutionary War. One of the questions which has intrigued me has been why British naval power could not crush the rebellion in America by cutting off the flow of arms and military supplies from Europe to the American rebels. During the course of studying the operations of the Royal Navy in American waters, I discovered that the problems confronting British naval power were much more complex than just blockading the American coast.

In studying the Royal Navy and the American Revolutionary War, one is confronted with a complex series of questions of strategy and policy. For example, how does one use warships to combat American concepts of their political rights? How does one deal with powerful neutrals on the high seas who are aiding the American rebels? How many warships should Britain send to America when confronted with powerful enemies in Europe, the West Indies and the Indian Ocean? What are the limits of British naval power? How does one deploy naval power to confront a continent in rebellion? Or what are the relationships, at any given time, between land and naval operations in America?

These questions and many others confronted British naval commanders during the American Revolutionary War, from the First Lord of the Admiralty down to the most junior master and commander, like an endless line of candles in a huge dark cavern. This book is a study of how the Royal Navy met the problems caused by the American revolt against British authority during the years 1775-83.

ACKNOWLEDGEMENTS

This book would never have been written without the assistance of many individuals and institutions in America, Canada and Britain. I want to thank the staffs of the Public Record Office; the National Maritime Museum; the William L. Clements Library of the University of Michigan; the British Library; the Library of Queens College, CUNY; and the University of London's Institute of Historical Research.

This project would never have come to pass without the support of my late wife, Betsy Blanchard Syrett, and my deceased parents, Professor H.C. Syrett and Dr P.M. Syrett.

Numerous individuals have helped me over the years in various ways to make this book possible. Among them are P.G.W. Annis, Royal Artillery Institute, Woolwich; Dr John Dann, Director of the William L. Clements Library; Dr Richard H. Kohn, Chief of US Air Force History; Dr Barbara Malament; Dr C.R. Middleton; David Lyons; Dr Roger Knight and A.W.H. Pearsall of the National Maritime Museum; Professor I.R. Christie; Dr W.A.B. Douglas, Director of the Directorate of History of the Canadian National Defence Headquarters; Miss Alice M. McCart; Mrs Dorothy Sondano, Mrs Ida Pizzo and Mrs Annita Giresi of Queens College, CUNY; Mrs Mary Kiffer; and Dr N.A.M. Rodger of the Public Record Office; my son Matthew D. Syrett who drew most of the maps. No doubt, I have omitted a number of names which should have been listed here. The only thing I can say is that I apologize for this oversight.

I am wholly responsible for any sins of omission or commission in this study.

D.S.
New York
December 1988.

STANDARD ABBREVIATIONS USED IN THE NOTES

ADM	Admiralty
ADM/L	Ships' logs
BL	British Library
CL	William L. Clements Library, University of Michigan
CO	Colonial Office (mostly military orders and dispatches)
G	Sir John W. Fortescue (ed.), *The Correspondence of King George the Third from 1760 to December 1783* (London, 1927–8)
HMC	Historical Manuscripts Commission
HOO	Hood Papers
MID	Middleton Papers
NDAR	*Naval Documents of the American Revolution* (Washington, DC, 1964–)
NMM	National Maritime Museum
NRS	Navy Record Society
NYHSC	New York Historical Society Collections
PRO	Public Record Office
SAN/T	Sandwich Papers
SP	State Papers
WO	War Office
PRO 30/20	Rodney Papers

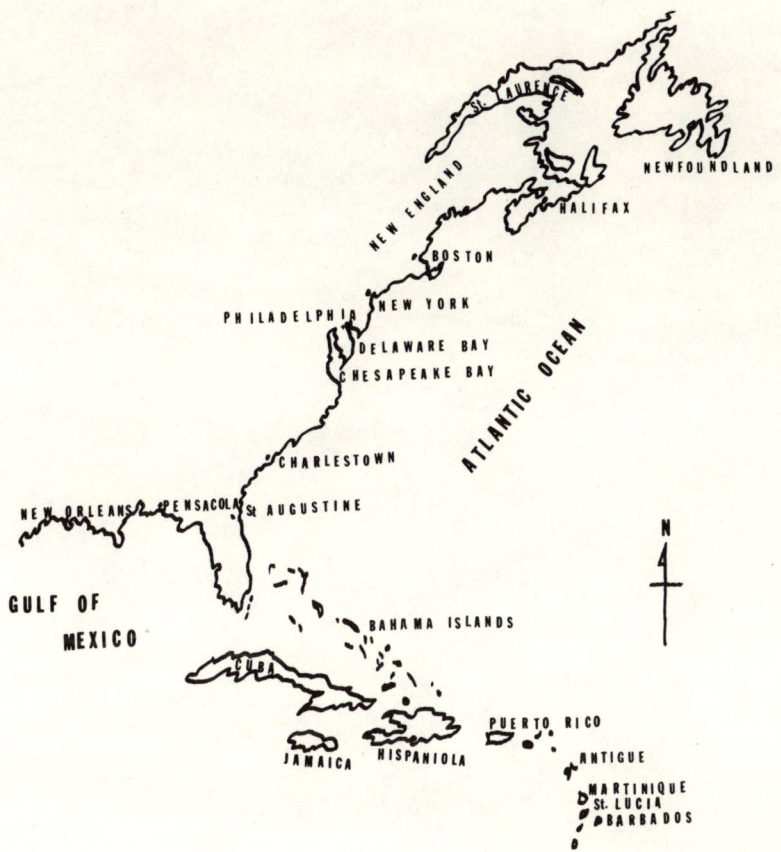

Map 1
East Coast of North America and the West Indies

1
AMERICAN COASTAL WATERS, 1775-76

The last vestiges of the British authority in America collapsed immediately after the clash between British troops and Massachusetts militia on 19 April 1775 at Lexington and Concord. Within hours of the beginning of hostilities the militia of Massachusetts laid seige to King George III's troops at Boston, and elsewhere in America governors and other royal officials were forced to seek refuge on board warships. By midsummer of 1775 the ships of the Royal Navy and the enclave at Boston were all that remained of the British empire in America.

The Royal Navy in America was completely unprepared for, and overwhelmed by, the outbreak of revolutionary war.[1] The squadron in North America was commanded by Vice-Admiral Samuel Graves, a man who although not very inspiring, has been much maligned. The main duty of his command was enforcing the Acts of Trade and Navigation, and on 16 June 1775 the squadron consisted of 30 warships, scattered along the entire length of the coast of America from Nova Scotia to Florida.[2] But with the advent of hostilities, Graves, whose flag flew from HMS *Preston* in Boston Harbor, suddenly found himself overtaken by events. The army was pinned down in Boston, and he commanded the only force capable of salvaging royal authority in America. Yet his weak and scattered squadron could not even attempt to contain or combat the revol-

---

[1] For an account of the activities of the Royal Navy in America before the beginning of hostilities see Neil R. Stout, *The Royal Navy in America, 1760-1775* (Annapolis, Md, 1973).

[2] PRO, ADM 1/485, Disposition of His Majesty's Ships and Vessels in North America, 16 June 1775. For an account of the problems faced by Admiral Graves see Donald A. Yerxa, 'Vice-Admiral Graves and the North American squadron, 1774-1776', *Mariner's Mirror* (November 1976) vol. 62, pp. 371-84.

utionary movement, so he was forced instead to use his ships to protect what little remained of the British position while awaiting the arrival of reinforcements.

Graves deployed about half of the ships under his command to defend Nova Scotia, Boston and the army's lines of communication; the remainder of the squadron was stationed either singly or in small flotillas at various American ports, such as New York, to show the flag and attempt to prop up what was left of royal authority. However, poor communications, coupled with the policy of stationing ships along the entire length of the American coast, resulted in Graves's not being able to command effectively a large proportion of his squadron. Thus, during the first year of the war, the British naval effort in America was a series of unrelated and often contradictory actions, ranging in intensity from concluding a local truce to destroying an entire city. Without instructions, hampered by poor communications and lacking co-ordination, Graves's small and ill-constituted squadron confronted a continent in rebellion.

To the British, Boston was the cradle of the rebellion, and it was here that the biggest strain was placed on the resources of the Royal Navy during the first year of the war. Believing that the town was the centre of resistance to royal authority in America, and hoping that if the inhabitants of Boston were intimidated by the presence of the military the rest of America would submit[3] the British had originally sent army and navy units to Boston after the Boston Tea Party. But with the beginning of fighting in America, the army at Boston became a strategic liability to the British. The town could not be evacuated owing to a shortage of transports[4] nor could it be defended against a determined attack, for it was dominated by heights that the British did not have the manpower to occupy. Moreover, Boston was thought to be unfit as a base for an offensive land campaign because it was besieged by the army of hostile Americans in extremely strong natural defensive positions.[5] Boston, though militarily worthless, severely strained the resources of the Royal Navy in American waters.

One of the most immediate and pressing problems confronting the British at Boston was the lack of supplies. Before the war, the British army in America obtained locally its provisions, fuel and forage. But

---

[3] See Bernard Donoughue, *British Politics and the American Revolution: The Path to War, 1773-75* (London, 1964).
[4] PRO, CO 5/235, ff. 177, 199.
[5] Ibid., ff. 171-2; Clarence Edwin Carter (ed.), *The Correspondence of General Thomas Gage* (New Haven, Conn., 1933), Vol. 11, pp. 418-19, 687.

when the fighting began, the Americans cut off the flow of supplies to the army at Boston, and the British were forced to 'have recourse to every means and artifice to procure provisions, money, forrage, and fuel'.[6] A request that provisions be sent from England was dispatched to London.[7] Graves wrote to Francis Legge and General Guy Carleton, the governors of Nova Scotia and Quebec respectively, requesting provisions.[8] The restrictions of the Boston Port Act were relaxed and monetary inducements were, to no avail, offered to Americans to ship provisions to Boston.[9] And on 14 May 1775, Graves ordered that vessels carrying supplies required by the army be confiscated on the high seas and sent into Boston for the use of the king's forces.[10] Yet none of these measures afforded immediate relief, so it was found necessary to dispatch expeditions in search of supplies for the garrison of Boston.

Throughout the summer and autumn of 1775 warships, transports and troops were sent to the coasts of Maine and the Bay of Fundy to procure firewood and forage;[11] on one of these expeditions to the coast of Maine the Royal Navy sustained its first casualty of the American War when, on 12 June, the Americans at Machias captured the tender *Margaretta*.[12] Other warships and transports were sent to Quebec and Nova Scotia for supplies.[13] The coasts of New England and Long Island in New York were scoured in search of livestock.[14] Arrangements were made to work the coal mines at Spanish River in Cape Breton.[15] Warships and transports sailed to Georgia for rice;[16] others went to the West Indies for provisions and rum.[17] Despite these efforts, the British garrison continued to be short of provisions, and as late as 10 March 1776 an army officer exclaimed 'provisions is our want.'[18]

[6] PRO, ADM 1/485, ff. 239, 334; CO 5/92, ff. 144, 166–7.
[7] BL, Add. MSS. 38343, f. 1.
[8] NDAR, vol. I, pp. 213, 231.
[9] Ibid., pp. 230, 502–3, 524.
[10] Ibid., p. 329.
[11] E.g. PRO, ADM 1/485, f. 365; CO 5/95, f. 296; BL, Add. MSS. 21680, f. 42; NDAR, vol. II, pp. 161, 194, 213, 225, 334, 967, and vol. III, p. 237; Carter, *op. cit.*, Vol. II, pp. 417, 420.
[12] For an account of this action see Gardener W. Allen, *A Naval History of the American Revolution* (New York, 1962 reprint), Vol I, pp. 7–11.
[13] E.g. PRO, ADM 1/485, f. 329; CO 5/92, ff. 145, 184.
[14] E.g. Carter, *op. cit.*, Vol. II, pp. 410, 413; NDAR, vol. III, p. 1191; NYHSC, *Kemble Papers*, vol. I, p. 55.
[15] PRO, CO 5/92, ff. 68, 184; Carter, *op cit.*, Vol. II, p. 417.
[16] See below, p. 20.
[17] PRO, CO 5/93, ff. 23–4; NDAR, vol. III, pp. 224, 557.
[18] BL, Add. MSS. 21680, f. 93.

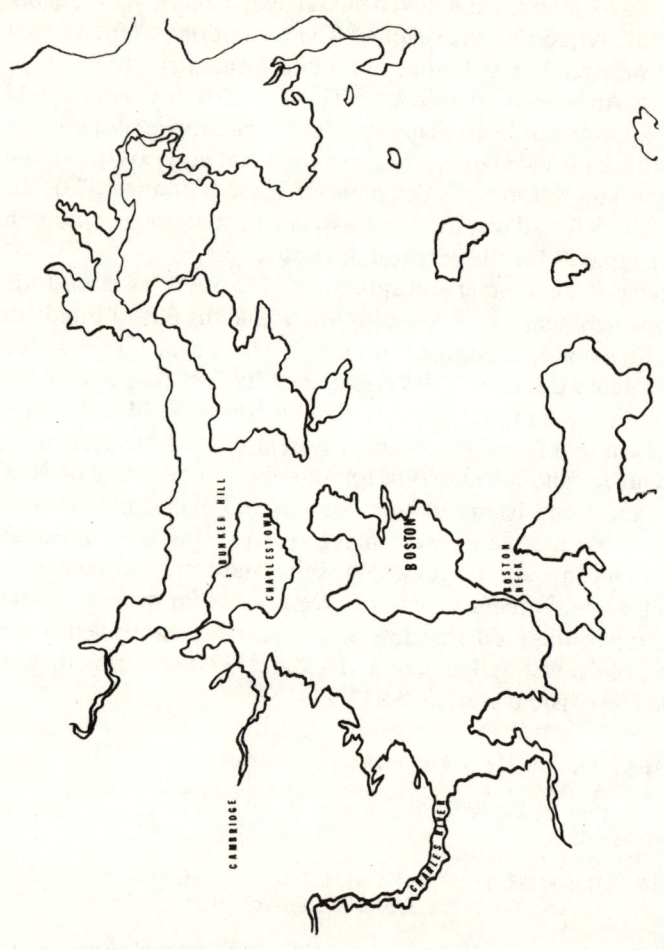

Map 2
Boston Harbor, 1775

In addition to supplying Boston, men and ships of the Royal Navy were required to defend the town and harbour as well. Located on a peninsula at the Western end of Massachusetts Bay, Boston was extremely vulnerable to waterborne attack. In order to protect the town from such an attack, Graves stationed warships and floating batteries on both sides of Boston, ordered that ships' boats patrol the harbour and placed HMS *Somerset* at Charlestown Ferry with orders to cannonade any American troops that attempted to occupy Charlestown. In addition, the movement of boats were forbidden at night.[19] However, soon learning that the Americans had a number of whaleboats and other small craft hidden around the shores of Boston Bay, the British greatly feared that the enemy would attempt to seize or destroy one of the warships guarding Boston while part of her crew was away manning guard-boats and floating batteries.[20] These fears were not without justification, for the British found that they could not prevent the enemy from carrying out numerous attacks on islands and boats in Boston Harbor. The most spectacular of these raids occurred on 31 July 1775, when the Americans destroyed Boston Lighthouse and captured the 40 marines guarding it.[21]

Graves believed that even if he deployed his entire squadron in Boston Bay, it still would be impossible to prevent such raids by the Americans, for, according to him, 'these excursions were always conducted with such secrecy and dispatch that the Flames were generally the first Notice of their Intentions'.[22] As it was, he deployed ten or more warships, or a third of the squadron, to assist in the local defence of Boston.[23] While placing so many ships in one area severely limited the Royal Navy, Graves thought it an absolute necessity, knowing the Americans had, in his words, 'A numerous and well appointed Army . . . which without the protection of the King's Ships can utterly destroy this town and the troops pent up in it'.[24]

Providing protection to vessels carrying supplies to the army was yet another task confronting the Royal Navy during the British occupation of Boston. Supply ships proceeding to Boston encoun-

[19] NDAR, vol. I, pp. 202-3.
[20] Ibid., pp. 961-2, 1059-60.
[21] HMC, *Hastings MSS*. vol. III, p. 158.
[22] NDAR, vol. I, p. 869.
[23] E.g. PRO, ADM 1/485, Disposition of His Majesty's Ships and Vessels in North America, 16 June 1775; NDAR, vol. I, pp. 47, 1350-1, vol. II, pp. 1250-1, and vol. III, p. 1007.
[24] NDAR, vol. I, p. 374.

tered difficulties neither foreseen nor understood by the British at the beginning of the war. There was a shortage of pilots, and the New England coast, especially during the winter months, is subjected to fogs and gales.[25] Moreover, ships entering Boston had to pass the American-held ports of Lynn, Marblehead, Salem, Beverly and Gloucester before reaching the comparative safety of Nantasket Roads. Compounding these difficulties was the American decision to send a number of armed schooners to sea for the purpose of attacking ships carrying supplies to the army at Boston.[26] As early as May 1775, intelligence reached the British that the Americans were fitting out armed vessels to attack British supply vessels, and Graves ordered HMS *St Lawrence* and HMS *Hope* to the coast of Maine to search for American armed vessels; other warships were directed to cruise in Massachusetts Bay to intercept supply ships and escort them into Boston.[27] Despite these measures, on 7 September the Americans made a prize of the unarmed British ship *Unity* off Cape Ann, and during the next few weeks three other British ships loaded with provisions blundered into American-held ports and were captured. In November the Americans extended their operations northward, and the armed schooners *Franklin* and *Hancock* captured several fishing boats off Cape Canso and landed seamen at Charlottetown, the capital of the Island of St John (now Prince Edward Island), and captured the acting governor and a member of his council.[28] However, the Americans made their most valuable capture within sight of Boston Harbor. On 28 November the armed schooner *Lee* took, without resistance, the ordinance storeship *Nancy* which was loaded with munitions.[29] The American Commander-in-Chief, General George Washington, looked upon the capture of the *Nancy* as an 'instance of Divine Favour'.[30] The loss of the storeship so enraged the British that there were allegations of treachery and negligence, and one British officer feared that the loss of the *Nancy* would result in the Americans burning 'Boston about our ears this winter'. Even though it was obvious that something had

---

[25] E.g. ibid., p. 177, and vol. III, p. 97.
[26] For an account of American naval operations in Massachusetts Bay during 1775–76 see William Bell Clark, *George Washington's Navy* (Baton Rouge, La, 1960).
[27] NDAR, vol. I, pp. 326, 587–8, 704, 820, 900, 961.
[28] Clark, *op. cit.*, pp. 7–8, 15, 17, 47–57.
[29] Ibid., pp. 60–1; according to an inventory made by the Americans the *Nancy*'s cargo consisted of, among other things, 2,000 muskets, 100,000 flints, 30,000-round shot, 11 mortar beds and a 3,000 lb brass mortar. See John C. Fitzpatrick (ed.), *The Writings of George Washington* (Washington, DC, 1931), Vol. IV, p. 128n.
[30] Fitzpatrick, *op. cit.*, Vol. IV, p. 130.

to be done to protect British storeships from American attack, it took Lord George Germain, the secretary of state responsible for the conduct of the war in America, several years to get all the relevant departments of the British government to take the necessary steps to ensure their safe passage.[31]

From the beginning of the fighting in America, Graves believed the British 'ought to act hostily . . . by burning and laying waste the whole country'.[32] By 29 August the admiral's belief had hardened into the resolve that the only way to prevent American attacks on British supply ships was to undertake a series of attacks against the New England ports in which the American armed vessels were based. However, he did not have under his command the necessary troops for this type of operation. Most of the marines belonging to the ships at Boston were serving ashore with the army, and Lieutenant-General Thomas Gage, the commander-in-chief of the army, would not release the troops needed for an operation of the size envisioned by Graves.[33] Nevertheless, the admiral did succeed in obtaining a small number of marines and some artillerymen. These troops were embarked on the transport *Symmetry* and the sloop *Spitfire*, both of which were armed with howitzers and mortars.[34]

On 8 October, Lieutenant Henry 'Mad' Mowat with HMS *Canceaux*, HMS *Halifax, Symmetry* and *Spitfire* left Boston with orders to destroy and 'chastize' the towns of Cape Ann, Marblehead, Salem, Newburyport, Portsmouth, Ipswich, Saco, Falmouth (now Portland, Maine) and Machias. Mowat sailed first to Cape Ann, but the buildings there were considered too scattered to be a proper subject for naval bombardment and the force proceeded to Falmouth. On the morning of 17 October the British ships anchored before Falmouth, and Mowat informed the inhabitants that the town would be destroyed unless all their munitions and the leading rebels of the region were surrendered by 9.00 a.m. the following day. The Americans failed to comply and at 9.40 a.m. on 18 October Mowat ordered Falmouth destroyed. The four British ships fired round after round of shot, shells and carcasses at the town, and parties of marines were landed to burn those buildings not destroyed by gunfire. When the attack ended at 6 p.m., four vessels were

---

[31] NDAR, vol. III, pp. 276-7; HMC, *Hastings MSS.*, vol. III, p. 161; David Syrett, 'Lord George Germain and the protection of military storeships, 1775-1778', *Mariner's Mirror* (November 1974), vol. 60, pp. 395-405.
[32] NDAR, vol. I, p. 193.
[33] Ibid., pp. 1252-3.
[34] Ibid., pp. 1282-3, and vol. II, 7-8.

British prizes, eleven others had been destroyed and most of the buildings and wharfs of Falmouth were either in ruins or on fire. The next day Mowat sailed from the still-burning Falmouth for Boston, where he arrived on 2 November.[35] The destruction of Falmouth was considered a barbaric act, even among some of the British.[36] Nevertheless, there was a brutal logic behind Graves's proposal to destroy every seaport in northern New England, for if the destruction were on a sufficiently large scale, the American ability to wage war at sea would be crippled in the first months of the contest.

The destruction of Falmouth was not followed by attacks on other New England ports. Lieutenant-General William Howe, who had replaced Gage as the army's commander-in-chief, had intended to use five battalions expected at Boston from Ireland to attack New England seaports;[37] but this reinforcement was sent instead on the Clinton-Parker expedition to the southern colonies. Therefore, on 26 November, Howe requested that Graves station warships in various harbours on the north shore of Massachusetts Bay, such as Marblehead and Cape Ann, to prevent their use by American armed vessels. Graves replied that his ships could not lie in those harbours because of American shore batteries and suggested instead that the general send troops to destroy the seaport towns on the north shore or to occupy the Cape Ann Peninsula.[38] On 12 December, Howe again expressed to Graves his fear that the American armed vessels would cut the army's seaborne communications and, again, the admiral restated his belief that the only way to prevent attacks on British supply ships was either to destroy or to occupy the seaports on the Cape Ann Peninsula, for naval measures alone would not be effective in preventing American attacks on British ships in Massachusetts Bay.[39] Since Howe felt that without reinforcements he could not spare the troops required to carry Graves's plan into effect, he suggested in a dispatch to London that supplies be sent to

---

[35] The British calculated that at Falmouth 11 ships, 139 dwelling and 278 other structures were destroyed and that the total damage amounted to £150,000; all the relative documents on the burning of Falmouth can be found in NDAR, vol. II, pp. 7–8, 324–6, 362, 374, 400, 433, 459, 471–2, 487–9, 500–2, 513–17, 590–2, 858, 877, 932–3, 1155–6. It was thought by some that Mowat picked Falmouth for destruction for reasons of personal revenge; cf. Robert Greenhalgh Albion, *Forests and Seapower: The Timber Problem of the Royal Navy* (Cambridge, Mass., 1926), pp. 279–80.
[36] E.g. NDA, vol. III, p. 468; CL, Germain Papers, Military Dispatches, pp. 315–16.
[37] PRO, CO 5/235, p. 10.
[38] NDAR, vol. II, pp. 1143–4.
[39] Ibid., vol. III, pp. 65, 82.

Boston, either in heavily manned and armed storeships or in warships whose guns had been removed from their lower decks.[40]

Having failed to obtain the troops necessary to seize or destroy the ports on the north shore, Graves was forced to fall back on what he considered to be weak, ineffectual measures for dealing with the problem of American attacks on ships entering Boston. The ships of the Royal Navy in Massachusetts Bay were ordered to cruise off Cape Ann, Salem Marblehead and Cape Cod, where Graves thought them best situated to blockade American naval bases and, at the same time, to intercept British supply ships as they approached Boston. Yet Graves knew, as he informed Howe, that 'it was impossible for Ships to keep their Stations or prevent the Rebels from making further captures'.[41] Nevertheless, on Graves's orders, throughout the winter of 1775–76 British warships patrolled the approaches to Boston. One of the few successes of this effort occurred on 5 December, when HMS *Fowey* captured off Cape Ann the American armed schooner *Washington*.[42] For the most part, however, patrolling Massachusetts Bay was a frustrating and dangerous task. Buffeted by winter gales, undermanned and in need of repairs, the ships were at sea almost continually, entering Nantasket Roads only for provisions and repairs.[43]

For the British at Boston, the winter of 1775–76 was a time of mounting frustration, humiliation and bitterness: the king's soldiers were hamstrung by what they considered to be a mob of country bumpkins; the Royal Navy appeared unable to protect British supply ships from American attack, the forces there were on short rations, surrounded by a sullen and hostile population, and cooped up in what was considered to be the centre of American rebellion and Puritanism. As the weather grew colder and wetter, and the American attacks on British ships became bolder, a feeling of blind rage and isolation gripped the British at Boston. Out of thirty-five ships dispatched from England with provisions for the garrison of Boston, only eight arrived at that port. The remainder were either captured or forced by bad weather to the West Indies.[44] The apparent lack of support from the authorities in London owing to the failure of provision ships to reach America gave rise to feelings of betrayal and

---

[40] Ibid., p. 82.
[41] *Loc. cit.*
[42] NRS, *Sandwich Papers*, vol. I, p. 96; D. Bonner Smith, 'The capture of the *Washington*', *Mariner's Mirror* (October 1934), vol. 20, pp. 420–5.
[43] E.g. NDAR, vol. II, pp. 475, 570, 1065–6, 1143, 1202–3, 1230, 1266, and vol. III, pp. 65, 276, 633, 835, 877–8, 1006.
[44] BL, Add. MSS. 38343, f. 2.

bitterness. One Scots officer exclaimed in a letter to his father, 'We are almost buried here'.[45] Another officer lamented, 'We are now almost as much blocked up by the sea as we have been for these eight months by land'.[46]

The humiliations and frustrations suffered by the king's forces at Boston caused the more thoughtful among the British to revise their attitudes towards their American enemies. Undoubtedly, Major John Pitcairn of the Marines stated a widely held belief among the British before the beginning of hostilities when he wrote, 'I am satisfied that one active campaign, a smart action, and the burning two or three of their towns, will set everything to rights'.[47] But such events as Bunker Hill, the burning of Falmouth and the capture of the *Nancy*, had a great impact on British thinking. An officer of the Royal Navy at Boston spoke for many others when he wrote to a London newspaper at the end of November 1775 that the Americans, 'whatever other vices they may have, *cowardice* is not one of them . . . like military Harlequins they attack us everywhere, God end this unnatural warfare'.[48] However, most of the anger and bitterness of the British at Boston was directed at the navy in general, and its commander, Admiral Graves, in particular. In an endless flood of letters to England, Graves was condemned for, among other things, nepotism, seizing provisions for his personal use, negligence and inactivity of all kinds and being unfair to the army.[49] Feelings in some quarters ran so high that Lord Rawdon thought that Graves 'deserves to be made an example of much more than ever Byng did'.[50] The cascade of complaints from Boston and the government's need to make a political sacrifice to atone for the failure of its policy in America resulted in Graves's being relieved at the beginning of 1776.

Had Graves been an abler commander, there could have been little difference in the effectiveness of the Royal Navy during the first year of the war. There simply were not enough ships for the vast command, and no amount of clever juggling could produce any more. Graves had to deploy what ships he had as best he could. His

---

[45] E. Stuart Wortley (ed.), *A Prime Minister and His Son* (London, 1925), p. 73.
[46] NDAR, vol. III, p. 84.
[47] NRS, *Sandwich Papers*, vol. I, p. 61.
[48] NDAR, vol. II, pp. 1203-4.
[49] E.g. ibid., vol. I, p. 1190, and vol. II, pp. 194, 811, 920, 995; HMC, *Hastings MSS.*, vol. III, pp. 158, 161; G.D. Scull (ed.), *Memoir and Letters of Captain W. Glanville Evelyn of the 4th Regiment ('King's Own') from North America, 1774-1776* (Oxford, 1879), pp. 64, 67-8; NYHSC, *Kemble Papers*, vol. I, p. 51.
[50] HMC, *Hastings MSS.*, vol. III, p. 161.

most taxing commitment was the defence of Boston, but it was only one of many.

Nova Scotia was the northernmost end of Graves's command. Located several hundred miles north-east of Boston across the Gulf of Maine, Nova Scotia was important because it was the only region in North America from which the British could mount a military counterstroke against the rebellion in America. The province's strategic importance was further enhanced by its location on the northern flank of the American coast, and Halifax, its capital, was the seat of the only royal dockyard in North America. Yet the defences of Nova Scotia at the beginning of the war were almost non-existent. There were few troops in the province, and the dockyard was undefended. The fighting in America and the fleeting appearance of American armed vessels off the coast, and the American invasion of Canada, threw into a panic Francis Legge, the Governor of Nova Scotia, and Commodore Marriot Arbuthnot, the commissioner of the royal dockyard at Halifax, for the safety of the province. Both officials bombarded authorities in London and Boston with requests for reinforcements.[51] Immediately after Lexington and Concord, Graves dispatched HMS *Tartar* to Halifax to defend the dockyard.[52] A small number of troops were sent to Nova Scotia from Boston, and at the beginning of December units of the 27th Regiment arrived at Halifax from England.[53] HMS *Merlin* and HMS *Senegal* were ordered to cruise in the Bay of Fundy and to spend the winter in the Nova Scotian ports of Liverpool and Windsor;[54] and on 10 December the third-rate *Somerset* was sent from Boston to reinforce Halifax.[55] By the end of 1775, Graves had committed five warships to Nova Scotian waters.[56] The defence of Nova Scotia was a strategic necessity, but these ships were desperately needed for other services.

During the winter of 1775-76 roughly half the ships of the Royal Navy in North America were either in Boston or Nova Scotia; the remainder were deployed along the American coast from Rhode Island to Florida.[57] These ships had the impossible task of attempting to blockade more than 1,000 miles of hostile coastline.

---

[51] E.g. NDAR, vol. I, pp. 1049, 1159, 1176-7, and vol. III, pp. 109, 180, 212, 251, 742-3, 792.
[52] Ibid., vol. I, p. 997.
[53] Ibid., vol. II, pp. 270, 360, and vol. III, p. 251.
[54] Ibid., pp. 68-9, 495, 1184, and vol. III, pp. 126, 152.
[55] Ibid., p.37.
[56] Ibid., pp. 1250-1.
[57] E.g. ibid., vol. III, p. 1008.

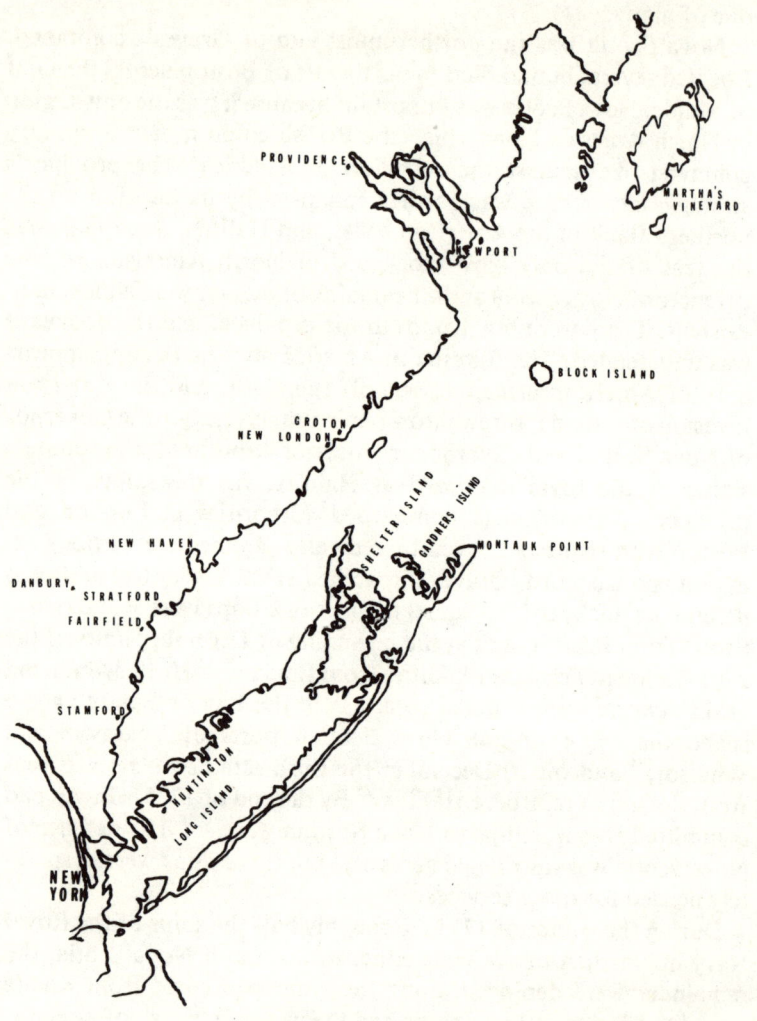

AMERICAN COASTAL WATERS, 1775-76

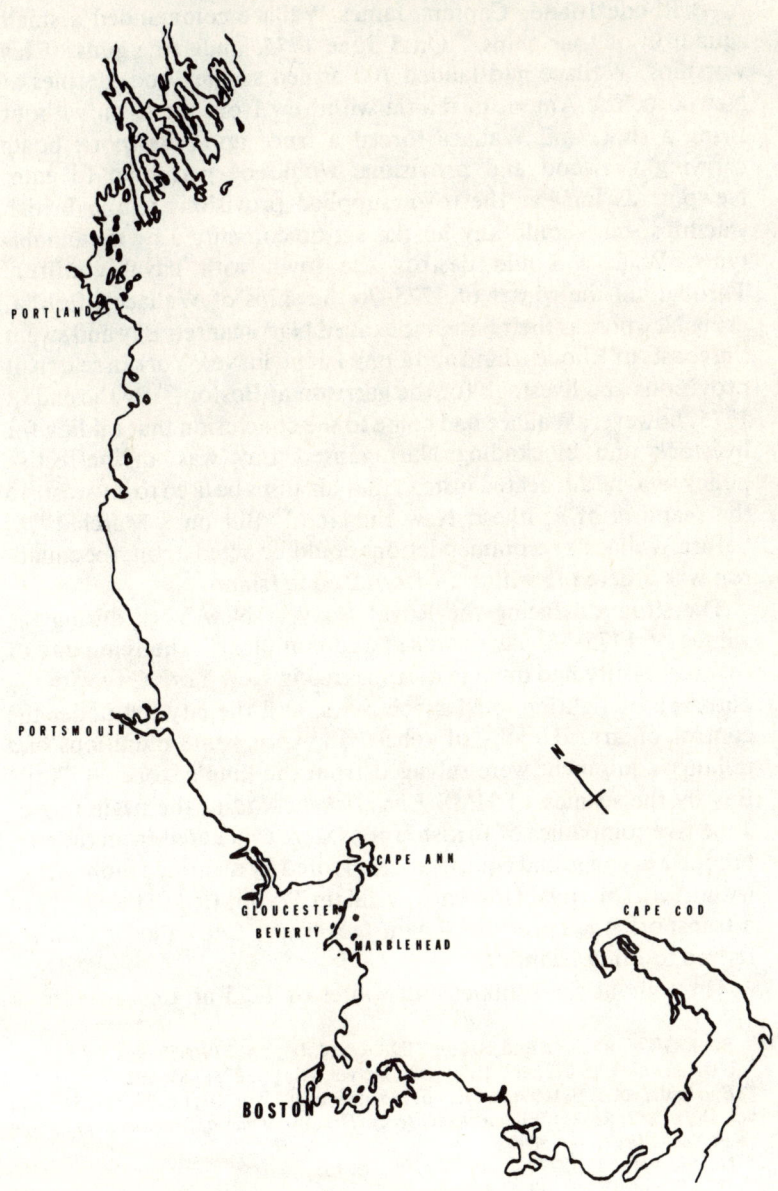

Map 3
The New England Coast Line

At Rhode Island, Captain James Wallace commanded a small squadron of four ships.[58] On 5 June 1775, under the guns of his warships, Wallace had landed 100 armed seamen and marines at Newport. The American militia withdrew from the town without firing a shot, and Wallace forced a truce upon Newport: boats carrying firewood and provisions would be permitted to enter Newport as long as the town supplied provisions to the British warships, but should any hostile act be committed by the inhabitants, Wallace would destroy the town with naval gunfire.[59] Throughout the winter of 1775–76 the ships of Wallace's flotilla, using Newport as their base, blockaded Narragansett Bay and swept the coasts of Rhode Island and Long Island in New York in search of provisions and livestock for the garrison at Boston.[60] By the end of 1775, however, Wallace had come to the conclusion that raiding for livestock and blockading Narragansett Bay was an ineffective policy, and he advocated instead that his ships be used to lay waste to the seaports of southern New England.[61] But on 8 March 1776, before Wallace's recommendations could be acted upon, the squadron was ordered to withdraw from Rhode Island.[62]

The situation facing the Royal Navy at New York during the winter of 1775–76 was confused and complex.[63] The remnants of royal authority had quickly disappeared in New York City with the outbreak of fighting in Massachusetts, and the city fell under the control of armed mobs of rebels. In April some munitions and military equipment were salvaged from the king's stores at Turtle Bay by the seamen of HMS *Kingsfisher*. And at the beginning of June five companies of British troops were evacuated from the city, but their baggage and equipage were looted by an armed mob as they withdrew. The royal Governor, William Tryon, fled to the safety of a transport; the royal Lieutenant-Governor, Cadwallader Colden, retired to Long Island.[64]

Throughout the summer and winter of 1775 an uneasy state of

---

[58] *Rose, Glasgow, Swan* and *Bolton*; NDAR, vol. III, pp. 278, 865, 902.
[59] NDAR, vol. I, p. 615, vol. II, p. 452, and vol. III, pp. 278, 865, 902.
[60] E.g. ibid., vol. I, p. 1099, vol. II, pp. 135, 451–2, 983, vol. III, pp. 37, 311, 575, and vol. IV, p. 283; Robert Wilden Neeser (ed.), *The Dispatches of Molyneux Shuldham* (New York, 1913), pp. 58–9.
[61] NDAR, vol. III, p. 278; Nesser, *op. cit.*, p. 133.
[62] NDAR, vol. IV, p. 230.
[63] *Kingsfisher* (withdrawn summer 1775); *Asia* (arrived 26 May 1775); *Viper* (ordered to New York but forced to the West Indies by bad weather); *Phoenix* (arrived end of 1775); and *Savage* (arrived spring 1776). NDAR, vol. I, p. 785, vol. II, pp. 373–4, 1250–1, vol. III, pp. 794, 1008, and vol. IV, pp. 1225–7.
[64] NDAR, vol. I, pp. 228, 616, 625, 691.

suppressed hostility existed between the city of New York and the Royal Navy. Captain George Vanderput of HMS *Asia* managed to reach an agreement with officials of New York, no doubt by offering not to bombard the city in exchange for being able to obtain provisions for British personnel on ships in New York Harbor.[65] But the truce between the city and the Royal Navy was an extremely frail one. On the night of 25 August a firefight broke out between HMS *Asia* and a group of Americans attempting to remove the guns from the Battery; and at the beginning of September the Americans seized and destroyed a ship's boat;[66] nevertheless, the truce continued through January 1776. The Americans did not cut off the supply of provisions to the British warships, and the Royal Navy did not bombard the city, nor did it attempt to prevent the flow of fuel and food to the inhabitants. In fact, in December 1775, the situation relaxed enough for HMS *Asia* and HMS *Phoenix*, under the supervision of city officials, to moor alongside wharves in the East River to escape from ice in the Hudson River.

On 5 February 1776 the situation at New York radically changed when General Charles Lee entered the city with several thousand American troops. Fresh from New England and full of patriotic zeal, they abruptly ended any hope on either side of continuing the truce.[67] At this point, Captain Hyde Parker, the senior Royal Navy officer at New York, was confronted with a classic dilemma: can such a movement be subdued with heavy weapons without destroying friend as well as foe in the process? The brutality of driving Lee's troops from New York City by levelling the city with naval gunfire was repellent to Parker and other British officials at New York; as Parker stated in a report:

> Firing upon the Town was judged by the Governor, General Clinton, and myself, too Severe a Measure, being Confident that the Majority of the Citizens, particularly those of *Property* are faithful to the King: . . . I must Sir, beg leave to remark, that I feel myself in a very difficult Situation to know how to Act, Convinced as I am of the Attachment to His Majesty of many Men of great Property in this Town, at the same time knowing that it is Garrisoned by Rebels. And they have even had the Audacity to place Centinels immediately before me, which I could never Submit to, was I not persuaded that my firing upon them

[65] For the terms of the agreement see ibid., vol. III, p. 978.
[66] Ibid., vol. I, pp. 1223-5, and vol. II, p. 40.
[67] Ibid., vol. III, pp. 653, 920, 1232.

would involve the City in ruins, which I must confess I cautiously Avoid, being determined if possible to make the Act of Committing Hostilities theirs not Mine.[68]

Forswearing the use of naval gunfire against the rebels, Parker moved the British warships from the East River. The *Asia* was stationed off Governors Island, and HMS *Phoenix* was placed in the Narrows.[69] But gradually the Americans were able to force the British from New York Bay. On 27 March the British seized one American ship and destroyed another; several days later, the Americans burned down the military hospital on Bedlows Island.[70] The Americans then cut off the flow of supplies to the British ships, and on 7 April began open hostilities by shooting up a number of ships' boats and occupying the British watering place on Staten Island.[71] In order to obtain a supply of fresh water and fearing attack by American fireships, Parker took over the wrecked lighthouse at Sandy Hook and withdrew his ships from New York Harbor and the Narrows to await the arrival of reinforcements.[72] By the end of April the maritime approaches to New York City had been surrendered to the Americans, who immediately began to fortify them in anticipation of a British invasion.

The operations of the Royal Navy in Chesapeake and Delaware bays during the first fourteen months of the war were greatly influenced by the quixotic military operations undertaken in Virginia by John Murray, Earl of Dunmore, the last royal governor of the Old Dominion.[73] On 7 June 1775, Dunmore and his family were forced to flee Williamsburg to the safety of a British warship. In the following weeks Dunmore spent his time on the one hand requesting military assistance from Boston, and on the other hand attempting to reinstitute his authority in Virginia. When the Americans rebuffed his attempts at reconciliation and he learned that Graves and Gage could not send reinforcements, Dunmore decided to take matters into his own hands. With two companies of the 14th Regiment, a motley handful of armed Loyalists and blacks, and the British ships *Fowey* and *Otter*, Dunmore seized the town of Norfolk.

[68] Ibid., vol. IV, pp. 75-6.
[69] Ibid., p. 76.
[70] Ibid., pp. 547, 647.
[71] Ibid., pp. 698-9; Neeser, *op. cit.*, p. 224.
[72] NDAR, vol. IV, pp. 1165, 1311-12; Neeser, *op. cit.*, p. 225.
[73] The best account of Dunmore's military actions during 1775-76 is W. Hugh Moomaw, 'The British leave colonial Virginia', *Virginia Magazine of History Biography*, vol. LXVI, pp. 147-60.

From Norfolk the royal governor issued a number of proclamations declaring martial law and emancipating black slaves, sent forth numerous parties on raids since described as 'chicken stealing expeditions' and dispatched to Boston and London a number of schemes calling for a winter campaign in Virginia to restore royal authority in the province.

Seeing Dunmore's actions and having learned of his plans, the Americans decided that the British position at Norfolk had to be destroyed. On 9 December 1775 they attacked Dunmore's small force and defeated it at Great Bridge, forcing the evacuation of Norfolk.[74] After the loss of Norfolk, Dunmore remained off the town with a fleet of merchant ships protected by several warships. Then on 1 January 1776 the Americans in the town and the British ships began to exchange small-arms fire. Accounts of this conflict differ, but it is clear that the firing quickly grew in intensity. Norfolk was bombarded by the *Kingsfisher, Liverpool* and *Otter*, set on fire and completely destroyed.[75]

On 16 February 1776, Captain Andrew Snape Hamond in HMS *Roebuck* arrived from Halifax off Norfolk with orders to protect the Loyalists in Virginia and to blockade the entrances of the Chesapeake and Delaware bays.[76] Together with Dunmore, Hamond seized and fortified Tucker's Mill Point in the Elizabeth River to use as a base and a place of refuge for the Loyalists under Dunmore's protection. By the beginning of March, Hamond had decided upon a course of action. He sent the *Otter* and a tender into the upper reaches of Chesapeake Bay and issued orders to the *Kingsfisher* to blockade the entrance of Delaware Bay and to the *Liverpool* to guard Dunmore's fleet of merchant vessels in the Elizabeth River; Hamond himself planned to cruise off Cape Charles in the *Roebuck*.[77] But before *Kingsfisher* could sail, Hamond received orders from Graves to send an expedition as far up the Delaware River as possible in order to destroy the American maritime defences of Philadelphia.

Hamond felt there were not enough ships at Virginia simultaneously to protect Dunmore's fleet, blockade the mouths of both the Chesapeake and Delaware bays and send a force up the Delaware

---

[74] Ibid., pp. 147-51.
[75] NDAR, vol. III, pp. 565, 580, 592, 704, 737-8; H.S. Parsons (ed.), 'Contemporary English accounts of the destruction of Norfolk in 1776', *William & Mary Quarterly* (October 1933), 2nd ser., vol. XIII, pp. 219-24.
[76] NDAR, vol. III, pp. 235, 276, 1324.
[77] Moomaw, *op. cit.*, p. 147; NDAR, vol. IV, pp. 56, 92, 274.

River. Moreover, there was a dangerous shortage of provisions, slops and naval stores aboard the ships at Virginia. He therefore sent the *Kingsfisher* to Boston with dispatches and requests for reinforcements and supplies. The *Liverpool* and the *Otter*, upon the latter's return to the Elizabeth River, were assigned to protect Lord Dunmore, while Hamond in the *Roebuck* was to blockade Delaware Bay and prepare to proceed up the Delaware River.[78] Thus, owing to the shortage of ships and the need to protect Lord Dunmore, the blockade of and operations in the Chesapeake Bay were abandoned, two out of three ships of Hamond's command were tied up on guard duty and Delaware Bay was inadequately blockaded.

On 25 March 1776, Hamond arrived off Cape Henlopen to begin a blockade of the mouth of Delaware Bay. No warship had operated there since HMS *Nautilus* had left the bay at the end of the summer of 1775.[79] The failure of the British to blockade Delaware Bay during the winter of 1775–76 was a serious omission. In this period, numerous shiploads of munitions had entered America through the bay, and before Hamond's arrival an American squadron of warships, under the command of Commodore Esek Hopkins, escaped from the Delaware River. For Hamond, the blockade of Delaware Bay must have been a frustrating task. Throughout April he chased many American ships but caught very few of them. It was extremely difficult for his single large frigate to blockade the many channels at the entrance of Delaware Bay and to capture small, fast vessels in the shoals.[80]

At the beginning of May the *Roebuck* was joined by the *Liverpool*, and on 5 May, together with the brig *Betsy*, the two ships headed up the Delaware River to attempt to carry out Hamond's orders to reduce the American maritime defences of Philadelphia. On 8 May the British force was attacked by a number of American armed galleys. The *Roebuck* ran aground but was refloated the next day, despite the presence of the Americans. Hamond then attempted to bring the American vessels to battle, but failing this, he returned down the Delaware River.[81]

On 16 May with the *Liverpool* blockading Delaware Bay, Hamond sailed for Cape Fear, where he knew General Henry

---

[78] Neeser, *op. cit.*, pp. 143–4; NDAR, vol. IV, pp. 182, 343, 427–8.
[79] NDAR, vol. II, p. 22.
[80] E.g. ibid., vol. IV, pp. 686, 1202, 1241, 1268.
[81] For an account of this action see W. Hugh Moomaw, 'The naval career of Captain Hamond, 1775–1779' (unpublished PhD dissertation, University of Virginia, 1955), pp. 167–82.

Clinton and Admiral Sir Peter Parker were to rendezvous. Hamond intended to convince Clinton and Parker to employ the forces under their command in a spring campaign in the Delaware and Chesapeake bays.[82] Hamond believed Maryland and Virginia ideally suited for such a campaign, for as he later wrote:

> on account of the navigable Rivers of the country, there is no part of the continent where ships can assist land operations more than this ... Whenever a thousand men can be spared, properly equipped ... with eight or 10 sail of small ships to act with them they may distress the colonies of Maryland and Virginia to the greatest degree, and employ more than ten times their numbers to watch them.[83]

But before Hamond could meet with Clinton and Parker, he was intercepted by a vessel that informed him that the Americans were about to overrun Dunmore's forces at Tucker's Mill Point.[84] He returned at once to Virginia.

Hamond found the situation at Tucker's Mill Point so grave that he was forced to evacuate Lord Dunmore's forces and the Loyalists under his protection. All were put aboard ships. Then before Hamond could decide where to relocate them, Dunmore, against his advice, seized Gwynn's Island as a base for further offensive operations. But within little more than a month the Americans forced the British from that island. A base was next established on St George's Island at the mouth of the Potomac River. Still hoping to mount an offensive campaign from Virginia, Hamond and Dunmore thought St George's Island would serve as a base from which British cruisers could operate in Chesapeake Bay. Short of supplies and without instructions, they doggedly maintained themselves there for the next several weeks while waiting for reinforcements. But at the beginning of August news arrived that the Clinton-Parker expedition had been repulsed before Charleston, South Carolina, and was going directly to New York. Since the king's forces in Virginia clearly were not going to be reinforced, Hamond's and Dunmore's hopes of mounting an offensive campaign in Virginia

---

[82] Moomaw, 'The naval career of Captain Hamond ...', pp. 182–5; NDAR, vol. IV, p. 1407.
[83] University of Virginia Libraries, Hamond Papers, Hamond to Sir Hans Stanley, 5 August 1776.
[84] Moomaw, 'The British leave ...' p. 158.

disintegrated. St George's Island was therefore evacuated and, on 5 August, Hamond and Dunmore sailed for New York with the *Roebuck, Liverpool, Otter*, about 100 troops and numerous Loyalist refugees aboard merchant ships.[85] From the beginning of the fighting to the evacuation of Virginia, the British naval effort in the Chesapeake and Delaware bays had suffered from a lack of ships. Compounding the shortage of ships and making it impossible to blockade Chesapeake and Delaware bays was the need to support Dunmore's unrealistic attempts to reconquer Virginia.

The few ships of the Royal Navy stationed on the coasts of the Carolinas and Georgia during the first year of the conflict stood by helplessly while royal authority collapsed in the South.[86] Not being strong enough to challenge the rebellious Americans, the king's ships in the Carolinas and Georgia served, for the most part, as places of refuge for royal officials.[87] The only offensive action undertaken by the Royal Navy in the South before the arrival of the Clinton–Parker expedition at Charleston, South Carolina, was a raid against shipping in the Savannah River. At the beginning of March 1776, HMS *Scarborough*, two transports and 170 troops arrived from Boston off the mouth of the Savannah River. The objective of this force was to obtain rice for the garrison of Boston. After attempts to purchase rice failed, Captain Andrew Barkley, RN, on the night of 3–4 March, raided Savannah and seized from the Americans eighteen merchant ships carrying 1,083 tierces of rice.[88] With the exception of this raid, units of the Royal Navy stationed along the coasts of the Carolinas and Georgia spent the winter of 1775–76 waiting for orders and reinforcements.

The fighting in North America quickly spread to the West Indies. In 1775 the British armed forces in the Caribbean were extremely weak, consisting of only 1,900 troops and ten warships.[89] It fell to this inadequate force to prevent the Americans from obtaining munitions at the Danish, Dutch and French West Indian islands. As early as 10 June 1775, Vice-Admiral James Young, navy commander-in-chief at the Leeward Islands, ordered HMS *Pomona* to

[85] Ibid., pp. 147–9, 158–60.
[86] On 3 December 1775 the *Cruiser, Scorpion, Tamer, St Lawrence* and *St John* were stationed on the American coast to the southward of Virginia, see NDAR, vol. II, pp. 1250–1.
[87] Ibid., vol. I, p. 712, vol. II, p. 114, vol. III, pp. 843, 1185, and vol. IV, p. 1239.
[88] Ibid., vol. IV, pp. 167, 172, 293–4, 443–4, 1437–8.
[89] Leeward Island squadron, *Argo, Hind, Lynx* and *Pomona*; Jamaica squadron, *Antelope, Maidstone, Squirrel, Florida* and *Diligence*: PRO, ADM 1/309, f. 375; WO 17/1154, f. 1; NDAR, vol. III, p. 980, NRS, *Sandwich Papers*, vol. I, p. 103n.

cruise off St Croix and seize any ships bound for North America with munitions.[90] And a day later, Young issued a general order to every ship under his command to seize any and all ships found conveying munitions to North America.[91] Then, in August, Young ordered that his ships stop every vessel, regardless of nationality, and search it for munitions. At the same time, the admiral requested that the governors of the British Leeward Islands prohibit the exportation of munitions.[92] The authorities at Jamaica were not as quick to react to the rebellion in America as did Young in the Leeward Islands, but on 29 November 1775 Rear-Admiral Clark Gayton, navy commander-in-chief at Jamaica ordered that the ships of his command seize all American vessels and property encountered on the high seas. At the same time, in an effort to intercept American ships leaving the Caribbean, Gayton ordered HMS *Squirrel* to cruise off the Caicos Island and HMS *Maidstone* to cruise near Great Inagua.[93] This was the beginning of an effort that would send the ships of the Royal Navy ranging throughout the West Indies, stopping, searching and seizing ships in a desperate attempt to prevent the flow of munitions to America.

The seizure in West Indian waters of munitions bound for North America was a policy full of difficulties. For several months neither Gayton at Jamaica nor Young in the Leeward Islands had what the courts considered to be the legal authority to detain American ships and seamen. Young ignored the legal niceties, pressing the American seamen and holding the ships while awaiting the arrival from England of the required authority to proceed against them in the vice-admiralty courts.[94] Gayton, while able to detain American ships, was sued and served with writs of habeas corpus that forced him to free the American crews.[95] Of far greater importance than these legal manoeuvers, however, was the shortage of ships. Nine or ten warships simply could not begin to search effectively an area as large as the West Indies, blockade all the non-British islands and suppress, to any meaningful extent, the huge American trade in munitions. Also at any given time, a number of ships were inactive owing to the need to be repaired, refitted and revictualled, or were

---

[90] NDAR, vol. I, pp. 653-4.
[91] Ibid., vol. I, pp. 659-60.
[92] Ibid., vol. I, pp. 1148, 1210-11, 1267.
[93] PRO, ADM 1/240, ff. 127-8.
[94] PRO, ADM 1/309, f. 413; NDAR, vol. III, p. 990.
[95] PRO, ADM 1/240, ff. 139-44, 158, 180; NDAR, vol. III, pp. 554-61, 868-9, 907, 1143.

tied up as escorts to military convoys.[96] Moreover, the growing fear of American privateers among British merchants and planters in the West Indies necessitated assigning a number of warships to escort the homeward-bound trade.[97] Throughout the winter of 1775-76 both Gayton and Young sent the Admiralty request after request for reinforcements, stating bluntly that they did not have the ships required to stop American importations of munitions and warning of disaster should American armed ships appear in the West Indies.[98]

Another problem confronting the British naval authorities in the West Indies during the winter of 1775-76 was the clandestine aid rendered to the Americans by the French. The French authorities not only permitted Americans to exchange North American produce for munitions in French West Indian ports,[99] they also supplied the Americans with the necessary papers and men to disguise the nationality of ships carrying munitions to America. In the Leeward Islands, Young quickly learned that American ships loaded with munitions were carrying French papers and clearances for voyages from Martinique to the French islands of St Pierre and Miquelon in the Gulf of St Lawrence. These vessels also had on board several Frenchmen to act as the ships' officers, should they be intercepted by British cruisers.[100] At first, Young tried to mitigate official French collaboration with the Americans by threatening to seize any American vessels found sailing under the cover of bogus French nationality.[101] Next he attempted pre-emptive buying by offering to purchase from the French merchants at Martinique gunpowder that would otherwise have gone to the Americans.[102] Finally, on 31 March 1776, Young issued orders to the ships of his command to seize all vessels carrying munitions that had French papers and 'nominal' French masters, but that in all other respects appeared to be American.[103]

Seizing American ships with French papers was extremely risky, for it called for stopping, searching and seizing ships sailing under

[96] E.g. PRO, ADM 1/309, f. 465; NDAR, vol. II, pp. 586-87, vol. III, pp. 708-9, and vol. IV, pp. 704-5.
[97] PRO, ADM 1/240, F. 216: ADM 1/309, f. 414; NDAR, vol. III, p. 1209, and vol. IV, pp. 155, 703-4.
[98] E.g. PRO, ADM 1/204, f. 217; NDAR, vol. I, p. 1268, vol. II, p. 1150, vol. III, pp. 53-4, and vol. IV, pp. 155, 703-4.
[99] E.g. NDAR, vol. II, p. 911, and vol. III, pp. 223, 232, 906.
[100] NDAR, vol. II, p. 585, and vol. IV, p. 188; PRO, ADM 1/309, f. 469.
[101] NDAR, vol. II, p. 354.
[102] Ibid., vol. IV, p. 280.
[103] Ibid., p. 604.

the protection of the French flag. Yet it was only one problem among many that American procurement of munitions in French, Dutch and Danish Caribbean ports created for the British. Most important, the rights and honour of neutrals in the West Indies were being increasingly disregarded by the Royal Navy as the British took increasingly harsh steps to cut off the flow of munitions, although orders were issued repeatedly to British navy officers 'not to offer any Insult to the Forts, Harbours, or Ships of War belonging to His Most Christian Majesty, His Danish Majesty, or the States General of Holland.[104] European neutrals in the West Indies felt more and more that the Royal Navy, in its search for American munitions, was subjecting their ships and possessions to inconveniences, insults and danger. The French, for instance, sent a diplomatic protest to London stating that British warships had repeatedly violated French territorial waters in the West Indies and that the Royal Navy had Martinique under blockade, with British warships hovering off the island and stopping every approaching ship with gunfire if necessary.[105] Young and other British officials knew they were running great risks, but when confronted with clandestine French aid to the enemy, they could see no other way to prevent Americans from obtaining munitions than to disregard diplomatic dangers.[106]

When Rear-Admiral Molyneux Shuldham arrived at Boston on 30 December 1775 to replace Graves as commander-in-chief of the North American squadron,[107] he was appalled by what he found. There were only fourteen warships in Massachusetts Bay,[108] and they were ill-manned, short of provisions, in a state of disrepair and constantly cruising to prevent the capture of British supply ships proceeding to Boston. Shuldham quickly saw that without a large reinforcement British ships sailing to Boston could not be further protected, for the Americans controlled the north shore of Massachusetts Bay.[109] On 16 February 1776, Shuldham reported to the Admiralty that the situation in Massachusetts Bay was hopeless:

> however Numerous our Cruisers may be, or however attentive our Officers to their Duty, it has been found impossible to prevent

---

[104] Ibid., pp. 1474–5.
[105] Ibid., vol. III, p. 179; IV, p. 957.
[106] Ibid., vol. IV, p. 704.
[107] For Graves's reaction to being relieved of command, see ibid., vol. III, p. 300.
[108] *Chatham, Lively, Halifax, Diligent, Dispatch, Tryal, Adventure, Spinkes, Renown, Centurion, Niger, Fowey, Halifax* schooner, *Nautilus* and *Hope*: NDAR, vol. III, p. 1007.
[109] PRO, ADM 1/484, f. 365; NDAR, vol. III, pp. 877–8.

some of Ordinance and other valuable Stores in small Vessels falling into the hands of the Rebels.[110]

Without reinforcements, Shuldham had no alternative but to continue Graves' policy of attempting to protect British supply vessels by keeping the ships of his command constantly cruising in Massachusetts Bay.

Then on the night of 4-5 March what the British at Boston had feared since the war began happening: the American army occupied and fortified Dorchester Heights, a position from which its artillery could bombard not only Boston, but the maritime approaches to the town as well. At first, the British planned to seize Dorchester Heights by means of a shore-to-shore amphibious assault, but the operation was called off at the last minute because of bad weather.[111] By the time the weather cleared, the Americans were well dug in, and it was then decided that since an assault on the Heights would be futile, Boston should be evacuated despite the shortage of transports.[112] By threatening to burn Boston to the ground if there were any interference with the withdrawal, the British obtained a truce from the Americans.[113] In the following days, 8,908 troops, 924 Loyalists and tons of military equipment and stores were crammed into seventy-eight transports and carried to the anchorage at Nantasket Roads, just outside Boston Harbor.[114] The British completed the evacuation by 17 March, but the shortage of ships and seamen forced them to abandon at Boston a quantity of military stores and forty-five vessels of various kinds.[115] From Nantasket Roads, Howe wrote the government on 21 March of his intention to proceed to Halifax:

> I am justly sensible how much more . . . it would be to His Majesty's Service if this army was in a situation to proceed immediately to New York; but the present condition of the troops crowded in transports without regard to conveniences . . . and all

---

[110] PRO, ADM 1/484, f. 399.
[111] NYHSC, *Kemple Papers*, vol. I, pp. 312-13.
[112] NDAR, vol. IV, p. 473.
[113] Ibid., pp. 229-30.
[114] David Syrett, *Shipping and the American War, 1775-83* (London, 1970), p. 207.
[115] For an account of the military equipment and vessels left at Boston see NDAR, vol. IV, pp. 445-6, 808-14. It was thought by some at the time that the equipment abandoned at Boston was the result of negligence: NYHSC, *Montressor Journals*, p. 418.

the incumberances with which [the army is] clogged, effectively disable me from . . . any offensive operations.[116]

The British army was immobilized at Halifax by a lack of shipping and provisions, and it was not until 7 June that Howe was able to obtain the transports and provisions required to undertake offensive operations.[117] He embarked his army in the second week of June and sailed for Sandy Hook, leaving behind 2,030 women and children because he lacked transports to carry them.[118] According to Colonel Charles Stuart, Howe originally intended to attack Long Island, but 'Owing to representations made by General Robertson', decided instead to capture Staten Island first.[119] On 3 July 1776, the day before the signing of the Declaration of Independence, the British army seized Staten Island without opposition.[120] Howe then suspended all further offensive operations against New York to await the arrival of stores from Europe, for he thought, 'the want of camp equipage particularly continues, so essential in the field, and without which too much is to be apprehended on the score of health'.[121]

When the army left Boston, Admiral Shuldham began to redeploy the ships of his squadron. In order to support the coming attack on New York and to prevent British ships that were unaware of the evacuation of Boston from attempting to enter that port, Shuldham deployed ships to blockade the coast of New England and the approaches to New York. Captain Francis Banks was ordered to remain off Boston with a small flotilla to blockade the town and to divert British ships to Halifax. But for reasons that are not clear, Banks lifted the blockade of Boston on 14 June and the next day the Americans captured two British transports that entered Boston Harbor on the supposition that it was still held by the British.[122]

Shuldham by the end of April had stationed cruisers off Liverpool and Cape Sable, Nova Scotia; on Georges Banks; in Boston Bay and on the coast of Maine; at the eastern end of Long Island Sound; and

[116] PRO, CO 5/93, f. 89.
[117] PRO, CO 5/235, pp. 278, 293.
[118] BL, Add. MSS. 34187, ff. 1-2; NYHSC, *Kemble Papers*, vol. I, p. 382.
[119] Wortley, *op. cit.*, p. 82.
[120] PRO, ADM 1/484, f. 658.
[121] PRO, CO 5/235, pp. 234-5.
[122] Nesser, *op. cit.*, pp. 167, 257-8. On 27 March, Banks's command consisted of *Renown, Lively, Niger, Fowey, Swan, Hope, Bolton* and *Dispatch*: NDAR, vol. IV, p. 536; David Syrett, 'The disruption of HMS *Flora*'s convoy, 1776', *Mariner's Mirror* (November 1970), vol. 56, pp. 423-7.

at Sandy Hook.[123] Such a small number of cruisers sparsely strung out along the American coast from Nova Scotia to New York made the British 'strong nowhere and weak everywhere'. But Shuldham, like every other British naval commander in America, faced the problem of stretching all too finite a number of ships to cover the seemingly infinite American coastline. Given the small number of warships available,[124] Shuldham had but two choices, both with serious weaknesses: he could concentrate the ships of his command in strong squadrons, or he could station them in ones or twos along the entire length of the coastline. If he chose the first alternative, he would have to lift the blockade from most of the American coast. He chose the second, yet he still lacked enough ships for an effective blockade and ran the risk of having his squadron destroyed piecemeal.

The tactical and strategic weaknesses of British naval deployments in America were revealed in the spring of 1776. On 17 February 1776 an American squadron consisting of eight vessels, under the command of Commodore Esek Hopkins, sailed from Cape Henlopen, which was not blockaded by the Royal Navy, and proceeded to New Providence in the Bahamas. Having scared away the only British warship in the Bahamas, HMS *St Johns*, the superior American force was left free to seize New Providence, on 5 March, and to strip it of munitions. Hopkins's squadron left the Bahamas for America on 17 March.[125] On 4 April as the American squadron approached the coast of southern New England, it captured the British armed schooner *Hawke* and the following day intercepted and took HM Brig *Bolton*. Then on 6 April off Block Island, Hopkins's squadron attacked and badly damaged the twenty-gun frigate *Glasgow*, and only British skill and American ineptitude saved the king's ship from capture.[126] Thus despite the presence of over thirty British warships in American waters, a small American force was able to escape from

---

[123] *Senegal* at Liverpool, NS; *Halifax*, at Cape Sable; *Centurion* and *Renown*, Georges Banks; *Lively, Milford, Swan, Hope* and *Bolton*, Boston Bay and Maine coast; *Diligent* and *Cerberus*, eastern end of Long Island Sound; and *Phoenix, Asia*, and *Savage*, Sandy Hook: Nesser, *op. cit.*, pp. 200-1.

[124] On 24 April 1776, Shuldham's squadron consisted of 44 ships stationed along the American coast from Quebec to St Augustine, Fla: Nesser, ibid., pp. 200-1.

[125] For an account of the raid on New Providence see Allen, *op. cit.*, vol. I, pp. 93-100; John McCusker, Jr, 'The American invasion of Nassau in the Bahamas', *American Neptune* (July 1965), vol. 25, pp. 189-217.

[126] Allen, *op. cit.*, vol. I, pp. 101-9; NDAR, vol. IV, pp. 679-81, 1157-9. For an account of the capture of the *Bolton* see J. H. Owen and Sir George Barnes, 'Lieutenant Edward Sneyd, Royal Navy, of Keele Hall, Staffordshire', *Mariner's Mirror* (November 1958), vol. 44, pp. 240-4.

Delaware Bay, seize the capital of a British colony, and capture two British warships and cripple a third upon returning to the American coast. The success of Hopkins's squadron should have showed that the British did not have the means to prevent American warships from leaving America or to protect from attack such isolated and vulnerable places as New Providence. Only by lifting the blockade of America and permitting the rebels freely to import munitions could the British prevent superior American forces from picking off individual British ships on blockade duty.

During the first year of the war the Royal Navy in American waters was confronted with the phenomenon of a continent in rebellion. With a mere handful of ships that were undermanned and short of supplies, Graves, and later Shuldham, had the impossible task of supporting the British army, protecting supply ships in American waters and policing over 1,000 miles of hostile coastline. In the first months of the conflict the Royal Navy destroyed Falmouth, Maine and Norfolk, Virginia, and between 1 June 1775 and 24 April 1776, warships under the command of Graves and Shuldham seized and brought into Boston and Halifax over 120 American ships.[127] Yet success in a conflict as complex as the American war is not always measured in terms of towns destroyed or ships taken, and the Royal Navy's effort during that first year was, at best, an ill-directed holding action, and, at worst, a failure. British warships were unable to prevent either the destruction of royal authority or the importation of munitions.[128] Rebel armed vessels appeared able to operate almost at will and captured a number of British ships. For the Royal Navy, it was a time of frustration and humiliation. The strongest navy in the world appeared to be rendered helpless by a rabble possessing a few whaleboats and armed schooners. Clearly the Royal Navy had to be massively reinforced if the rebellion was to be suppressed. What was less apparent was the need for a rational plan for the re-establishment of royal authority, for the first months of the war had shown that there are limitations to the effectiveness of naval power when applied against a political movement such as the American Revolution.

---

[127] NDAR, vol. II, pp. 1373-7, and vol. IV, pp. 1228-31. This figure is an approximation and does not, for example, include American ships captured in the West Indies: see ibid., vol. IV, pp. 517, 1375.
[128] Cf. C.W. Stephenson, 'The supply of gunpowder in 1776', *American Historical Review* (January 1925), vol. 30, pp. 271-81.

2
ONE DECISIVE CAMPAIGN, 1776

The British government abandoned its policy of coercing the American rebels by a display of military force at Boston during the summer and autumn of 1775, when dispatches arrived in London telling of the beginning of hostilities in Massachusetts and the route of royal authority throughout America. No longer could the government view the American problem simply as one of crushing a dominant minority or a single province: it now confronted a continent swept by revolutionary war. There was no question that the government would fight what amounted to a civil war within the British empire to reassert royal authority, for it was firmly believed in London that the loss of America would result in Britain's being reduced to a second-rank European power. Unaware of the grave dangers and great difficulties of attempting to restore royal authority in America by force of arms, the resolve to resist the revolution came easily to the government in 1775.

The potentially most dangerous aspect of the situation in the long run lay not in America, but in Europe. Gone was the Prussian alliance of the Seven Years' War, and France, with a rejuvenated navy and the strongest army in Europe, was closely observing the progress of the rebellion with the idea that British problems in America could be used as means of overturning the humiliation of the Peace of Paris. As British authority disappeared and fighting began, the French Foreign Minister, the Comte de Vergennes, came to the conclusion that the British could never retain control of America by force. Thus, France's foreign policy began – secretly and slowly – to set the stage for intervention against the British. Care had to be exercised, for the surprise opening of hostilities in 1755 between Britain and France was still remembered in Paris, and to the

French at the beginning of the American War, an Anglo-American reconciliation coupled with a pre-emptive attack on the French West Indies was not beyond possibility. Furthermore, Spain, coveting Minorca and Gibraltar but having a vast empire to protect, had to be courted and brought into the scheme, for the combined French and Spanish navies would outnumber the Royal Navy.[1] As France stealthily moved towards intervention, it was perceived in London that unless the Americans were quickly crushed, the conflict would grow into a world war in which Britain would be at a serious disadvantage.

As hostility to royal authority grew and fighting broke out in Massachusetts, the strength of a squadron in America was steadily increased. This naval build-up began on 3 October 1774 when the Cabinet decided to mobilize and send three guard-ships and 600 marines to America.[2] And during 1775 the Admiralty dispatched twenty-four additional warships to America as quickly as they could be fitted and manned. By the end of 1775 the squadron in America numbered fifty-one warships manned by 7,555 men, or roughly a third of the total strength of the Royal Navy.[3]

Lord Sandwich, the first lord of the Admiralty, declared that 'we are at war with the rebels of America'.[4] Nevertheless, while reinforcing the Royal Navy in America, the Admiralty always kept one eye on Paris, for it saw from the beginning that a French war was the great danger to Britain. Therefore, the central and overriding aim of the Admiralty was to keep in Britain a force of ships of the line capable of dealing with the French navy, and possibly that of Spain as well. Admirals, generals and secretaries of state might protest and demand that ships of the line be sent to America, but the Admiralty would not change its policy. On 3 August 1775, HMS *Somerset*, HMS *Asia* and HMS *Boyne* – the three guard-ships ordered to America in October 1774 – were directed to return to England, to be replaced by forty-four- and fifty-gun ships. The Admiralty, led by Sandwich, was prepared to, and actually did, strip Britain of sloops of war, frigates, fifty-gun ships and other small warships in order to reinforce America, but the ships of the line were

---

[1] Samuel F. Bemis, *The Diplomacy of the American Revolution* (New York, 1935), pp. 11–27.
[2] *Asia, Boyne*, and *Somerset*: NMM, SAN/T/6, 4 October 1774; Clarence Edwin Carter (ed.), *The Correspondence of General Thomas Gage* (New Haven, Conn., 1933), Vol. II, p. 174.
[3] NRS, *Sandwich Papers*, vol. I, pp. 42, 64–6
[4] Ibid., p. 70.

to remain in Britain.[5]

The dangers that Britain faced in Europe because of the revolution quickly became apparent when the government attempted to prevent arms from reaching the rebels. On 15 October 1774 a dispatch arrived in London from the British ambassador at The Hague stating that the Americans were secretly purchasing munitions in Amsterdam.[6] Four days later an Order in Council was issued prohibiting the export from Britain of gunpowder, arms and all other forms of military equipment; at the same time, orders were issued to the Admiralty to seize any ship carrying munitions to America.[7] But the British found it extremely difficult to prevent Americans from importing munitions from Europe, and by the middle of 1775, according to Lord Suffolk, a secretary of state, 'an extensive, illicit, and dangerous commerce is carrying on by vessels belonging to His Majesty's Colonies under Foreign Colours'.[8] While still nominally at peace, however, the Royal Navy could not do much about American ships with false foreign papers. The American colonies had not yet been declared in a state of open rebellion, and a foreign ship could only be seized when it fell within the prescription of the Hovering Act, that is when intercepted within two leagues of British territory.[9] Nevertheless, despite legal obstacles, ships of the Royal Navy were stationed on the Thames and in the Downs to assist customs officials in the search for munitions bound for America.[10] Other ships cruised in the English Channel in an attempt to prevent the flow of munitions to America.[11] In the autumn of 1775, HMS *Atlanta*, HMS *Pallas*, and HMS *Weazle* were ordered to 'range' along the West African coast and seize any American ships there in order to prevent the rebels from obtaining arms on the Slave Coast.[12] It was not until 22 December 1775 that Parliament passed the Capture Act, which proclaimed the colonies in a state of open rebellion, prohibited all trade with America and authorized the

---

[5] PRO, ADM 3/81, 3 August 1775; NDAR, vol. I, pp. 592, 1305–6, 1318, 1349.
[6] PRO, ADM 1/4129, f. 163. In 1768 all British diplomats were ordered to report the arrival and departure of ships thought to be carrying illegal or suspicious cargoes to America.
[7] PRO, ADM 1/4129, f. 169; Carter, *op. cit.*, vol. II, p. 176.
[8] PRO, ADM 1/4130, f. 72.
[9] 5 Geo. I, c. 11, s. 8; PRO, ADM 1/4130, f. 18.
[10] PRO, ADM 3/81, 17 August 1775; NDAR, vol. II, pp. 676, 678–9.
[11] E.g. PRO, ADM 2/100. pp. 18–20, 258, 287; ADM 2/1332, pp. 227–34; ADM 2/1333, pp. 22–4; AD, 3/81, 10 August and 13 November 1775; NDAR, vol. III, pp. 367, 401.
[12] PRO, ADM 1/4130, f. 82; ADM 2/100, pp. 171–2, 247–8; NDAR, vol. III, p. 722.

seizure of all American ships.[13]

London quickly saw that stopping the flow of munitions to America was as much a diplomatic problem as a naval one. The British, with varying degrees of success, brought diplomatic pressure to bear on European nations to prohibit the export of munitions to America.[14] But diplomacy was not a very effective means of preventing Americans from obtaining munitions. Even in those countries that were supposed to have prohibited the traffic in arms, the Americans still managed to obtain them; moreover, France – and to a lesser degree Spain – secretly supported the Americans' procurement efforts. The British government had good information on the activities of American ships loading munitions in French ports but could do no more than rather ineffectually protest;[15] and attempts by the Royal Navy to intercept American ships outside of French and Spanish ports brought forth violent protests from Spain and France.[16]

Even if the British had managed to prevent American ships from leaving European ports with munitions, the problem would not have been solved. There was no way to stop American agents from sending munitions in neutral bottoms to the French, Dutch or Danish West Indies, where they could then be trans-shipped to America.[17] The only truly effective way of stopping the flow of arms to America would have been to seize all munitions found on the high seas, regardless of the nationality of the ship carrying them. Therein lay the British dilemma: to stop the traffic they would have to seize neutral ships and run the risk of a European war, while not stopping it would result in the rebellion in America being fed by a flow of munitions from Europe. The British government, however, would not risk a European war in 1775–76 and adopted the ineffectual policy of diplomatic protest and seizing only those neutral ships carrying arms that were clearly contravening the laws and usages of war.

In the last weeks of 1775, as news arrived in London that the Americans were fitting out armed vessels,[18] the government began to take the steps necessary to protect British shipping from attack.

---

[13] 16 Geo. III, c. 5. NDAR, vol. III, pp. 453–4.
[14] NDAR, vol. II, pp. 679–80, 684, 749–50.
[15] E.g. ibid., pp. 718, 744, and vol. II, p. 471.
[16] E.g. ibid., vol. IV, pp. 1012, 1076, 1089.
[17] E.g. PRO, ADM 1/4131, f. 64; G, no. 1810; NDAR, vol. I, p. 1346, and vol. III, pp. 403, 409–10; Gardener W. Allen, *A Naval History of the American Revolution* (New York, 1962 reprint), Vol. I, pp. 196–7.
[18] E.g. PRO, ADM 1/4130, f. 171; G, no. 1810; NDAR, vol. III, p. 345.

An Order in Council was issued authorizing the arming of British Merchant ships,[19] orders were sent to Graves at Boston to destroy any American ships being fitted as armed vessels[20] and a limited system of convoys was instituted. Ships carrying stores to the king's forces in America were placed under naval escort.[21] Five warships were ordered to Ascension Island and St Helena to intercept the homeward-bound East India trade and escort it to England.[22] Acting on a petition of the merchants of Poole, the government ordered that the Newfoundland trade be convoyed and the squadron there be increased to eight warships to protect the fisheries from American attack,[23] and orders were also sent to the Leeward Islands and Jamaica directing that the homeward-bound trade be escorted 80–120 leagues into the Atlantic as a means of protecting it from American cruisers.[24] For the most part, these limited and not very systematic trade protection measures were designed to allay the fears of merchants, but they were the beginning of an effort that, before the war was two years old, would see the strength of the Royal Navy stretched almost to breaking-point.

By the end of 1775, however, the importance of preventing the Americans from obtaining arms and the protection of trade was superseded by the more pressing need for a plan quickly to reassert royal authority in the colonies before France could intervene. During the Stamp Act crisis, royal authority in America, which rested on the consent of the populace, had for the most part vanished and could only be re-established by force of arms. But subduing America – a continent in rebellion 3,000 miles from the centre of British power – presented the ministry in London with a military and political problem without precedent.

In 1775, in many respects, revolutionary America was to the British government the unknown viewed by the uncomprehending. The rebellion was a unique event to which the lessons of previous wars and revolutions did not apply, for a conflict with an ideologically motivated and armed insurgent population was unknown to contemporary Europe. Furthermore, there was no society in Europe

[19] PRO, ADM 1/4168, 13 October 1775.
[20] PRO, ADM 3.81, 14 September and 23 October 1775.
[21] E.g. CL, Douglas Papers, vol. S1, 28 September 1775; PRO, ADM 2/100, pp. 86–7, 128–9, 183–4; ADM 2/101, p. 422.
[22] PRO, ADM 2/1332, pp. 248–9; ADM 2/1333, ff. 34–7, *Arethusa, Thetis, Pallas, Atlantic* and *Weazle*.
[23] *Romney, Fox, Deal Castle, Surprise, Martin, Cygnet, Fowey* and *Egmont* schooner, plus 2 armed vessels and 4 shallops: PRO, ADM 1/4131, ff. 32, 64; NDAR, vol. III, p. 534, and vol. IV, pp. 993–4.
[24] NDAR, vol. IV, pp. 918–9.

similar to that in America, so the rulers of Britain in 1775 found it nearly impossible to determine the military potential of the American rebels. Those British officials, with the possible exception of Lord Amherst, who had had contact with the American loathed them and underrated their military ability. General James Wolfe thought that Americans could not be 'trusted',[25] and Admiral Sir George Rodney became disgusted with Americans and their 'republicanism' while serving as Governor of Newfoundland.[26] General James Murray, who had succeeded Wolfe at Quebec, believed as late as the summer 1776 that 'the native American is an effeminate thing, very unfit for and very impatient of war'.[27] And Lord Sandwich had the incredible theory that the more Americans who took up arms against the British, the easier would be the victory for the king's forces.[28] Clearly, Sandwich, who had never been to America, had not thought out the maritime aspects of the problem, for the ability to wage war at sea was one of the few aspects of American military potential that, in 1775, was susceptible of rational analysis.

America in 1775 did not have a navy, but it did have a large merchant marine and well-developed shipbuilding industry.[29] Its large maritime population, which had continually engaged in such activities as fishing and the carrying trade, had a long history of privateering and smuggling. In fact, Americans were so skilled at smuggling that in the years after the Seven Years War the Royal Navy had found itself incapable of suppressing American illegal seaborne trade.[30] From even the most superficial analysis, which apparently was not made, it should have been evident that the outbreak of hostilities would pose serious problems for the Royal Navy. The length of the American coast and the great skill of Americans as smugglers would make it extremely difficult, if not impossible, to prevent the rebels by means of naval blockade from importing from Europe and the West Indies the arms and munitions required to carry on the war. Moreover, if the rebellion were not quelled quickly, the Americans would undoubtedly dispatch armed vessels to attack Britain's far-flung seaborne commerce and thus the

[25] Beckles Willson, *The Life and Letters of James Wolfe* (New York, 1909), p. 394.
[26] David Spinney, *Rodney* (London, 1969), p. 98.
[27] HMC, *Stopford-Sackville MSS.*, vol. I, p. 371.
[28] Bernard Donoughue, *British Politics and the American Revolution: The Path to War* (London 1964), p. 253.
[29] It has been estimated that, at the beginning of the American war, at least one out of every four ships in the British merchant marine was American-built: Ralph Davis, *The Rise of the English Shipping Industry in the Seventeenth and Eighteenth Centuries* (London, 1962), p. 68.
[30] Cf. Neil R. Stout, *The Royal Navy in America, 1760–1775* (Annapolis, Md, 1973).

Royal Navy, the most powerful naval force in the world, would conceivably find itself bogged down in an endless maritime guerrilla war.

The rebellion in America presented the British government with a unique strategic problem. America was not Ireland, which had been repeatedly terrorized into submission by relatively small military forces. Nor was America similar to Scotland, which in 1745 had been blockaded by the Royal Navy, overrun by the king's army and pacified by the construction of forts and military roads. Neither could guidance be drawn from the conquest of Canada in the Seven Years War. Then the British had with one blow aimed at Quebec – the strategic nerve centre of Canada – reduced the French forces to impotency in a manoeuver analogous to placing a cork in the top of a bottle. But in 1775 America was a vast, sprawling decentralized country without a strategic, economic or political centre. There was in America no London, Paris, or Vienna, the capture of which would signal the defeat of the country. In the course of the war the British would occupy every urban centre in America, only to find that the country was like Russia, in that the capture of a city became a meaningless victory swallowed up by the vastness of the land itself. The strategies of previous eighteenth-century conflicts simply did not apply to revolutionary America.

While only dimly perceiving the strategic difficulties posed by America, the British government knew it would take a massive effort to crush the rebellion. Reasoning that if the Americans were decisively beaten by an overwhelming force of European troops they would then see the futility of further resistance to the king's forces, the government decided to attempt to end the rebellion in one campaign by invading New York with a huge army in the spring of 1776. Seizing New York would not only demoralize the rebels, but provide the British with a refuge for Loyalists, an area from which to draw supplies and a military base for which further operations could be undertaken. It would also open to British amphibious forces the Hudson River, which is navigable for more than 100 miles along the western flank of New England. New England – believed by the British to be the centre of the revolt – would then be cut off from the rest of America and caught between the Royal Navy and British forces in Canada and New York.[31]

---

[31] PRO, CO 5/92, ff. 290-1; CL, Sackville-Germain Papers, vol. 5, 1 July 1775; Carter *op. cit.*, Vol. I, pp. 404, 413-14, 418-19, and Vol. II, pp. 205, 678; NDAR, vol. II, pp. 11, 703; HMC, *Stopford-Sackville MSS.*, vol. I, pp. 135-7, and vol. II, pp. 1, 3, 6.

Some people in 1775 argued that the committing of massive British military power to quell the rebellion was probably futile and certainly dangerous. Lord Barrington, the secretary at war, thought that the Americans could and should be subdued by the Royal Navy and that the bulk of the British army should not be committed to America.[32] Others maintained that the army would be destroyed piecemeal, or that it was impossible to conquer such a country.[33] But if these doubts were ever considered, they were quickly cast aside by the government, and preparations for the invasion continued unabated throughout the summer and autumn of 1775.

However, the principle of concentration of force was soon partially abandoned by the government. In the autumn of 1775 reports began to arrive in Whitehall from the governors of Virginia, North Carolina and South Carolina, optimistically telling of the great Loyalist strength in the South. The belief quickly grew in London that with a modest amount of aid, Loyalists would flock to the support of the royal governors in the South, the rebels would be easily subdued and royal authority restored.[34]

At first, it was intended to aid the Loyalists in the South by sending a shipload of munitions from Britain and dispatching to North Carolina a small detachment of troops from the army at Boston. But as more and more optimistic reports of Loyalist strength in the region reached London, the idea of sending a shipment of munitions began to expand into a scheme to dispatch a major expedition. The plan that was finally formulated in October 1775 called for the 32nd and 36th Regiments to be sent from Portsmouth to Cork to reinforce Ireland; while the 15th, 37th, 53rd, 54th and 57th Regiments, which were in Ireland, were to be sent from Cork to North Carolina. On 1 December 1775 they were to sail from Cork with attached artillery and an escort of seven warships,[35] in order to reach North Carolina in the first months of 1776, at which time the loyalists were to rise against the rebels. General Henry

---

[32] Shute Barrington, *The Political Life of William Wildman Viscount Barrington* (London, 1814), pp. 140–50. Perhaps Barrington was against sending an army to America because he thought that it would be difficult to find the required number of men; see Bonamy Dobrée, (ed.), *The Letters of King George III* (London, 1935), p. 111.
[33] E.g. *Parliamentary History*, vol. XVIII, p. 209; J. W. Fortescue, *A History of the British Army* (London, 1902), Vol. III, pp. 168–71; Eric Robson (ed.), *Letters from America, 1773–1780* (New York, 1950), pp. 17–18.
[34] Eric Robson, 'The expedition to the southern colonies, 1775–1776', *English Historical Review* (October, 1951), vol. LXVI, pp. 538–9.
[35] *Solebay, Bristol, Active, Sphinx, Actaeon, Friendship* and *Thunder* (bomb).

Clinton, who was at Boston, was to meet the expedition off Cape Fear and take command of the troops.[36]

At this point, all the weaknesses in British military planning and administration began to assert themselves, for the ministry's military plans had outrun the administrative ability of the government to equip promptly and dispatch the intended expedition to the southern colonies. In 1757 it took more than six months to raise and send 3,000 troops to America.[37] In 1775 the government was attempting to dispatch five regiments in a month. This left the government with no margin of error for administrative delays or delays occasioned by bad weather. The organization of the expedition began smoothly enough: by the beginning of November twenty-one transports, a total of 5,959 tons, had been assembled to move the two regiments from England to Ireland and the five regiments from Cork to North Carolina. But the ordnance Board failed to produce the required ordnance transports and one of the naval escorts had to be repaired. Then on 25 October, the 28th Regiment and seven companies of the 46th Regiment were added to the expedition. The 32nd and 36th Regiments did not leave Portsmouth until 12 December, and only to encounter bad weather in the Channel, which delayed the arrival of the transports in Ireland. Finally, on 8 January 1776 all the troops of the expedition were embarked, but the force did not sail until 17 February because the naval escort failed to appear promptly. Still their problems were not over. A few days after leaving Cork, the expedition encountered bad weather; the ships were dispersed and three transports were forced back to the British Isles. It was not until May 1776 that the force from Cork began to assemble off Cape Fear.[38]

Ill-conceived and mismanaged, the expedition to the southern colonies proved a waste of time, ships and lives. The force from Cork arrived too late to help the Loyalists of North Carolina who, according to plan, had taken up arms only to be crushed by the Americans on 27 February 1776 at the Battle of Moore's Bridge. General Henry Clinton, who met the expedition off North Carolina, and Commodore Sir Peter Parker, the naval commander of the force, were to transform what was already a fiasco into a débâcle by deciding to attack Charleston, South Carolina. This decision was

[36] Robson, 'Expedition . . .', pp. 539–43.
[37] C. R. Middleton, 'A reinforcement for America, 1757', *Bulletin of the Institute of Historical Research* (May 1968), vol. XLI, pp. 57–72.
[38] PRO, ADM 1/486, f. 51: Robson, 'Expedition . . .', pp. 543–54; David Syrett, *Shipping and the American War, 1775–83* (London, 1970), pp. 194–5.

without strategic logic and could only have been made with an eye to personal glory. Their instructions called for them to proceed to New York in time to take part in the invasion, but having some time to kill and a large expedition to play with, Clinton and Parker set off to take the largest city in the South. They must certainly have been aware, if only dimly, of the folly of attacking Charleston. Clinton did not believe that Charleston, if it was fortified, could be captured without a seige, which the British force had neither the time nor the artillery to undertake. And if Charleston could be taken, how was it with the means at Clinton's and Parker's disposal to be garrisoned, supplied and held? Further, the expedition from Cork, if it managed to take Charleston, would find itself in much the same situation as the army at Boston, that is penned up to no purpose in an American city. The seizure of some offshore island, such as Sullivan's Island, would be ridiculous, for it could neither be supplied nor defended. In 1776 a British base on an island off the coast of South Carolina would be isolated, and would most likely suffer the same fate as the garrison of Fort Sumter in 1861. Yet on 31 May, the Clinton–Parker expedition, without a meaningful strategic objective, sailed from Cape Fear for Charleston.[39]

On 1 June 1776 the British force arrived off Charleston Bar, and with the advantage of surprise might have captured the city if the British warships had entered Charleston Harbor immediately. However, the chance was lost, bad weather set in and it was not until 9 June that Clinton's troops landed on Long Island (now the Isle of Palms). The choice of Long Island was a mistake. The objective of the landing was a fortification on Sullivan's Island, which guarded the entrance to Charleston Harbor. Clinton's plan called for landing first on Long Island, because there was less surf there than on Sullivan's Island, and then for the army to pass across the narrow body of water between the two islands and attack the American fort from behind. But the channel between the two islands turned out to be not 18 inches but 7 feet deep at low water; and before Clinton could collect the boats required to undertake a shore-to-shore assault on the northern end of Sullivan's Island, the Americans emplaced two field-pieces to prevent any attempt at landing. At this point, with his troops immobilized on Long Island, all desire for further offensive action appears to have left Clinton.[40]

---

[39] Robson, 'Expedition . . .', pp. 553–5; William B. Willcox, *Portrait of A General: Sir Henry Clinton in the War of Independence* (New York, 1964), pp. 77–86; Williard M. Wallace, *Appeal to Arms* (New York, 1951), pp. 90–1.
[40] Willcox, *op. cit.*, p. 87.

Parker apparently did not desire, nor see the need for, the assistance of the army in forcing an entrance into Charleston Harbor. The commodore made almost no attempt to co-ordinate his actions with Clinton and resolved to overpower the American fortification at the southern end of Sullivan's Island with naval gunfire.[41]

On the morning of 28 June, with a favourable wind and floodtide, Parker began the naval attack on Sullivan's Island. Parker's plan called for a heavy division consisting of HMS *Solebay*, HMS *Bristol* and HMS *Active* to bombard the American fort from the south, while another division consisting of HMS *Sphinx*, HMS *Actaeon* and HMS *Syren* was to proceed past the heavy division in order to enfilade the western side of the fortification. HM Bombship *Thunder* and HMS *Friendship* were to fire on the American position from the south-east.

As the British warships approached the crude log fortification on Sullivan's Island, it must not have appeared to be a very impressive position. However, the fort was commanded by Colonel William Moultrie, an old Indian fighter not given to panic because of a mere display of force. Armed with thirty heavy cannon mounted behind palmetto logs enclosing dirt walls 16 feet thick, the American fortification would not be easy to subdue with naval gunfire alone.

From the start of the attack everything went wrong for the British. After firing several rounds, the *Thunder's* mortar became dismounted. The division of ships assigned to attack the west side of the fort ran aground on the Middle Ground Shoal, where later Fort Sumter would be built, and it took several hours to refloat them. The *Actaeon*, a new twenty-gun frigate which could not be got off, had to be burnt by her crew. Under Parker's personal direction, the heavy division anchored at 11 a.m. within half a musket shot of the American fort and opened fire. At close range, naval gunfire, because of its great weight and volume, is awesome; yet the American guns under the command of Moultrie returned slow but extremely destructive fire directed mainly at the *Experiment* and the *Bristol*, both of which suffered heavy casualties and great damage. At one point during the engagement, the *Bristol's* cable was cut, the ship swung stern to Sullivan's Island and the American artillery raked her with such effect that every man, with the exception of Parker, who had his trousers shot off and suffered wounds in his

---

[41] Parker sent copies of all his correspondence with Clinton to the Admiralty: NRS, *Sandwich Papers*, vol. I, pp. 129–43.

legs, was cleared from the quarterdeck. The British losses were heavy: 64 dead and 161 wounded. They would have been far greater had not the Americans run short of ammunition, for owing to the unfavourable state of the tides, Parker was not able to withdraw his shattered force from before Sullivan's Island until 9 p.m.[42]

The attack on Charleston failed because it was hastily organized and badly executed. While the object was the American fort on Sullivan's Island, Clinton landed his soldiers on Long Island without bothering to find out if a ford between the two islands did indeed exist. And when Parker decided to attack the fort with his ships, he made almost no effort to enlist the support of the army. In fact throughout the whole campaign Clinton and Parker scarcely met each other, much less attempted to plan a joint course of action. Aside from the loss of the *Actaeon* and the casualties suffered, the whole affair made the British throughout America look ridiculous. For the Loyalists in the South, Moore's Bridge and Charleston crushed any hopes they had of military assistance. After the beating Parker' squadron took off Sullivan's Island, there was nothing else to do but embark Clinton's troops and proceed to New York, where on 2 August the force arrived.

While the expedition to the southern colonies had weakened the British plan to concentrate their ships and troops in one massive campaign directed at New York, the American invasion of Canada forced the government to abandon altogether the principle of concentration of force. At the end of December 1775 news arrived in London of the American invasion of Canada. On 23 December 1775, dispatches arrived from Quebec stating that the main British force in Canada had been shattered by American invaders before Montreal, another American force had burst from the wilderness at Port Levis and Quebec City, with its small garrison and weak defences, was under siege. This news forced the government to alter radically its plans for the forthcoming campaign in America. The relief of Quebec and the reconquest of Canada now had to take priority over the invasion of New York.[43]

On 26 December 1775, Lord George Germain, the secretary of state responsible for the conduct of the war in America, and Sir Hugh Palliser, a lord of the Admiralty, met to plan the immediate relief of Quebec. They decided that the city should be succoured as soon as possible by a small force,[44] so on 4 January 1776 orders were

---

[42] Willcox, *op. cit.*, p. 88; Wallace, *op. cit.*, pp. 92–6.
[43] Piers Mackesy, *The War for America, 1775-1783* (London, 1964), pp. 56–7.
[44] NMM, SAN/T/7, 27 December 1775.

issued for the 29th Regiment to embark on a fifty-gun ship, two frigates, one sloop of war, two transports and three victuallers.[45] This force sailed from the Nore on 10 February and broke the American siege of Quebec on 6 May, when HMS *Isis*, HMS *Martin* and HMS *Surprise* reached the city.[46] This marked the opening of the campaign of 1776.

While undertaking the reconquest of Canada, the government's primary objective remained the crushing of the rebellion in America in one campaign. It could not be the massive concentration of force originally planned; none the less, they hoped to end the rebellion and retake Canada as well by reinforcing the squadron in North America to seventy ships and by transporting 27,480 infantry, the 16th Light Dragoons and 1,000 horses from Europe to North America in time to begin operations in the spring of 1776. As the scheme was explained to Sandwich, the troops were to be dispatched in four divisions. The first division was to be sent to Quebec aboard 15,880 tons of transports and to be comprised of 5,300 British and 2,280 Brunswick troops. The second division was to proceed to New York and to be made up of 8,200 Hessians, 3,500 Highlanders and 1,000 Guards requiring 27,000 tons of transports. The third division, consisting of Brunswick and Hanau troops, was to be sent to Quebec. The fourth and last group was destined for New York and would be made up of 4,000 Hessians, the 16th Light Dragoons and 1,000 horses embarked on 28,000 tons of shipping.[47] The success of this plan depended absolutely on skilful administration and speed, for everyone in authority agreed that the force had to arrive in North America in the early spring of 1776 if the rebellion were to be crushed in one decisive campaign.[48] This trans-Atlantic troop movement was an unprecedented administrative and military challenge.

General Eisenhower is reputed to have exclaimed in 1942: 'Ships! Ships! All we need is ships!'[49] A similar cry must have echoed throughout Whitehall in the first weeks of 1776. On 6 January 1776, Palliser stated the problem when he informed Sandwich, 'we are now required to provide (as it were instantly) more transports than the greatest number employed in the last war, which were years in

---

[45] PRO, ADM 1/14, 31, f.5.
[46] CL, Sackville-Germain Papers, vol. 4, 14 May 1776.
[47] NRS, *Sandwich Papers*, vol. p. 77; NMM, SAN/T.1, 6 February 1776.
[48] CL, Sackville-Germain Papers, vol. 4, 17 December 1775; PRO, CO 5/92, f. 312; CO 5/93, ff. 33-4; G, nos 1699, 1760; Carter, *op. cit.*, Vol. II, p. 203.
[49] Quoted in Arthur Bryant, *The Turn of the Tide, 1939-1943* (London, 1957), p. 344.

growing to that number'. The lord of the Admiralty then went on to say that everything 'that can be effected by zeal, duty, and money, will be done'.[50] The government departments that chartered transports – the Treasury, Victualling, Ordnance and Navy Boards – co-ordinated, for the first and only time, their procurement policies in an effort to obtain the required transport tonnage. Advertisements for chartering ships to the government for use as transports appeared in the London newspapers. Agents were sent to the outports and to Holland and Germany in an effort to hire additional transport tonnage, and the freight rates offered for shipping by the government were steadily increased during the first months of 1776 in an effort to attract ships into government service.[51]

Despite titanic efforts on the part of such government departments as the Navy Board and the Treasury, the chartering and fitting out of the shipping required to carry the army to North America were subject to a number of delays, some of which delays were avoidable while others were not. The unusually severe winter of 1775–76 slowed up the fitting out of transports at Deptford, but a number of delays were the result of administrative ineptitude: the Customs Service systematically impeded the fitting out of transports by subjecting the vessels to such customs procedures as extensive searches; the regulations banning the shipment of munitions by sea retarded the arming of transports; and Germain's office put forward a number of schemes for sending transports to the West Indies that would divert badly needed tonnage from the main task of conveying troops to North America.[52] But above all, it was the sheer size of the task that tended to make difficulties that resulted in delays.

By 2 February the Navy Board had assembled at British ports 101 transports totalling 38,996 tons. The majority of these ships were to be used to transport the first division of troops bound for Canada. Nineteen of the transports were sent to the Elbe River to embark 2,932 Brunswick and Hanau troops. The embarkation was completed on 26 March, and at the beginning of April the German troops were joined at sea off Plymouth by transports carrying the 21st Regiment. Then on 20 April, off Cork, the force was met by thirty-four transports carrying six regiments from Ireland and one from

[50] NRS, *Sandwich Papers*, vol. I, p. 97.
[51] For an account of the measures taken to charter transports see Syrett *op. cit.*, pp. 90–3.
[52] For an account of the obstacles encountered in assembling transports at the beginning of 1776 see ibid., pp. 198–200.

Scotland. Escorted by four warships,[53] this force proceeded to Quebec where it arrived on 20 May. The arrival of this reinforcement from Europe, in addition to the 47th Regiment which had arrived from Halifax, increased the number of king's troops in Canada to over 11,000.[54]

The sailing of the Hessians and Guards for America was delayed by a shortage of shipping. Until the end of April enough transports had not been assembled in the Weser River to embark the Hessian troops, and even then two regiments and a part of a third, as well as a quantity of baggage and stores, had to be left in Germany. The transports with the Hessians arrived at Portsmouth at the beginning of May and joined other transports carrying 1,103 Guards, a year's supply of camp equipage for 26 battalions of British infantry and large numbers of wagons and flat-bottomed boats. But again, owing to a shortage of shipping, 107 wagons and some camp equipage had to be left at Portsmouth. On 7 May, embarked on 70 transports, 2 storeships, 2 ordnance transports and 9 navy victuallers escorted by 7 warships[55] commanded by Commodore William Hotham, the force sailed from Portsmouth and arrived at Staten Island on 12 August. The arrival of the Guards and the Hessians at Staten Island brought the strength of the British army before New York up to 25,000 men; one British officer thought that it was 'for its numbers . . . one of the finest that ever was seen'.[56]

The second group of reinforcements to be sent to America and Canada was assembled at Spithead in June. The 16th Light Dragoons, 950 horses, 4,200 Hessians and 680 Waldeckers were to go to New York, while 2,148 Brunswick and Hanau troops were bound for Canada. The embarkation having been completed by late June, and then the second echelon of reinforcements sailed for North America. The German troops arrived at Quebec on 14 September, and the second division of Hessians, the horses and the 16th Light Dragoons were off Sandy Hook on 18 October 1776.[57]

The conveyance of reinforcements to North America in 1776 was a considerable achievement in the organization of seaborne transport. By the summer of 1776 the Navy Board had 416 transports engaged

---

[53] 9th, 20th, 24th, 34th, 62nd, and 53rd Regiments from Ireland and the 31st Regiment from Scotland; the naval escort consisted of *Juno, Pearl, Carysfort* and *Blonde*: NDAR, vol. IV, p. 1048.
[54] Syrett, *op. cit.*, pp. 200-2.
[55] *Preston, Rainbow, Emerald, Brune, Jersey, Carcass* and *Stromboli*: NDAR vol. IV, p. 1103.
[56] Syrett, *Shipping*, pp. 202-4.
[57] Ibid., pp. 204-5.

in carrying troops, while the Treasury had another 76 ships transporting army provisions across the Atlantic.[58] According to an official at the Treasury, 'The country is drained of ships for transport purposes'.[59] Yet the undertaking was a failure. Great efforts were made to procure shipping and great success was achieved in obtaining, fitting out and organizing transports, but the troops intended for America did not arrive at New York until August, which was very late in the summer and perhaps too late for a decisive campaign to be conducted.

The late arrival of reinforcements at New York in 1776 was, for the most part, a result of the British government's administrative failures and strategic miscalculations. The major military objective in 1776 was to form a large army at New York in the early spring. However, the American invasion of Canada forced the ministry to choose between New York and Canada. Because of the shortage of ships, the government could not mount campaigns simultaneously for the invasion of New York and the relief of Canada. The strategic mistake in 1776 was to allow the expedition to the southern colonies to sail. News of the invasion of Canada reached London on 23 December 1775, which was more than enough time to prevent Parker from sailing. If the expedition to the southern colonies had been cancelled, over 20 transports would have been available and, perhaps, the relief of Canada and the reinforcements for American could have sailed simultaneously.[60] Compounding strategic errors was the fact that the ministry's strategic plans for 1776 were beyond the administrative capabilities of an eighteenth-century government. In 1776 it was impossible to avoid delays when assembling and co-ordinating the movements of thousands of troops and hundreds of ships in such separated and distant places as the Thames, Cork, the Clyde and Germany.

The British bid to crush the rebellion in America with one mighty campaign opened on 22 August 1776 when, under the guns of the Royal Navy, British infantry landed at Gravesend, Long Island. The American Declaration of Independence had been issued more than a month before when the summer was almost over and only a few months of the campaigning season remained. The question in everybody's mind was whether there was enough time left before the onset of winter to inflict a decisive defeat on the Americans or whether the reinforcements from Europe had arrived so late as to

---

[58] Ibid., p. 249.
[59] HMC, *American MSS.*, vol. I, p. 37.
[60] Syrett, *Shipping*, pp. 206–8.

preclude a decisive victory. If Rommel's famous dictum that before the fighting proper, the battle is fought and decided by the quartermasters[61] is correct, then the British bid for decisive victory in 1776 had already failed. Only the generalship and statesmanship of the British commanders in chief in America – General Sir William Howe and Admiral Lord Howe – could prove otherwise.

Infant insurgent nations are not inevitably triumphant on the field of battle. The Confederacy was crushed by force of arms and the Boer Republics were destroyed by military power. And perhaps in 1776 the rebellion in America could have been crushed if the British had waged war with the relentlessness of a Grant, a Sherman or a Kitchener. But the Howes, the only British commanders to have an opportunity to destroy the rebellion in America by force of arms, proved themselves singularly incapable of waging a war of annihilation. Ambivalent at best towards the revolution in America, the Howes in 1776 were confronted with a problem the military solution of which, if it existed at all, could only be obtained by waging war with ruthlessness and determination. The Howes were products of the *ancien régime*, and as such they were probably doomed to failure when confronted by revolution in America.[62]

Admiral Howe had one of the longest and most distinguished careers in the history of the Royal Navy: he quelled the mutiny at Spithead, was the victor of the Glorious First of June and, during the American war, began the reformation in tactics and signalling that made possible the great naval victories of the French Revolutionary

---

[61] Robson, *Revolution*, p. 102.
[62] The enigma surrounding the Howes is greatly enhanced because there is no collection of Howe papers. For the period of the Howes' command in America there are the official dispatches in PRO, ADM 1/487-8; CO 5/93-5, 177, 236; there are scattered throughout the papers of contemporary military, naval and political figures Howe letters. These documents, whether they are in the PRO or elsewhere, for the most part tell what happened, but almost never why. In addition, there has been little of worth written about the Howes in America. The few modern studies consist of T.S. Anderson, *The Command of the Howe Brothers during the American Revolution* (New York, 1933); Ira D. Gruber, *The Howe Brothers and the American Revolution* (New York, 1972); Maldwyn A. Jones, 'Sir William Howe: conventional strategist', in George Athan Billias (ed.), *George Washington's Opponents* (New York, 1969), pp. 39–72; Worthington C, Ford, 'Parliament and the Howes', *Massachusetts Historical Society Proceedings* (October, 1910), vol. XLIV, pp. 120–43. After exhausting this small list, one is left with such works as Bellamy Partridge, *Sir Billy Howe* (London, 1932), a popularized and unreliable work, and the biography by Sir John Barrow, *The Life of Richard Earl Howe* (London, 1838), which is not much use to modern students of the American war; see also David Syrett, 'A checklist of Admiral Lord Howe Manuscripts in United States Archives and Libraries', *Mariner's Mirror* (August 1982), vol. 67, pp. 273–84.

and Napoleonic Wars.[63] But Admiral Howe viewed the rebellion in America as a personal as well as a political tragedy, for his family had close ties with Massachusetts. Howe's older brother, George, was one of the most popular British officers to serve in America during the Seven Years War, and when he was killed before Ticonderoga, the General Court of Massachusetts had a monument to George Howe erected at Westminster Abbey.[64] Remembering this gesture, wishing above all for reconciliation between America and Britain and, at the same time, having the ambition to think of saving the British empire in terms of his own personal glory, as early as 1774 Howe offered his services to the government as a peacemaker and mediator. He did not want to negotiate a major constitutional settlement, but rather believed that the right words stated in a kindly tone by a person of obvious good intentions would go a long way towards settling the dispute. The government, believing that the rebellion had to be defeated by armed might, repeatedly rejected Howe's offer until the autumn of 1775. At this time, thinking that the king's forces would destroy the rebellion in 1776, the government decided to employ Howe simply as a commissioner to accept American surrender. But Howe, not wanting merely to accept the surrender of the Americans and hoping to reach a true reconciliation, immediately began demanding wider powers from the ministry.[65]

At this point, fate, politics and personal ambition all combined to make Admiral Lord Howe the navy's commander-in-chief in America, as well as a peace commissioner. At the beginning of December 1775, Admiral Sir Charles Saunders died, vacating the office of Lieutenant-General of the Marines, a sinecure worth about £1,200 a year that Lord North had already promised to Howe. Forgetting his promise, North permitted Admiral Sir Hugh Palliser, Sandwich's right-hand man at the Admiralty, to be appointed to the position, whereupon Howe, who was on good personal terms with King George III and politically well connected, threatened to resign his commission in the navy.[66] Something had to be done to pacify Howe, and after several weeks of negotiation, the admiral indicated that he would be satisfied with an appointment as the navy's commander-in-chief in America. Over the strong objections of

---

[63] For an account of Lord Howe's tactical and signal innovations, see NRS, *Fighting Instructions 1530-1816*, and NRS, *Signals and Instructions, 1776-94*.
[64] [J. A. Holden], 'Description of the Howe Monument, Westminster Abbey', *New York State Historical Association Proceedings* (1911), vol. X., pp. 323-5.
[65] The best account of the negotiations resulting in Lord Howe's appointment as navy commander-in-chief in America is Gruber, *op. cit.*, pp. 50-71.
[66] NRS, *Sandwich Papers*, vol. II, pp. 201-2.

Sandwich, who did not want to relieve Shuldham, the ministry accepted the offer, and Shuldham became, as he put it, 'the football of Fortune'.[67] The appointment of Howe to the American command was not without its ironies and difficulties. Of the admiral's two immediate superiors, it is said that Howe hated Sandwich and had refused to speak to Germain since the raid on St Malo in 1758.[68] No doubt, Howe sought the American command not only to further his naval career, but also as a means of strengthening his hand as a peace commissioner, while the ministry appointed the admiral to pay off a political debt and also to place a highly competent professional in the American command.[69]

The ministry must have understood Howe's attitude towards the American rebellion, but it also expected him to do his duty, and when it came to drafting the admiral's orders the government clearly indicated that the rebels be crushed by force of arms. Under the terms of the peace commission, Howe along with his brother, General Sir William Howe, could accept the surrender of the Americans but could not discuss the terms of reconciliation or suspend hostilities until the American rebels had restored royal authority, dissolved their illegal governments and disbanded their military forces.[70] Admiral Howe was ordered to blockade the American coast in order to destroy American seaborne trade and to deny the rebels arms from Europe and the West Indies while, at the same time, directly assisting the army in smashing the revolt. Furthermore, Howe was specifically ordered to destroy American armed vessels, protect Loyalists, attack towns that were in a state of open rebellion, impress rebel seamen, remove all obstacles and fortifications from American ports and seize supplies for the king's service.[71]

The British at New York in the summer of 1776 had the best opportunity of the entire war for inflicting on the Americans a decisive defeat. By the third week in August the British forces at Staten Island had grown to an army of some 25,000 highly trained and well-equipped troops supported by thirty-three warships, scores

---

[67] NRS, *Sandwich Papers*, vol. I, pp. 44, 119–20. Shuldham's disappointment was somewhat lessened by being promoted to a vice-admiral of the blue and made an Irish baron.
[68] G. Cornwallis-West, *The Life and Letters of Admiral Cornwallis* (London, 1927), pp. 55–6.
[69] Gruber, *op. cit.*, pp. 64–71.
[70] HMC, *Sixth Report of the Royal Commission on Historical Manuscripts, Pt. I*, pp. 400–1.
[71] PRO, ADM 2/1332, pp. 216–72; ADM 2/100, 4 May 1776.

of transports and all the special equipment required to conduct large-scale amphibious operations.[72] New York, on the other hand, was held by 19,000 ill-trained, poorly led and badly equipped Americans without naval support. The American forces were stationed in extremely exposed and weak positions, for New York City was indefensible against a combined naval and land attack. Guns mounted on Brooklyn Heights commanded the city, but in order to maintain that position General Washington had to occupy Brooklyn, which in itself was indefensible. The Americans could not prevent the British from landing on Long Island in overpowering strength, while units of the Royal Navy entered the East River to block the retreat of the garrison at Brooklyn. Furthermore, if the British boldly exploited their amphibious mobility, not only the enemy garrison at Brooklyn, but also the entire American army at New York possibly could be enveloped and destroyed. The effects of the capture or destruction of Washington's army at Manhattan in August 1776 would be beyond calculation. Since the Americans had only one army, the Declaration of Independence had been issued only a few weeks before, and Loyalism was still a political power, the rebellion in America might not have been able to withstand military ruin at New York.

As early as July 12 the extreme strategic weakness of the American position at New York was revealed when HMS *Phoenix*, HMS *Rose* and HMS *Trial* ran the American batteries at the entrance of the Hudson River and broke into the Tappan Zee, threatening American east-west communications south of the Hudson Highlands and demonstrating the vulnerability of the western flank of the American forces at New York.[73] However, with the exception of Clinton, who was not the most brilliant of soldiers, no one appears to have seen the importance of forcing the mouth of the Hudson as a prelude to enveloping the entire American army. Of the top British commanders, Clinton alone saw that the strategic key to New York was Kingsbridge in the Bronx. If a British force could occupy

---

[72] On 13 August 1776 there were at New York the *Eagle, Asia, Chatham, Preston, Centurion, Renown, Rainbow, Emerald, Repulse, Flora, Greyhound, Solebay, Swan, Tamar, Stromboli, Thunder, Carcass, St Lawrence, Adventure, Senegal, Brune, Niger, Kingsfisher, Halifax, Phoenix, Rose* and *Trial*; in American waters and en route for New York were *Bristol, Experiment, Syren, Roebuck, Fowey and Otter*: PRO, ADM 1/487, ff. 55–6. For an account of British amphibious techniques see David Syrett, 'The methodology of British amphibious operations during the Seven Years War and the American war', *Mariner's Mirror* (August 1973), vol. 58, pp. 269–80.
[73] NRS, *Sandwich Papers*, vol. I, pp. 149–54.

Kingsbridge before Washington managed to evacuate Brooklyn, New York City and Fort Washington, the American army would be trapped. Following this line of reasoning, Clinton proposed that British naval power and amphibious capabilities be exploited by passing a corps up the Hudson, landing at Spuyten Duyvil at the western end of the Harlem River and seizing Kingsbridge.[74] Although General Howe at first seemed quite taken with Clinton's scheme, in the end it was discarded, for as early as 7 June the commander-in-chief had decided to attack New York by way of Gravesend and Brooklyn.[75]

The British campaign at New York opened on 22 August 1776, when under the guns of warships British infantry from Staten Island, in a superbly executed shore-to-shore amphibious assault, landed at Gravesend Bay on Long Island. Then, on the night of 26 August, the British army went on the offensive. In a masterly series of manoeuvres the American forces in Brooklyn were outflanked, surprised, beaten on the field of battle and driven in panic into the weak fortifications at Brooklyn Heights. The only thing that saved the Americans from being killed, captured or driven into the East River was that General Howe ordered, though there were several hours of daylight left, that the attack be broken off and that the American position at Brooklyn Heights be reduced by regular siege operations. In an attempt to divert the attention of the Americans, Lord Howe had ordered five warships[76] to proceed 'higher up the Channel towards the Town of New York' as the army advanced towards Brooklyn Heights. In the face of a north wind, the effort was only halfheartedly carried out, and only the *Roebuck* got near enough to the Americans to exchange a 'few random' shots with an enemy battery at Red Hook. Shortly thereafter, with the onset of the ebb tide, the admiral called off the operation. As a result, on the night of 29–30 August, while the British army was still preparing for the 'siege' of Brooklyn Heights, Washington evacuated Brooklyn under the cover of bad weather without the slightest hindrance from the Royal Navy.[77]

With the American evacuation of Brooklyn Heights, New York City became the next British objective. The American army on Manhattan was in a desperate situation, and some British observers

---

[74] Willcox, *op. cit.*, p. 104.
[75] HMC, *Stopford–Sackville MSS.*, vol. 11, p. 33.
[76] *Asia, Renown, Preston, Roebuck* and *Repulse*.
[77] PRO, ADM 1/487, ff. 60–1.

ONE DECISIVE CAMPAIGN, 1776

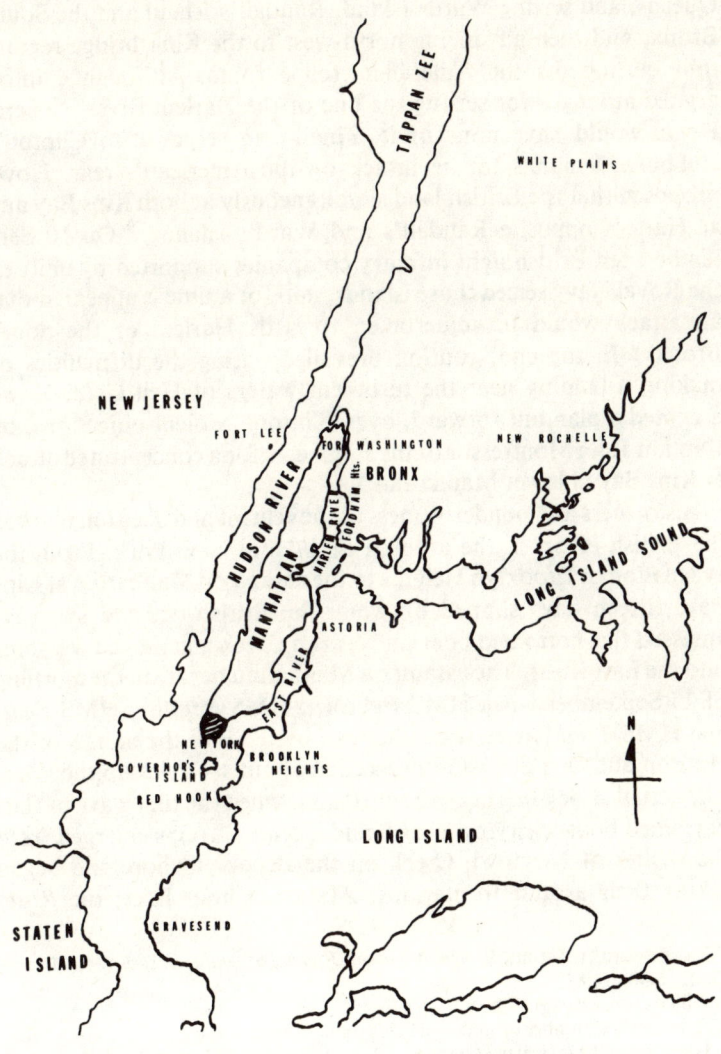

Map 4
New York in 1776

believed that Washington was already withdrawing from the city.[78] Clinton, however, thought that the opportunity still existed to trap the entire American army on Manhattan if the British moved quickly and exploited their amphibious mobility to seize Kingsbridge. Clinton advocated launching an amphibious attack from Astoria and Queens, and seizing Wards Island, Randall's Island and the South Bronx, and then advancing north-west to the Kingsbridge region, thus cutting off the American escape route. Although Clinton argued at length for seizing the line of the Harlem River, General Howe would have none of it. Finally, in response to Clinton's stubborn demands for an attack on the American's rear, Howe proposed that the British land simultaneously at both Kips Bay and at Harlem opposite Randall's and Ward's islands.[79] On 10 September, ten British light infantry companies supported by units of the Royal Navy seized those islands, and for a time it appeared that an attack would be undertaken towards Harlem or the South Bronx.[80] In the end, caution prevailed; citing the difficulties of making a landing near the turbulent waters of Hell Gate, Howe accepted a plan put forward, over Clinton's violent objections, by Captain John Montressor of the Engineers for a concentrated attack at Kips Bay in lower Manhattan.[81]

A slowness and ponderousness of movement and decision marked the British effort in the autumn of 1776 at New York. From the evacuation of Brooklyn Heights to the assault on Manhattan at Kips Bay, fifteen days slipped by while the British debated strategy, amassed flat-bottomed boats in Newton Creek and moved warships into the East River. The assault on Manhattan began on the morning of 15 September when HMS *Renown*, HMS *Repulse*, HMS *Pearl* and HMS *Trial* passed the American batteries at the mouth of the Hudson and as a diversion proceeded about six miles up the river. The actual attack began at about 10 a.m. when the first wave of flat-bottomed boats carrying British and German troops emerged from the shelter of Newtown Creek on the Brooklyn shore and began taking their assault formations. About an hour later, the *Rose*,

---

[78] E.g. Edward H. Tatum, Jr, *The American Journal of Ambrose Serle* (San Marino, Calif., 1940), p. 88.
[79] Willcox, *op. cit.*, pp. 108–9.
[80] Apparently a number of junior officers thought that an attack on the south Bronx or Harlem was the logical next step: e.g. *Diary of Frederick Mackenzie: Giving a Daily Narrative of His Military Service as an Officer of the Regiment of Royal Welch Fusiliers during the years 1775-1781 in Massachusetts, Rhode Island and New York* (Cambridge, 1930), Vol. I, pp. 38, 42–3, 46.
[81] NYHSC, *The Montressor Journals*, p. 121.

Roebuck, Phoenix, Orpheus and *Carysfort*, which had been anchored under cover of darkness in a line broadside to the shore, opened an extremely heavy and rapid fire at the landing-site. In 45 minutes of firing the *Orpheus* expended 5,376 lb of gunpowder. This violent bombardment drove the American defenders from the landing-site; and at noon the first wave of king's troops, under the command of Clinton, landed at Kips Bay without opposition. The British advanced as far inland as Murray Hill (now about 38th Street and Park Avenue), cutting the Post Road and then halted for several hours until the rest of the army had landed and the position was consolidated before resuming the advance. The failure of the British to drive immediately across Manhattan to the Hudson River, cutting both the Bloomingdale Road and the Post Road, gave several thousand American troops the opportunity to escape from New York City. The British resumed the offensive at about 5 p.m. and by the end of the day had cleared Manhattan of American troops south of McGown's Pass (roughly the present 96th Street). At this point, the advance of the British army halted for nearly a month while a way was found to manoeuvre the American forces out of their strong positions in northern Manhattan.[82]

The opportunity to trap and destroy the American army at New York by means of an amphibious envelopment had passed forever. After Brooklyn and Kips Bay, Washington had had enough of open battles and resolved: 'We should on all occasions avoid a general action, or put anything to the risk, unless compelled by a necessity into which we ought never to be drawn.'[83] This doctrine became the cornerstone of Washington's strategy. After the loss of lower Manhattan, the American army occupied strong positions at Harlem Heights, Washington Heights, Inwood and Kingsbridge while waiting for the British to make the next move and prepared to retreat into Westchester at a moment's notice.

After the seizure of New York City and lower Manhattan, General Howe concluded that it would take at least another year of fighting to crush the rebellion.[84] Therefore, the British spent the next few weeks consolidating their hold on lower Manhattan by constructing fortifications and in figuring out how to force the Americans from their strongholds in northern Manhattan and Kingsbridge. Finally, after almost a month of inaction, it was decided to dispatch warships

---

[82] PRO, ADM 1/487, ff. 85-6; Willcox, *op. cit.*, pp. 110-12; NRS, *The Journal of Rear-Admiral Bartholomew James*, p. 31; HMC, *Hasting MSS.*, vol. III, pp. 183-4.
[83] Quoted in D.S. Freeman, *George Washington* (New York, 1951), Vol. IV, p. 217.
[84] CL, Sackville-Germain Papers, vol. 5, 25 September 1776.

once more into the Hudson above Fort Washington to threaten and, if possible, cut American east-west communications and to outflank the American army by means of an amphibious landing in the east Bronx. On the morning of 9 October the *Phoenix, Roebuck* and *Tartar* broke through the American river defences at Fort Washington and entered the Tappan Zee, capturing two American armed galleys and driving two others into shallow water. The warships, then out of range of American guns off Tarrytown, effectively stopped American waterborne movement on the Tappan Zee.[85] Then on the night of 11 October, troops, artillery and supplies were embarked on flat-bottomed boats and other small craft at Kips Bay. The force then proceeded up the East River and, in a brilliant feat of seamanship, negotiated the treacherous currents of Hell Gate during a thick fog with only two boats upsetting and two artillery pieces being lost and three men. At 9 a.m. the next morning, British infantry landed on Throgs Neck in the east Bronx and quickly overran the tip of the peninsula, virtually an island connected to the mainland by a bridge. Here the British offensive was checked, for a small detachment of Americans that could not be dislodged had destroyed the bridge and were blocking the only exit from Throgs Neck. Thus, General Howe found himself in a ludicrous position, similar to that of Clinton on Long Island during the attack on the fort at Sullivan's Island. After waiting penned up on Throgs Neck for supplies and reinforcements on the morning of 18 October, the British force re-embarked and then re-landed a short distance up the coast at Pells Point, just below New Rochelle. After another short delay, the British army marched towards White Plains in an attempt to surround the American army between the Bronx and Hudson rivers before it could retreat from Manhattan and Kingsbridge. Washington, however, quickly perceived General Howe's intention, evacuated Manhattan and Kingsbridge with the unwise exception of the garrison of Fort Washington and with the bulk of the Continental Army marched to White Plains, reaching the area before the British and in time to take up a strong defensive position. Here the Americans fought an indecisive defensive battle on 28 October, after which they withdrew northward beyond the Croton River into a strong defensive position.[86]

---

[85] PRO, ADM 1/487, f. 118; see also William Hugh Moomaw, 'The naval career of Captain Hamond, 1775-1779' (unpublished PhD dissertation, University of Virginia, 1955), pp. 270-5.
[86] PRO, ADM 1/487, ff. 118-9; CO 5/236, pp. 2-3; *Diary of Frederick Mackenzie* Vol. I, pp. 76-7, 80, 84-5; Willcox, *op. cit.*, pp. 112-13.

After the battle of White Plains, Howe withdrew southward towards the Bronx in order to attack the isolated American strongholds at Fort Washington and Fort Lee and to drive American troops from New Jersey. On 16 November, Fort Washington was stormed by British and German troops, who mounted amphibious assaults across Spuyten Duyvil and the Harlem River while another body of troops attacked the fortress from the south. Over 2,000 prisoners were taken, and some of the victors argued that Howe should have had them put to the sword, an act of savagery permitted by the laws and customs of war in the eighteenth century. As one British officer noted, 'it would have struck such a panic as would have prevented the Congress from ever being able to raise another army'.[87] Two days later, the Royal Navy landed Lord Cornwallis with 4,500 men eight miles above Fort Lee on the New Jersey shore of the Hudson River. Troops, artillery and supplies were moved rapidly up the Palisades; then the British advanced quickly on Fort Lee, forcing the American garrison to evacuate the position so hurriedly that it left its tents still standing.[88]

While British and German troops were capturing Forts Washington and Lee, Clinton and Commodore Sir Peter Parker at New York City were preparing an expeditionary force to seize Newport, Rhode Island, which was to be used as a base by the Royal Navy. Clinton objected to the entire project as a strategic blunder. He still thought that enveloping and destroying the American army was the best way to obtain victory. With the American forces in New Jersey rapidly retreating towards the Delaware River and hotly pursued by General Lord Cornwallis's troops, Clinton put forward a number of schemes to have the force intended for Rhode Island transported instead to the Delaware River, Chesapeake Bay or the coast of New Jersey ahead of the retreating Americans, thus trapping them.[89] However, Clinton's strategic advice was rejected once more, and the expedition to Rhode Island sailed from New York on 29 November. As the British invasion force approached Newport, Commodore Esek Hopkins's small squadron[90] fled up Narragansett Bay to Providence. On 9 December, Clinton, with 7,000 troops supported

---

[87] *Diary of Frederick Mackenzie*, Vol. I, p. 111.
[88] PRO, ADM 1/487, ff. 119-20; Willcox, *op. cit*, pp. 122-3.
[89] Willcox, pp. 115-16. Clinton was not the only British officer thinking along these lines; see, for example, NYHSC, *Kemble Papers*, vol. I, pp. 104-5; *Diary of Frederick Mackenzie*, Vol. I, p. 99.
[90] PRO, ADM 1/487, f. 153.

by fifteen warships,[91] landed on Rhode Island and occupied Newport without opposition.[92]

The British effort to crush the rebellion in America in one campaign at New York ended in December 1776 with the occupation of Newport and the flight of an apparently disintegrating American army into Pennsylvania. The king's troops went into winter quarters and set up a string of posts in New Jersey along the Delaware River. The British had swept all before them, for with the exception of a skirmish at Harlem Heights, in every battle of the campaign the Americans had been driven from every position they had occupied, and at the end of the campaign General Howe's soldiers controlled Staten Island, Long Island, the Bronx, Manhattan, a large region of New Jersey, and Newport, Rhode Island. But the campaign around New York was not a decisive victory, for the Continental Army had not been destroyed. In fact the conduct of the British commanders during the campaign was, at the very least, puzzling.

The campaign around New York in 1776 raises questions not only about the Howes, but also about the entire British conduct of the war, that have continued to defy answers. Perhaps the answers will never be found, for the Howes in word or deed never fully revealed their intentions. Were the Howes interested solely in occupying strategic points, such as New York City, or was their objective the destruction of the American army, something they failed to achieve because of their caution, lack of vigour or bad generalship? Why did the Howes never attempt fully to exploit the advantages of British naval power and amphibious mobility at New York to envelop the enemy as proposed by Clinton on several occasions? Why before the opening of the land attack at Brooklyn, did not Admiral Howe move warships into the East River, so that the British army could drive the Americans into the guns of the Royal Navy? And why did General Howe halt the British attack on Brooklyn Heights just at the moment of victory? Perhaps the easiest answer to these questions and the many others raised by the campaign around New York was that the Howes did not see that an absolute prerequisite for ending the rebellion in America by force of arms, was the destruction of Washington's army. Maybe it is too much to ask that the Howes, who were so far removed in time and thought from the advent of

---

[91] *Sphinx, Kingsfisher, Ambuscade, Mercury, Chatham, Preston, Renown, Centurion, Asia, Experiment, Emerald, Brune, Cerberus, Carysfort* and *Diamond*: PRO ADM 1/487, f. 151.
[92] PRO ADM 1/487, ff. 149–50, 155–6, CO 5.236, pp. 23–4.

total war, should have waged a campaign of annihilation against the Continental Army at New York in 1776.

Both contemporaries and historians have put forward a number of theories to explain the enigma of the Howes. Sir John Fortescue, characteristically, blames the ministry in London for the failure of the campaign.[93] On the other hand, there is a whole school of thought that maintains that the Howes did not want to fight the Americans, but rather to conciliate them, and they at times let their desire for peace override their military judgement.[94] But there are two other factors that must certainly have influenced the Howes to be cautious. American militiamen could be easily replaced, British seamen and the king's soldiers could not. Schemes such as storming fortifications without adequate reconnoitring or moving heavy warships into the confined waters of the East River in the face of American shore batteries could very possibly have resulted in heavy British casualties. A bloodbath such as Bunker Hill was too high a price to pay for a battle that did not break the back of American resistance. Furthermore, they needed to avoid anything that might appear to be a check or defeat. The British advantage was moral and lay in the skill and discipline of their troops and seamen. In many respects, the Continentals were still an armed rabble, but anything that tasted of victory might turn them into an army. Also, in 1776, a British setback or débâcle at New York could have had huge political repercussions. All of this was well understood by the British at New York. As one of them noted, 'One daring attempt, if unsuccessful, would ruin our affairs in this part of the world. And the difficulty of getting troops – and such troops – is so great that we ought not to hazard our men without the evident prospect of accomplishing our purpose.'[95] Exceptionally great commanders see the need for casting these arguments aside at times, but the Howes did not.

Yet the greatest failure for the British in 1776 was not their inability to destroy the American army, but rather the total lack of success of the Royal Navy's effort to blockade the coast. The failure of the blockade in 1776 was the direct result of a number of geographical and strategic problems. There are those, however, who believe that the failure of the blockade can be traced in part to the

---

[93] Fortescue, *op. cit.*, Vol. III, p. 195.
[94] Gruber, *op. cit.*, pp. 350–68; Anderson, *op. cit.*, p. 13; see also E. Stuart Wortley (ed.), *A Prime Minister and His Son* (London, 1925), p. 98; NYHSC, *Montressor Journals*, p. 136.
[95] HMC, *Hastings MSS.*, vol. III, p. 186.

reluctance of Lord Howe to deal harshly with the Americans.[96] His instructions to Commodore William Hotham, dated 15 January 1777, are usually cited as evidence of Howe's unwillingness to conduct ruthlessly the blockade of the southern colonies. In these instructions,[97] Hotham is simultaneously ordered to enforce the Capture Act by seizing or destroying all American ocean-going vessels, and authorized:

> to grant, and it is advisable to take all suitable opportunities to allow, the Inhabitants dwelling upon the Coasts adjacent to the Stations of the Ships under your Orders, to use of their ordinary Fishing-Craft, or other means of providing for their daily subsistence and support; where the same does not seem liable to any material abuse.[98]

These instructions, which by modern standards are conciliatory and moderate in tone, can be interpreted in several different ways. Perhaps Lord Howe was walking a fine line between conciliation and coercion. But then, of course, attacking small fishing-craft would arguably be counterproductive because it would force, by economic necessity, a large section of the American maritime population to seek employment as privateersmen. A similar argument can be applied to schemes for burning American seaports. Mowat reduced Falmouth to ashes and Norfolk was destroyed, but a good case can be made that these acts did not deter or coerce the Americans, but rather hardened their resolve to resist royal authority. More likely, Howe issued these instructions simply because he was not an ideologically inflamed American Loyalist, nor a practitioner of total war, but a man who did not think in terms of total destruction as a means of achieving a military or political objective. In many respects, it is futile to speculate about Lord Howe, for in the last analysis the effectiveness of the blockade of America was determined by factors that did not rest on a desire for a policy of conciliation or coercion.

To show how effective a British blockade of the American coast could be, many have compared the British effort in 1776–77 to the blockade during the War of 1812, but such comparisons are meaningless. At the outbreak of war in 1812, the Royal Navy simply

---

[96] E.g. Gruber, *op. cit.*, pp. 150–2; Anderson, *op. cit.*, pp. 223–4; Don Higginbotham, *The War of American Independence: Military Attitudes, Politics, and Practices, 1763–1783* (New York, 1971), p. 171.
[97] PRO, ADM 1/487, ff. 172–6.
[98] Ibid., f. 172.

transferred the units to America as men and ships became free from operations in Europe. A close blockade could be kept on those islands in the West Indies that were not either allied with or under the control of the British. And in Europe the great focal points of maritime trade, such as the Straits of Gibraltar, the Western Approaches and the Skagerrak, were dominated by the British. Moreover, those ports in Europe that in 1776 served as American depots for the export of munitions had by 1812 been under blockade for years by the Royal Navy.[99] Unlike the beginning of the War of 1812 when the Royal Navy was unrivaled in its control of the seas, the British in 1776 were fighting a major war in America while facing the possibility of war with equal, or possibly superior, European naval powers.

More than anything else, the failure of the coastal blockade in 1776 was the result of a shortage of ships. With only a limited number of ships, the Royal Navy could not with any success simultaneously blockade America, maintain forces in England to guard against the possibility of a French war and deploy ships and men in support of the army in Canada and New York. Because of the danger of a French war, the Admiralty could not commit ships of the line to America;[100] yet Lord Howe's squadron consisting of about 70 warships (for the most part, small ones), 50-gun ships, frigates, sloops of war and other small armed vessels lacked the necessary ships and manpower. Lord Howe had to choose between deploying the bulk of his ships in support of land operations at the expense of the blockade, or strengthening the blockade at the expense of the British army's mobility in America. In many respects, it was not really a choice, for the government's policy called for crushing the rebellion in a single blow at New York in 1776, and clearly the army's operations would not be decisive unless massively supported by the Royal Navy. As General Howe noted in a dispatch to Germain, the shortage of 'Land carriage' made the army in America almost totally dependent upon waterborne transport and incapable of operating more than a few miles from navigable bodies of water.[101] Therefore, Lord Howe had to commit a large number of ships and men in support of land operations in 1776 if the campaign were to be decisive.[102] At the time, it seemed a fair gamble, for if the British army crushed the rebellion during the 1776 campaign, then the

[99] For a discussion of the differences between the British blockades of America in 1776–77 and during the War of 1812 see Mackesy, *op. cit.*, pp. 98–100.
[100] See above, pp. 28–32.
[101] HMC, *Stopford-Sackville MSS.*, vol. II, p. 30.
[102] E.g. PRO, ADM 1/487, ff. 86–7.

blockade was not very important. On the other hand, if the land campaign proved to be indecisive, the lack of an effective blockade would be of the highest importance.

The campaigns during 1776 in Canada and New York, being largely amphibious in nature, required the lifting of the blockade along sections of the American coast. In order to provide the large number of seamen needed to conduct amphibious operations, warships had to be concentrated at New York and in the St Lawrence River. As one Naval officer explained:

> The ships are ill manned and very short. You can have no idea of the number of men it takes to attend upon such an army as this; with the ships we have (which is two thirds of those employed in America) when all the flat boats, galleys, gondolas, horse stages &c &c are mann'd there is scarce men enough left on board many of the ships to move them so that we really want six or eight line of battle ships; not so much perhaps for the use of the ships; as for their large complements of men for the purposes before mentioned.[103]

During the campaign of 1776 the strength of Lord Howe's command averaged 70 ships, of which only two were ships of the line. On 13 August 1776, 27 warships (with an additional six expected to arrive) of Lord Howe's squadron were deployed at New York supporting the army, while 12 more were supporting land operations in Canada; only 24 warships, mostly small ones, were scattered along the coast from Prince Edward Island to St Augustine in what amounted to no more than a token effort to blockade America. By 18 September no ships of the Royal Navy were blockading the entrances of the Chesapeake and Delaware bays, while 33 ships were at New York and nine more in the St Lawrence supporting the army; only 42 ships were left to blockade the entire coast of America. The situation did not change as the campaign of 1776 drew to a close, for on 24 November only 20 ships were on blockade duty while the remaining 54 were deployed in support of the army.[104]

With the end of offensive land operations in December 1776, a number of ships were released from the task of supporting the army. However, because of a lack of repair facilities in America and the need to defend the British positions at New York, Newport and

[103] University of Virginia Libraries, Hamond Papers, Hamond to Stanley, 24 September 1776.
[104] PRO, ADM 1/487, ff. 55-6, 89-90, 135-6.

Halifax, the blockade of the American coast did not markedly increase in effectiveness. New York was the only city in America of great strategic importance: it stood between New England and the middle colonies at the mouth of the Hudson River, which was navigable as far inland as Albany. After its capture in the autumn of 1776, New York became the centre of British operations in America. Based here and utilizing interior lines of communication, British forces could threaten American north-south communications by advancing up the Hudson with amphibious forces. With its large harbour, New York also became the main logistical base for British naval and military forces. However, in order to defend New York, which is laced with navigable waterways, a number of warships had to be stationed there permanently. Newport, Rhode Island and Halifax also required warships for their defence. The number of ships available for blockade duty was further reduced during the winter of 1776-77 by the need to send vessels for careening either to Halifax or Antigua, or to Jamaica, and if a dockyard repair was required, to England. Thus, at any given time during the winter of 1776-77, a substantial number of ships of Lord Howe's squadron were either deployed in static defence or undergoing repairs.

On 5 January 1777, out of 80 ships under the command of Lord Howe, 24 (of which three were under orders to proceed to the West Indies for refitting) were stationed in the New York area. Another 11 were either en route to or about to depart for England. Six were in the St Lawrence River. Another 24 ships based at Rhode Island and Halifax were deployed to blockade the coast of New England or to protect Newport and Nova Scotia. The remaining 15 ships (of which five were under orders to refit in the West Indies and one was unfit for further employment) were assigned the impossible task of attempting to blockade the coast southward from New York to St Augustine. By 1 March 1777 there were 72 ships under Lord Howe's command and still no effective coastal blockade. Twenty-three warships (six of which were refitting) were stationed in the New York area. Two were en route for England. Twenty-four others (of which one was ordered to the West Indies for refitting) were blockading the coasts of New England and protecting Newport and Halifax. Seven other ships were in the St Lawrence, while south of New York the coast was virtually unblockaded with only 16 ships stationed there, of which eleven were either about to depart for, or already proceeding to, the West Indies for refitting.[105] Hence the blockade of the American coast during the winter of 1776-77 failed because of a

[105] Ibid., ff. 178-9, 350-3.

shortage of ships. The need to protect with warships places, such as the St Lawrence River, Halifax, Newport and New York, when coupled with the necessity of sending ships to England, Halifax or the West Indies owing to the lack of careening wharfs and dockyards in America, reduced the force blockading the American coast to the mere rump of the squadron stationed in America.

The failure of the blockade during 1776 had a huge effect on the conduct of the war in America. Even if one measures the success of a blockade simply in terms of ships taken or lost, it was a failure. None of the new Continental frigates got to sea during 1776 partly due to the Royal Navy's blockade, Hopkins's squadron was bottled up at Providence as a result of the occupation of Rhode Island[106] and, between 10 March and 31 December 1776, Lord Howe's squadron recaptured 26 British vessels and took at least 140 American ships;[107] during 1776 American warships and privateers captured or destroyed at least 347 British vessels, including several loaded ordnance storeships and six troop transports.[108] However, the real failure of the Royal Navy's blockade can best be measured by the degree to which the British were able to cut off, or at least retard, the flow of munitions to America from Europe and the West Indies. During the first two years of the war American armies were sustained by foreign munitions, and failure of the coastal blockade in 1776–77 gave the Americans the opportunity to obtain the necessary materials with which to continue the war.[109]

Above all, the attempt to crush in one campaign the rebellion in America during 1776 failed because of the great size and complexity of the enterprise. It was an undertaking without precedent and, in many respects, beyond the physical and administrative capacity of an eighteenth-century government. But when considering the elusiveness of the objective, the unique nature of the conflict, the necessity of conveying thousands of troops across the Atlantic and the vast size of America, and the physical, administrative and strategic problems of the undertaking, the astonishing fact about the British effort in 1776 is not that the campaign failed, but rather that it came so close to succeeding.

---

[106] Allen, *op. cit.*, Vol. I, p. 158.
[107] PRO, ADM 1/487, ff. 334–8.
[108] Allen, *op. cit.*, Vol. I, pp. 181–2.
[109] O. W. Stephenson, 'The supply of gunpowder in 1776', *American Historical Review* (January 1925), vol. 30, pp. 277–81.

3
THE FAILURE OF THE BRITISH EFFORT IN AMERICA, 1777

At the conclusion of the campaign of 1776 the British had the illusion of victory in America. A seemingly fatally weakened American army had disappeared into Pennsylvania, while the king's troops went into winter quarters and set up a string of posts along the Delaware River. The British had carried all before them. In every encounter Washington's army had been routed, and there were many who believed that the revolution in America would be crushed in 1777.[1] But the reality behind an illusion is often cruel, and in 1777 the apparently victorious British were going to flounder into a strategic quagmire. In 1777 the stage would be set for French entry into the conflict; one British army would surrender to the Americans; another army would be confined to a few enclaves in America; and the strength of the Royal Navy would be absorbed by an inconclusive effort to prevent munitions from reaching America and attempts to suppress American cruisers. By the end of 1777 it was clear that even without French intervention, the war in America had become a futile undertaking for the British.[2]

The first and one of the most decisive defeats of the war for the British came at the very end of 1776 when the Americans mounted a surprise winter campaign. On 25 December 1776 the Continental Army crossed the Delaware River, and in a surprise attack overwhelmed the Hessian garrison at Trenton, and on 3 January the Americans attacked and mauled a British infantry brigade at Prince-

---

[1] E.g. HMC, *Hastings MSS.*, Vol. III, p. 188.
[2] Cf. Eric Robson, *The American Revolution* (London, 1955), pp. 103, 143, 162, 174.

ton.[3] These American victories at Trenton and Princeton imperilled the king's troops stationed along the Delaware River and forced the British to evacuate most of New Jersey.

Politically the evacuation of New Jersey was a disaster. When the king's forces occupied New Jersey in the fall of 1776, the Loyalists of the region had made their presence known by attempting to regain political control of the province. However, with the British evacuation of New Jersey, the Loyalists were given the stark choice of either fleeing with the British army to New York or remaining in New Jersey to face political retribution at the hands of the rebels. This withdrawal and the earlier evacuation of Boston clearly showed that the British were unable to protect their political supporters in America and thus made it impossible to form the Loyalists into a meaningful political movement.[4]

Logistically the loss of New Jersey deprived the British of a source of supplies. One of the main objectives of the occupation of New Jersey had been to gain a region from which the British forces could obtain provisions, fuel and forage.[5] But the losses at Trenton and Princeton and the threat of future American surprise attacks on isolated detachments forced the British, for the rest of the war, to concentrate their forces for the most part in a few well-defined defensive regions such as New York City. This made it impossible to obtain sufficient quantities of supplies in America.[6]

In 1775 when the government began preparing to dispatch an army to America, a few officials wondered how it was going to be supplied;[7] but apparently the government thought that the necessary supplies could be obtained in America.[8] By the beginning of 1777, however, the British faced a logistical catastrophe. With New Jersey lost, not only troops and munitions, but also the bulk of the provisions required to sustain the kings's troops in America, now had to be supplied from Europe. Transporting across the Atlantic Ocean all the supplies required by the army in America placed a huge burden on the maritime resources of the British. The need for ships ever increased, and by 1782 rations for 72,000 men in North America

---

[3] For an account of the winter campaign of 1776–77 see William S. Stryker, *The Battles of Trenton and Princeton* (Cambridge, Mass., 1898).
[4] The political consequences of failing to protect Loyalists were seen by only a few British officers in 1776–77; see E. Stuart Wortley (ed.), *A Prime Minister and His Son* (London, 1925), p. 112.
[5] PRO, CO 5/92, ff. 290–1; CO 5/93, ff. 304–5; CO 5/94, f. 2.
[6] David Syrett, *Shipping and the American War* (London, 1970), pp. 125–8.
[7] NRS, *Sandwich Papers*, vol. I, p. 88.
[8] HMC, *American Manuscripts*, vol. I, p. 46.

were being supplied from the British Isles. Throughout the war scores of warships and thousands of tons of victuallers were employed in supplying the army in America.[9]

The problems caused by the dependence of the British forces in America on European sources of supply possibly could have been overcome if the Royal Navy maintained control of the Atlantic supply lines. But at the end of 1776 the Americans intensified and enlarged the war at sea by conducting naval operations in European waters.[10] Perhaps the first American cruiser to appear in European waters was the privateer *Rover* of Salem, which was reported on 31 August 1776 by the British consul at Faro to have captured four British merchant ships off Cape St Vincent.[11] The *Rover* was quickly followed to Europe by a number of other American privateers and warships.[12] The American objectives in sending cruisers to Europe were threefold: to capture and destroy British shipping; to force a redeployment of units of the Royal Navy away from America by turning European seas into a major theatre of maritime war; and most important, but rarely noted, to assist in precipitating conflict between Britain and France by using French ports as sanctuaries from which to stage attacks on British ships on the high seas.[13]

The British soon realized that the French intended to give the American cruisers all possible aid while ostensibly remaining neutral. Commanders of American cruisers found that it was generally possible to dispose of prizes and obtain supplies, refits and seamen in French ports.[14] The British authorities viewed the opening of French ports to American cruisers as an act of French duplicity that posed a grave threat to British seaborne commerce and probably preceded French intervention in the American war. The arrival of American cruisers in European waters thrust a grim choice

---

[9] For an account of the obtaining and transport of army provisions to America see Norman Baker, *Government and Contractors* (London, 1971), and Syrett, *op. cit.*, pp. 129-80, 248-50.
[10] Gardener W. Allen, *A Naval History of the American Revolution* (New York, 1962 reprint), Vol. I, pp. 250, 279-80.
[11] PRO, ADM 1/386, Extract of a letter from the Council at Faro . . . dated at Faro 31 August 1776.
[12] E.g. Allen, *op. cit.*, Vol. I, pp. 158, 234. For an account of one of the first American privateers in European waters see William Richard Cutter (ed.), 'A Yankee privateersman in prison in England, 1777-1779', *New England Historical and Genealogical Register* (April and July 1876), vol. XXX, pp. 175-7.
[13] Francis Wharton (ed.), *The Revolutionary Diplomatic Correspondence of the United States* (Washington, DC, 1889), Vol. II, pp. 262-3, 325-7, 329, 348, 399-400.
[14] Ibid., Vol. II, pp. 364-5, 377, 379-82, 388-9; see also Ruth Y. Johnston, 'American privateers in French ports', *Pennsylvania Magazine of History and Biography* (October 1929) vol. LIII, pp. 352-74.

upon the British: if harsh and decisive measures were not taken, Britain's merchant marine would suffer greatly from American attack; yet the only firm action the British could take against the American cruisers in Europe would be to deny them the use of French ports, which could only be done by means of a naval blockade that would precipitate a war with France.

From the beginning of the war, British authorities – especially those at the Admiralty – had been observing events in France with growing suspicion and fear. As reports of French and Spanish preparations for war and of clandestine aid rendered to the Americans reached London, Lord George Germain, the secretary of state responsible for the conduct of the war in America, and other British officials persisted in the belief that the French would not intervene as long as the British appeared to be victorious in America.[15] But the first lord of the Admiralty, Lord Sandwich, strongly believed that the possibility of French intervention posed an immediate and grave danger. He feared that France might attempt, secretly and quickly, to mobilize her navy and seize control of the English Channel before the Royal Navy could muster sufficient ships to oppose such action. Therefore, throughout the summer of 1776 the first lord of the Admiralty urged the mobilization of the Channel Fleet as a means of countering any possible French naval threat.

On 20 June 1776, in response to intelligence reports of naval preparations in French and Spanish ports, the government decided on a limited mobilization. It would increase the number of guardships in England to 24, recruit additional seamen and marines and secretly plan for a general press in the event of a total mobilization of the fleet.[16] By the autumn of 1776 intelligence reports on the expected operations of American cruisers[17] and especially those on naval preparations in French ports further alarmed Sandwich and Lord North:

> The accounts of French armaments multiply so fast that I must tell your Lordship that every hour is precious, as the French are certainly greatly ahead in their preparations, and I dread the consequence of their being at sea before us.[18]

On 23 October 1776, Sandwich drew up and submitted to the king

[15] E.g. CL, Sackville-Germain Papers, vol. 5, Germain to W. Howe, 18 October 1776 and 14 January 1777; Germain to Gloserter, 1 July 1777.
[16] G, nos 1894, 1895; NRS, *Sandwich Papers* vol. I, pp. 212-13, 215-16.
[17] E.g. PRO, ADM 1/4134, f. 20.
[18] NRS, *Sandwich Papers*, vol. I, p. 216.

a memorandum setting forth the measures necessary for the mobilization of the Channel Fleet,[19] and consequently several days later the government decided to place the entire Royal Navy on a war footing. On the night of 28 October a general press was conducted, and orders were issued for readying 34 ships of the line for Channel service.[20] However, despite the mobilization of the Channel Fleet in the autumn of 1776 to meet the French threat, the Royal Navy in European waters would be unprepared for the onslaught of American cruisers in 1777, for according to Sandwich, all the smaller types of warships suitable for the protection of commerce protection and hunting down cruisers were serving in America.[21]

The British attempted to employ diplomatic pressure to deprive American cruisers of the use of French ports. Under the terms of the Treaty of Utrecht, France was not to permit the cruisers or prizes of Britain's enemies to enter French ports. Nor was France to allow her territory to be used to fit out cruisers. Although these articles had been specifically renewed by the Anglo-French Treaty of 1763, the French government's policy artfully violated them. According to the American commissioners in Paris, this policy was one of professing:

> to England a resolution to observe all treaties, and prov[ing] it by restoring prizes too openly brought into their ports, imprisoning such persons as are found to be concerned in fitting out armed vessels against England from France, warning frequently those from America to depart, and repeating orders against the exportation of warlike stores. To us [the American commissioners in Paris] it privately professes a real friendship, wishes success to our cause, winks at the supplies we obtain here as much as it can without giving open grounds of complaint to England, privately affords us very essential aids, and goes on preparing for war.[22]

The spectacular career of Captain Gustavus Conyngham of the Continental Navy is illustrative of the obstacles and frustrations that the British encountered in attempting to make the French abide by the definition of neutrality as stated in the Treaty of Utrecht. On 1 May 1777, Conyngham sailed from Dunkirk in a cruiser disguised as a smuggler. Outside French territorial waters, Conyngham hoisted American colours and, on 3 May, he captured the Harwich—Helvoetsluis packet *Prince of Orange*. The following day he intercepted

---

[19] G, no. 1918.
[20] PRO, ADM 2/101, pp. 381-9, 399-400, 418-20, 429.
[21] G, no. 1894.
[22] Wharton, *op. cit.*, Vol. II, pp. 388-9.

and took the British brig *Dove*. On 7 May, Conyngham and his two prizes returned to France. The next morning Lord Stormont, the British ambassador to France, successfully demanded that the two British vessels be restored and that Conyngham and his men be jailed and tried as pirates. In a speech to the House of Commons, Lord North dwelt at length on the apparently satisfactory conclusion of the 'Conyngham affair', but several weeks later the British received information that American agents were fitting out two cutters at Dunkirk as cruisers and that Conyngham was to be released from prison. British spies swarmed over Dunkirk in an attempt to gain the information necessary to get the French government to prevent the sailing of the cutters. While the British repeatedly protested this breach of French neutrality, the Americans used various subterfuges to hide the ownership of the cutters and their purpose. On 17 July one of the cutters, the *Revenge*, with a passport stating that her destination was Bergen, Norway, sailed from Dunkirk. Once outside the French port, Conyngham took command of the vessel. For two months, without touching land, Conyngham cruised in the North Sea, the English Channel and the Irish Sea capturing or destroying British merchant ships. Insurance rates for English ships shot up and British officials fumed at the French for permitting the *Revenge* to sail from Dunkirk. When it was discovered that most of Conyngham's crew were not American, but French, Stormont threatened to break relations with the French unless some action was taken by the Paris government. Thereupon, to placate the British, an American agent was thrown into the Bastille for a short time; the French official supposedly responsible for the escape of the *Revenge* was ordered as a 'punishment' to attend court; and directions were issued for the arrest of Conyngham should he appear again in a French port. In the meantime, Conyngham had shifted the base of his operations to Spain and then to the West Indies, leaving in his wake a series of diplomatic incidents.[23] Conyngham was only one of many American commerce raiders operating from French ports, but he was the most daring and successful among them. He and the other raiders did much to accelerate and ensure the deterioration of Anglo-French relations.

Having failed to close French ports to Americans by diplomatic means, the British were forced to use the Royal Navy to combat American cruisers in European waters. Great 64- and 74-gun ships of

[23] For a full account of the activities of Conyngham see R. W. Neeser (ed.), *Letters and Papers Relating to the Cruises of Gustavus Conyngham: A Captain of the Continental Navy, 1777-1779* (New York, 1915).

the line were dispatched to cruise in the Bay of Biscay, the Western Approaches and the Irish Sea in search of American commerce raiders. From the autumn of 1776 onwards, a succession of ships from the Channel Fleet sailed between such points as Cape Clear, Ushant and Cape Ortegal, others were stationed off commonly frequented landfalls, such as Cape Finisterre, and others were dispatched far into the Atlantic to intercept and escort safely to Britain homeward-bound trade.[24] Month in and month out, the great ships of the Channel Fleet lumbered across the eastern Atlantic in a vain search for small American armed vessels. One of the few successes of this effort occurred on 15 April 1777, when HMS *Terrible* chased and captured the privateer *Rising States* off Belle Isle.[25] But for the most part, the ships suffered damage from the elements and the cruises were fruitless.[26]

The few small warships, such as sloops of war and cutters, which were not serving overseas were deployed by the Admiralty in the seas around Britain to search for American raiders. For example, in July 1777, HMS *Arethusa* was ordered to cruise in St George's Channel; HMS *Pelican* and HMS *Cameleon* were stationed off the Shetland Islands; and HMS *Drake*, HMS *Hound* and HMS *Alderney* were cruising between England and the Dutch coast.[27] Some sloops of war and cutters ranged along the coasts of Britain,[28] others were stationed to protect such ports as Waterford, Dublin, Dartmouth, Penzance, Milford, Shields, Hull, Liverpool and Glasgow[29] and still others regularly searched the coasts of Portugal and Spain;[30] and from time to time warships were dispatched off ports such as Dunkirk[31] and Brest.[32] But from the beginning, the situation was hopeless owing to the shortage of warships.[33]

The British instituted further measures to protect their shipping

---

[24] E.g. PRO, ADM 2/101, pp. 65-6, 124-5, 234-6, 253, 336-40; ADM 2/102, pp. 300-21, 324-5, 400-11, 423-4, 439-40, 449, 453-4, 480-3, 516, 522-3, 525-6, 530, 533, 542; ADM 2/103, pp. 8, 22-5, 37-8, 42, 44-5, 126, 146-7, 170-1, 183, 223-4, 237-8, 300-1, 306-8, 413-14, 488-9; ADM 3/82, 2, 16, 20-1, 23 and 27 May 1777, 4, 11, 19, 20 and 28 June 1777, 11, 17, 19, 23 and 31 July 1777, 6, 27, 28 August 1777, 18 September 1777 and 15 December 1777.
[25] Cutter, *op. cit.*, p. 1777.
[26] E.g. CL, Douglas Papers, vol. V, 16 February 1777.
[27] PRO, ADM 2/103, pp. 85, 143, 151-4; ADM 3/82, 2, 10, 19 and 22 July 1777.
[28] E.g. PRO, ADM 2/103, pp. 19-20, 49-50; ADM 3/82, 20 June 1777.
[29] PRO, ADM 2/103, p. 19; ADM 3/83, 9 December 1777.
[30] E.g. PRO, ADM 2/103, pp. 220-1.
[31] E.g. PRO, ADM 3/83, 14, 16-17, October and 12, 15 and 21 November 1777.
[32] E.g. PRO, ADM 2/102, pp. 488-90, 529-30; ADM 2/103, p. 21; ADM 2/1332, pp. 307-14, 330-51; ADM 3/82, 7 and 16 May 1777 and 28 June 1777.
[33] See e.g. NRS, *Sandwich Papers*, vol. I, p. 250.

from attack in European waters. Orders were issued to speed the construction of frigates and sloops of war and to charter a number of armed vessels to be employed in commerce protection.[34] The Navy Board was directed to purchase a number of former East Indiamen, which were to be heavily armed, to serve as military storeships,[35] and other steps, such as carrying parties of army recruits, on transports and storeships, were taken to protect military stores.[36] At the request of various groups of merchants the system of convoys was greatly enlarged, and by the end of 1777 nearly every major branch of British seaborne trade was conducted under naval escort. Convoys were organized to protect the West African trade,[37] and warships were sent to intercept merchant ships returning from Greenland and Hudson Bay and to escort them to British ports.[38] Moreover, on 31 July the Admiralty began planning to set up a comprehensive system of coastal convoys throughout British waters.[39] All military storeships, transports and victuallers were placed under naval escort,[40] as were East Indiamen in the North Atlantic.[41] Also naval escort and convoys were provided for the West Indian,[42] Newfoundland,[43] Canadian[44] and Baltic trades[45] and an elaborate system of convoys was instituted between British, Spanish and Portuguese ports and the Mediterranean.[46] However,

---

[34] PRO, ADM 3/82 16 July and 9 August 1777; CL, Shelburne Papers, vol. 138, Admiralty to Navy Board, 19 November 1777.
[35] PRO, ADM 3/83, 25 and 29 November 1777; CL, Shelburne Papers, vol. 142, Admiralty to Navy Board, 28 August 1777.
[36] E.g. PRO, ADM 1/4134, f. 49; ADM 2/101, pp. 284–5; ADM 2/103, p. 4; ADM 3/83, 23 and 30 September and 27 December 1777; HMC, *Various Collections*, vol VI, p. 138.
[37] PRO, ADM 2/102, pp. 128–9, 260–9.
[38] PRO, ADM 2/1332, pp. 325–6; ADM 3/83, 25 July 1777.
[39] PRO, ADM 1/4133, f. 146; ADM 2/102, pp. 518–20; ADM 2/103, p. 28, 128–9, 154–6; ADM 3/82, 16 May 1777, 16, 25, and 31 July 1777 and 21 August 1777; NRS, *Sandwich Papers*, vol. I, p. 224.
[40] E.g. PRO, ADM 2/102, pp. 416–18, 357–9; ADM 2/103, pp. 212–13, 218–19.
[41] PRO, ADM 2/101, pp. 317–20, 412; ADM 2/102, pp. 319–21; ADM 2/103, pp. 66–7, 108–9; ADM 2/104, pp. 91–3; ADM 3/82, 26 June 1777; ADM 3/83, 31 December 1777.
[42] PRO, ADM 2/101, pp. 335–7, 346–7; ADM 2/102, pp. 504–7; ADM 2/103, pp. 343–4, 383–7, 484–5; ADM 2/1333, f. 42; ADM 3/82, 10 May 1777 and 4 and 17 July 1777; ADM 3/83, 13 and 30 September 1777.
[43] PRO, ADM 2/102, pp. 318, 349–50; ADM 2/103, pp. 93–4; ADM 3/82, 16 May and 3 July 1777.
[44] PRO, ADM 2/103, pp. 4–6, 166–7, 463–7; ADM 3/83, 23 December 1777.
[45] PRO, ADM 2/103, pp. 148, 173–4, 186–7; ADM 3/82, 31 July 1777.
[46] PRO, ADM 1/368, 3 October and 26 December 1776; ADM 2/101, pp. 345–6; ADM 2/102, pp. 145–9, 307–10, 373–5; ADM 2/103, pp. 187–8, 197, 317–20, 346–9, 350–2, 357–9; ADM 3/82, 6 and 9 August 1777; ADM 3/83, 2 October 1777.

despite the dispatch of warships to hunt for American commerce raiders and the institution of convoys, the Admiralty was flooded with complaints about the shipping losses sustained at the hands of American cruisers.[47]

The Admiralty believed that no decisive measures could be taken to protect British shipping from attack as long as the majority of the Royal Navy's sloops of war and frigates were stationed overseas and French ports remained open to American cruisers.[48] Germain, however, thought that if harsh measures were adopted by the British forces in America, 'a salutary check will unavoidably be put to the successes of the Rebel privateers'. Therefore, on 3 March 1777 the American secretary directed that the Howes consider attacking and destroying or occupying major seaports in New England as a means of destroying the bases of American cruisers and of immobilizing the manpower of New England in local defensive efforts.[49] It was a scheme similar to the plan advocated by Admiral Graves in 1775. However, the Howes rejected absolutely any proposals for attacking New England seaports on the grounds that they did not have the necessary ships and troops to undertake such projects 'without interfering materially with more important operations of the campaign'.[50]

The Howes believed that the best way to end the cruiser problem was to end the rebellion by means of regular military operations aimed at the destruction of the Continental Army, the occupation of American cities and the maintenance of an effective blockade. Further, the Howes had concluded at the end of 1776 that the Americans could be decisively beaten in the campaign of 1777 if the British forces in America were reinforced with 15,000 additional troops and ten ships of the line with a number of 'supernumerary seamen for manning boats'.[51] The brothers intended to use the additional ships of the line with their large crews to supply the naval manpower required to support amphibious operations and thus end the necessity of having to lift the blockade of the American coast in order for the army to undertake offensive operations. However, they would not get the number of ships of the line they wanted.

The Admiralty violently opposed sending additional ships of the

---

[47] E.g. PRO, ADM 1/4134, f. 14; ADM 3/82, 17 May 1777 and 1-2, 8 and 17 July 1777; NRS, *Sandwich Papers*, vol. I, pp. 223, 225, 227.
[48] PRO, ADM 3/82, 28 June 1777.
[49] CL, Sackville-Germain Papers, vol. 5, Germain to W. Howe, 5 March 1776.
[50] PRO, CO 5/236, p. 81.
[51] CL, Sackville-Germain Papers, vol. 5, W. Howe to Germain, 25 September 1776; HMC, *Stopford-Sackville MSS.*, vol. II, p. 50.

line to America, for it was believed that France and Spain posed a greater danger to Britain in the long run than the rebellion. It was Sandwich's maxim 'that England ought for her own security to have a superior force in readiness to anything that France and Spain united have in readiness on their side'.[52] Hence, because of French and Spanish naval rearmament in Europe, most of the Royal Navy's ships of the line would be kept in England; only five would be dispatched to reinforce America.[53]

The British were torn: without naval support, the army in America would be rendered ineffective, but because of the shortage of warships to adequately support the army, they would have to abandon either the two-power standard in Europe or the blockade of America and efforts to destroy the ports from which American cruisers came. The Admiralty would not give up the two-power standard in Europe and Germain and the Howes would not tailor military operations in America to fit the requirements of the naval war. Therefore, the blockade of America in 1777 was doomed to be ineffective, and the Royal Navy would be incapable of suppressing the raiding of commerce by the Americans.

Lord Howe has been severely criticized for his conduct of the blockade of America.[54] One of his many contemporary critics was Germain, who called the Admiral 'the most disinterested man I know ... when he might avail himself of so many rich prizes'.[55] But much of this criticism is unfair and overlooks the great difficulties in blockading America: the shortage of ships, the great length of the American coastline and the need to support the army. In an apologia written after leaving the American command, Howe answered his critics by noting that the great length of the American coast and the shortage of ships forced him to concentrate his efforts off the maritime sections of America, such as New England, while neglecting such regions as the coast of the Carolinas.[56] But even off New England where, for example, in March 1777 there were some 27 warships,[57] counting those ships stationed in Long Island Sound, the blockade was not effective. For instance, during a cruise in the

---

[52] NRS, *Sandwich Papers*, vol I, pp. 234–8, 250.
[53] *Augusta, Nonsuch, Raisonable, St Albans* and *Somerset*: NRS, *Sandwich Papers*, vol. I pp. 279–80, 285.
[54] E.g. [Joseph Galloway], *A Letter to the Right Honourable Lord Viscount H—e* (London, 1779).
[55] HMC, *Various Collections*, vol. IV, pp. 131, 137.
[56] Gerald Saxon Brown (ed.), *Reflections on a Pamphlet entitled 'a Letter to the Right Honble Lord Vict. H—e* (Ann Arbor, Mich., 1959).
[57] PRO, ADM 1/487, ff. 350–1.

Gulf of Maine in the summer of 1777, HMS *Orpheus* sighted some 90 American vessels but was only able to intercept 33.[58] Fogs, storms, shoal water and equipment failures dogged British efforts to blockade the coast of New England.[59] Yet despite wear and tear on men and ships, Admiral Howe kept warships cruising either singly or in small squadrons off the coast of New England in an effort to prevent the escape of American cruisers and the importation of munitions.[60]

The policy of stationing ships on blockade duty singly or in small groups along the American coast was potentially one of considerable risk. There was always the possibility, as had been shown by the sortie of Hopkins's squadron in 1776, that a superior American force might, without warning, put to sea and overpower blockading British ships before they could be effectively concentrated to oppose the American force. On 21 May 1777 the strategic weakness of British naval deployments in America became apparent when an American squadron commanded by Captain John Manley of the Continental Navy escaped from Boston. Manley's force consisted of the continental frigates *Boston* and *Hancock*, along with nine privateers, including several of considerable force. This American squadron looked to be extremely powerful and dangerous, but in fact owing to the weakness of the American command structure, the squadron all but disintegrated as a fighting force several days after leaving Boston.[61] Manley's departure from Boston greatly alarmed the British, for the American force appeared to be capable of destroying piecemeal the ships of the British blockade.

When news of the escape of the American squadron reached Lord Howe at New York, there were no effective countermeasures that the admiral could take. Howe had 29 warships in the New York area,[62] but they were assigned to support pending military operations in New Jersey. Howe explained his helplessness:

> The attendance of the ships of war which might otherwise be spared from occasional service within the limits of this port, being necessary to co-operate in the expected movements of the army, I am not able, at this crisis, to make any detachments from the

[58] NRS, *Journal of Rear-Admiral Bartholomew James, 1752–1828*, p. 45.
[59] For an account of service on a warship on blockade duty off the New England coast in 1776–77 see ibid., pp. 35–50.
[60] PRO, ADM 1/487, ff. 388–9.
[61] Allen, *op. cit.*, Vol. I, pp. 202–3.
[62] PRO, ADM 1/487, ff. 388–9.

number, to proceed in pursuit of the enemy, which under other circumstances would be proper.[63]

The blockade of New England had to be abandoned while the blockading ships concentrated and began searching for the American squadron.

Manley, after a brush with the escort of a British military convoy, proceeded to raid the Grand Banks fishery; on 7 June the *Boston* and the *Hancock* intercepted and captured the 28-gun frigate HMS *Fox* of the Newfoundland squadron.[64] News of the loss of *Fox* and the appearance of the American raiders on the Grand Banks threw the British into a panic, and the ship of the line *Bienfaisant* was dispatched from England to reinforce Newfoundland.[65] After cruising for several weeks without result on the Grand Banks, Manley with the *Boston*, *Hancock* and their prize proceeded towards the coast of New England. But on 7 July off Cape Sable the American force was intercepted by HMS *Flora*, HMS *Rainbow* and HM Brig *Victor*. A running battle ensued, lasting 39 hours, during which the British captured the *Hancock* and Manley and retook *Fox*.[66] While resulting in little material damage, Manley's raid demonstrated the strategic weakness of the British blockade of America. When coupled with the success of other American cruisers, the sortie forced the Admiralty to realize that it simply did not have the ships required simultaneously to wage war in America and protect British seaborne trade.[67]

The 1777 campaign in America is one of the most appalling examples of strategic planning in British military history. In fact there was no plan for the campaign of 1777 but rather two uncoordinated and mutually exclusive plans. The disaster at Saratoga was the result of the failure of the government in general, and Germain in particular, to provide strategic direction to the British commanders in America and to co-ordinate the widely differing and totally exclusive schemes submitted by Generals Howe and Burgoyne. The astounding fact that no one in authority seemed to comprehend what the consequences would be if the plans of the two generals were carried out simultaneously has been debated endlessly. There is no

[63] Ibid., ff. 401-2; cf., ADM 2/104, p. 427.
[64] Allen, *op. cit.*, Vol. I, pp. 204-6.
[65] PRO, ADM 2/103, pp. 168-70; CL, Sackville-Germain Papers, vol. 6, Montagu to Germain, 11 June 1777; NRS, *Sandwich Papers*, vol. I, p. 234.
[66] For an account of this action see Allen, *op. cit.*, Vol. I, pp. 206-15; NRS, *Sandwich Papers*, vol. I, pp. 296-301.
[67] PRO, ADM 3/82, 20 August 1777.

simple explanation, but a partial answer lies in the lack of intellectual effort expended on the campaign by its three principal planners – General Howe, Germain and Burgoyne – and the way in which the plans were conceived.[68]

In 1777, Burgoyne was a man travelling down a fixed route towards an undetermined objective. Burgoyne's plan, which was drawn up in London and submitted to Germain in February 1777, called for Burgoyne to lead an army overland from Canada to Albany on the upper Hudson. Here the plan became so general as to be worthless: upon reaching Albany there was no stated objective for Burgoyne's force other than 'to effect a junction with General Howe, or after co-operating so far as to get possession of Albany and upon the communication to New York, to remain upon Hudson's river and thereby enable that General to act with his whole force to the southward'.[69] As a statement of a military objective, this is meaningless. If and when the armies of Howe and Burgoyne joined at Albany, what was the combined force to do next? Perhaps Burgoyne expected not to join with Howe's army at Albany, but simply to draw American troops northward, so that Howe could invade New Jersey or Pennsylvania without confronting the bulk of Washington's army. Or did Burgoyne hope to draw Washington to the upper Hudson and there fight a decisive battle? The possible interpretations of Burgoyne's intentions are nearly infinite. Most likely, Burgoyne did not know what he would do upon reaching Albany other than be, as he said, 'on the high road to glory'; and before Saratoga a case can be made that he was indifferent at best to the movements of Howe's army. However, had Burgoyne indeed reached Albany, clearly the only course open to him, unless he received at least logistical support from New York City, would have been to retreat as Napoleon would later do at Moscow.[70]

From November 1776 to April 1777 at New York, General Howe

---

[68] The origins and evolution of the strategy followed by the British in America during the 1777 campaign is a subject clouded by polemics. Perhaps the best modern treatment is William B. Willcox, 'Too many cooks: British planning before Saratoga', *Journal of British Studies* (November 1962), vol. II, pp. 56–90.
[69] Quoted in Hoffman Nickerson, *The Turning Point of the Revolution* (Boston, 1928), pp. 86–7.
[70] One of the problems of studying Burgoyne is that his memory is subject to change according to the demands of a given circumstance. See Lieutenant-General John Burgoyne, *A State of the Expedition from Canada as Laid before the House of Commons by Lieutenant-General Burgoyne* (London, 1780). For the most balanced modern study see George Athan Billias, 'John Burgoyne: ambitious general', in George Athan Billias (ed.), *George Washington's Opponents* (New York, 1969), pp. 142–92.

drew up plans for the campaign of 1777. The first scheme put forward by Howe in the fall of 1776 called for King George's forces in America to be reinforced by 15,000 men and 'eight or ten' ships of the line and for simultaneous offensives to be undertaken in New Jersey, New England and in the Hudson River Valley. But with the rapid collapse of the American position in New Jersey following the battles of Trenton and Princeton, Howe's concept of what form the campaign of 1777 should take gradually began to turn away from New England and the Hudson River and to evolve into a fixation to capture Philadelphia. At the beginning of 1777, Howe proposed that the main army should move across New Jersey towards Philadelphia while a corps went by sea to the Delaware River; if he did not receive enough reinforcements from Europe to carry out a double offensive against Philadelphia, then he would attack the city overland through New Jersey. Yet upon learning that he was in fact not going to receive any major reinforcements, Howe's plan underwent another drastic change. On 2 April 1777, Howe wrote Germain that he was going to leave a garrison at New York City and transport the bulk of his army by sea to Philadelphia.[71]

The decision to move on Philadelphia by sea appears to have been made without regard to the strategic consequences. It was the greatest single mistake made by Howe, for he forfeited every strategic advantage enjoyed by the British forces in America. The plan to move overland across New Jersey, while not particularly brilliant, had several features to recommend it: fighting a campaign in New Jersey was not likely to result in a disaster; and still occupying the interior position, Howe's army would thereby be able to protect New York, to prevent Washington from reinforcing the forces opposing Burgoyne and, if necessary, to support Burgoyne by undertaking an attack up the Hudson towards the Highlands. Moreover, an overland campaign against Philadelphia would not require large-scale naval support and would thus release ships for blockade duty and the suppression of American cruisers. But in changing the campaign to a seaborne one, Howe split the British forces in America into three separate groups and relinquished the interior position, giving Washington the opportunity to move troops across New Jersey to the Hudson River and thus to proceed against either New York City or Burgoyne. Also, in order to supply the naval support required to hold New York and at the same time mount a seaborne invasion of Pennsylvania, the blockade would for all

[71] William B. Willcox, *Portrait of a General: Sir Henry Clinton in the War of Independence* (New York, 1964), pp. 147–68.

practical purposes have to be lifted. Thus with a single decision Howe sacrificed the naval blockade of America, the advantages of operating from the interior position of New York City and the ability to assist Burgoyne's army on the upper Hudson.

By opting for an invasion of Pennsylvania from the sea, Howe made not only a strategic but a tactical mistake, and one which may have forfeited the possibility of ever bringing Washington to a decisive battle. Howe did not, it appears, understand that one of the great tactical advantages enjoyed by the British forces in America was amphibious mobility. In the campaign of 1776 he never exploited this advantage to the full, and in 1777 he again missed the opportunity to use amphibious mobility and naval power as a means of inflicting a decisive defeat on the Americans. Perhaps the best course that Howe could have adopted in 1777 was to have undertaken an amphibious offensive up the Hudson River directed at the Highlands of the Hudson. This would have had several advantages. It might have resulted in the decisive battle that the British had vainly sought because if Washington would fight for anything it would be for the forts in the Hudson Highlands. Further, such an offensive would have permitted Howe to protect New York City, maintain the advantages of interior lines of communication and, at the same time, assist the operations of Burgoyne's army. Also by advancing up the river Howe would have been able to exploit the tactical advantages of naval support and amphibious mobility. In hindsight, the advantages of such an attack appear so obvious that it is extremely difficult for the modern reader to comprehend the motives behind the invasion of Pennsylvania.

When Howe submitted the plan for the seaborne invasion of Pennyslvania, he knew that the campaign would not be decisive, for he informed Germain at the time, 'My hopes for terminating the war this year are vanished'.[72] Howe also knew that Burgoyne was going to march on Albany from Canada. Moreover, he was aware of the strategic dangers involved in a seaborne invasion of Pennsylvania because Clinton had pointed them out at great length in private discussions.[73] Why, then, the expedition to Philadelphia? Perhaps the answer is twofold? First, he believed that Burgoyne's campaign, even though it would not be decisive, would not need his support and so was not his concern. After all, Carleton's drive on Lake Champlain in 1776 did not require Howe's assistance, nor did it influence

[72] HMC, *Stopford-Sackville MSS.*, vol. II, pp. 63–4.
[73] Willcox, *Portrait of a General*, pp. 154–64.

the outcome of the campaign around New York City. Secondly, Howe was a cautious, slow and conservative general who thought that the best way to win the war was systematically to increase the region of British control by striking at and holding limited and clearly defined objectives rather than trusting at abstract points in the interior, as Burgoyne's campaign seemed designed to do. Thus when the government refused to give Howe the troops and ships that he thought necessary to occupy the Hudson River Valley, he set his sights on a more limited, practical and rational objective, Philadelphia. It was the seat of the Continental Congress, the largest city in America and purportedly the site of a large Loyalist population. But above all, Philadelphia was a distinct, tangible objective that could easily be grasped by a conventional eighteenth-century military mind like Howe's.

Commanders in the field are expected to exhibit a degree of strategic myopia, but one of the most conspicuous aspects of the campaign of 1777 is the general lack of strategic direction provided by the government in London. The main responsibility for this failure rests with Germain. Indeed there is no evidence that the American secretary ever understood or thought out the strategic consequences if both the Howes and Burgoyne were given a free rein. While authorizing Burgoyne's offensive from Canada, Germain took almost no positive steps to ensure that the northern army would be supported by the forces at New York City. Germain's office believed during the spring of 1777 that General Howe would attack Philadelphia overland at the beginning of the campaigning season and then, after quickly capturing the city, turn northward to support Burgoyne if necessary. It was not until 18 May 1777 when news of Howe's intention to capture Philadelphia from the sea reached London that Germain issued a directive calling for assistance to be given to Burgoyne. But by the time that order arrived in America, Howe's army was already committed to the seaborne invasion of Pennsylvania.

Not only was Germain lax in overseeing the planning of the campaign of 1777, but the few calculations he did make concerning it were based upon misconceptions. First, he believed that the armies of Howe and Burgoyne were capable of acting independently. Secondly and paradoxically, he assumed that Howe would keep Burgoyne in mind and see the possible need to support him. A copy of Burgoyne's instructions were sent to Howe; but although Germain wrote to Howe eight times between 3 March and 19 April, never once did he refer to the need to support the northern army. A third misconception was the belief that Washington's army was the major military danger to the British forces in America. The fourth and crowning misconception was a double one: that Howe would advance across New Jersey to attack Philadelphia and thereby pin down Washington's army in the middle colonies. In fact none of the above came to pass. Howe invaded Pennsylvania by sea, Washington's army remained in the middle colonies defending Pennsylvania and Burgoyne's army was overpowered by a horde of New England militia in the wilds of upper New York State.[74]

British strategic thinking in 1777 was inept, unco-ordinated and unrealistic. Generals Howe and Burgoyne were permitted to put into effect two mutually exclusive plans, and no effort was made by the ministry in London to fit the plans for the campaign in America into an overall scheme embracing Britain's total strategic commitments in 1777. The campaign was conceived in a vacuum without any real thought given to naval and diplomatic considerations. If French intervention were to be forestalled and American attacks on British seaborne trade were to be stopped, Britain needed a decisive victory in 1777; only the destruction of Washington's army could give the British that. Colonel Charles Stuart, an able Scots officer, stated the problem clearly when he wrote: 'If we wish to conquer them we must attack him [Washington], or if his posts are too strong, by a *ruse de guerre* place ourselves in that situation that he may expect to attack us to advantage'.[75]

Faced with an elusive Continental Army, the British were forced to fall back on a strategy of attrition, although it was never recognized as such. But wars of attrition take time and resources and the British had not enough of either owing to the very unstable diplomatic situation in Europe. Then, too, the Howes lost whatever chance there might have been for a gradual wearing down of American resistance and resources by naval blockade and the slow extension of British control over population centres such as Philadelphia. But Washington would not be forced or enticed into a battle that risked the destruction of the Continental Army, not even to save Philadelphia and certainly not to prevent an army from wandering around in the wilderness. The way in which the Howes carried out the invasion of Pennsylvania forced the lifting of the blockade of the

[74] Gerald Saxon Brown, *The American Secretary: The Colonial Policy of Lord George Germain, 1775–1778* (Ann Arbor, Mich., 1963), pp. 81–128; Willcox, 'Too many cooks . . .', pp. 56–90; Piers Mackesy, *The War for America, 1775–1783* (London, 1964), pp. 103–27.
[75] Wortley, *op. cit.*, p. 112.

78 THE FAILURE OF THE BRITISH EFFORT IN AMERICA, 1777

American coast because of the large numbers of warships required to support the army, and without an effective blockade, there could be no effective war of attrition.

The British forces at New York expended almost half the summer of 1777 waiting for the arrival of new camp equipage from Europe[76] and conducting a series of desultory manoeuvres in New Jersey in a vain attempt to draw Washington into a battle. It was not until 23 July that the invasion of Pennsylvania got under way when almost 14,000 rank and file were embarked on 267 ships, and escorted by twenty-two warships, sailed from Sandy Hook.[77] Colonel Stuart, who was on board one of the hot, crowded transports, thought the undertaking ill-conceived and believed that the army should either attack Washington in New Jersey or drive up the Hudson to support the northern army. To Stuart, General Howe seemed blinded by the supposed importance of Philadelphia as the 'capital' of America.[78] But Stuart was not in command; and for the next six days, beset by calms and in the face of prevailing southwesterly winds, the fleet crawled along the coast of New Jersey towards the entrance of Delaware Bay.[79]

The invasion force arrived off Cape Henlopen on the morning of 30 July and was joined by Captain Andrew Snape Hamond, commander of the squadron blockading Delaware Bay.[80] Hamond had an extremely precise knowledge of Delaware Bay and the Delaware River and had for several weeks, on the order of Lord Howe, been making preparations for landing the British army on the banks of the Delaware. But General Howe had not settled on a landing-site; he was waiting to see what move Washington would make. On 16 July, before leaving New York, the general wrote to Germain explaining that he:

> proposed going up the Delaware in order to be nearer this place [New York City] then I should be by taking the course of Chesapeake Bay which I once intended and preferred to that of the Delaware provided the enemy had discovered a disposition to defend Pennsylvania.[81]

---

[76] PRO, CO 5/94, ff. 180, 194, 211.
[77] *Eagle, Nonsuch, Augusta, Somerset, Sphinx, Dispatch, Swift, Stromboli, Vigilant, Haerlem, York, Cornwallis, Stanley, Adventure, Richmond, Apollo, Raisonable, Isis, Emerald, Solebay, Otter* and *Senegal*: PRO, ADM 1/487, ff. 480, 483.
[78] Wortley, *op. cit.*, p. 113.
[79] PRO, ADM 1/487, f. 480.
[80] *Roebuck, Pearl, Camilla* and *Merlin*: PRO, ADM 1/487, ff. 388-9.
[81] PRO, CO 5/94, f. 432.

That is, if Washington crossed the Delaware and moved south of Philadelphia, General Howe would invade Pennsylvania by way of Chesapeake Bay; but if Washington remained in New Jersey, the British would go up the Delaware River.

On the morning of 30 July, Hamond went on board HMS *Eagle* and conferred informally with the Howes at some length. The meeting began with Hamond stating erroneously that Washington's army had crossed the Delaware and was marching on Wilmington, when in fact the Continental Army was just crossing the Delaware north of Philadelphia. Hamond and the Howes then discussed the relative merits of conducting a landing either in Chesapeake Bay or in Delaware Bay. According to Hamond's account of the meeting, General Howe opposed landing on the shores of the Delaware for the following reason:

> As General Washington, by the long passage of the Fleet from New York, had got his army over the Delaware before the fleet arrived, great opposition was expected to be given the Troops at landing at Newcastle or Wilmington the places intended. That the Enemy expecting the Fleet to come into the River had made uncommon preparations to annoy the Men of War & Transports with Fire Ships, fire rafts, and had besides a considerable number of Row Galleys, Xebecks, & Floating Battery's, which in the narrow navigation & rapid tides of the River might do great damage among the transports.

Hamond reports Howe was in favour of proceeding to the head of Chesapeake Bay where:

> The troops would be put ashore without any molestation, have time to recover the Horses after the fatigue of the Voyage before they entered Service, and where the Transports could remain in perfect security.

The discussion ended when the two Howes stepped out on to the stern galley of the *Eagle* for a short private talk. When they returned to the cabin, Hamond was informed by General Howe that: 'Since there was no doubt what the Enemy was apprized of the plan of the Expedition . . . it confirmed him to his design of landing his army at the Head of the Elk in the Chesapeake rather than the Delaware'. Hamond was surprised by this decision and attempted to persuade the Howes to land in the Delaware. But General Howe refused to reconsider the decision, and on the afternoon of 30 July the fleet sailed from Cape Henlopen. Unfortunately, General Howe seems to have decided to land at the head of the Elk River instead of in the Delaware River because he thought the American army was approaching Wilmington.[82]

For the next fifteen days, during the hottest season of the year, the ships carrying General Howe's army crept slowly southward along the coast of America towards the entrance of Chesapeake Bay. They encountered nothing but calms and southwesterly winds; water ran short and all but a few of the army's horses died. It was not until 15 August that the fleet entered the Chesapeake. With Hamond in HMS *Roebuck*, leading the way and acting as a guide, the force proceeded slowly up the bay to Turkey Point, Maryland. Finally, on 25 August General Howe's army landed without opposition on the eastern side of the Elk River near Cecil Court House.[83] Thirty-two days in all had been consumed reaching the head of the Elk River, a point almost as far from Philadelphia as the port of embarkation, New York City. During this time General Howe's army and its naval escort of over twenty warships were a strategic neuter, removed from the campaign.

The ponderous and indecisive actions of the Howes in 1777 enraged some British officers, Colonel Charles Stuart among them, and the apparent futility of the whole effort was beginning to be seen by some of the brighter young officers. For example, several days after the landing a young Scots officer wrote his sister from the head of the Elk River, 'It is a barbarous business and in a barbarous country. The novelty is worn off and I see no advantages to be reaped from it'.[84] But despite misgivings in some quarters, General Howe marched on Philadelphia. After fighting an indecisive action with Washington at Brandywine Creek, on 26 September the city was occupied without opposition. At this point, all offensive operations in Pennsylvania halted while ships of the Royal Navy, supported by troops, fought a bitter battle to open the Delaware River to British shipping.

---

[82] This account of the decision to land in Chesapeake Bay is primarily based on H. W. Moomaw, 'The denouement of General Howe's campaign of 1777', *English Historical Review* (July 1964), vol. 79, pp. 498–512; the quotations are on page 504. Before the publication of Professor Moomaw's article, the reasons for General Howe's decision were unknown for the simple fact that neither the Howes nor Hamond revealed them. The whole problem is further confused by the parliamentary inquiry into the Howes' conduct of the war in America because a number of people, such as Hamond, told less than the complete truth.

[83] PRO, ADM 1/487, ff. 480–2; CO 5/236, pp. 121–2.

[84] Eric Robson (ed.), *Letters from America, 1773–1780* (New York, 1950), p. 48.

The American forces had to be cleared from the maritime approaches to Philadelphia if General Howe's army were to be supplied. This task proved to be extremely difficult, for the Americans had placed six lines of underwater obstacles, or *chevaux-de-frise*, in the Delaware River, effectively blocking navigation below Philadelphia.[85] The American *chevaux-de-frise* were defended by a number of gunboats, fire-rafts and galleys. In addition, the obstacles were covered by the guns of a number of forts and batteries that were difficult to approach because they were protected by shoal water and swamps. The American underwater obstacles, small craft and forts formed an extremely strong interlocking defensive system that, at considerable cost in men and materiel, would take the king's forces almost two months to reduce.

The forcing of the Delaware began on 2 October when two regiments of infantry, supported by a small squadron[86] under the command of Hamond, seized without resistance the American fort at Billingsport, New Jersey, which defended the first two lines of *chevaux-de-frise*. On 4 October, Hamond's seamen began clearing a passage through the obstacles at Billingsport. It was not any easy task. The working parties were hampered and harassed by long-range fire from Fort Mifflin on Fort Island, and the British warships were forced almost daily to withdraw temporarily down river by frequent American sorties with galleys and fire-rafts. On 15 October, Hamond at last managed to clear a passage through the *chevaux-de-frise* at Billingsport.[87]

Lord Howe arrived in the Delaware on 6 October and soon perceived, even before Hamond succeeded in breaching the first two lines of American underwater obstacles, that the remaining four lines of *chevaux-de-frise* could not be cleared until Fort Mifflin was seized.[88] But as General Howe confessed in a letter to Germain, simply getting near enough to attack Fort Mifflin was a 'tedious operation', for it was thought that the only way to do so was to gain control of both banks of the Delaware River opposite the American fort.[89]

On the night of 8 October, British army engineers began con-

---

[85] For a detailed account of American river obstructions see C. R. Harte, 'The river obstructions of the revolutionary war', *Annual Report of the Connecticut Society of Civil Engineers* (1946), vol. 62, pp. 135-186a.
[86] *Merlin, Roebuck, Liverpool, Carysfort, Pearl* and *Camilla*.
[87] William Hugh Moomaw, 'The naval career of Captain Hamond, 1775-1779' (unpublished PhD dissertation, University of Virginia, 1955), pp. 355-60.
[88] PRO, ADM 1/488, f. 74.
[89] PRO, CO 5/236, p. 159.

82 THE FAILURE OF THE BRITISH EFFORT IN AMERICA, 1777

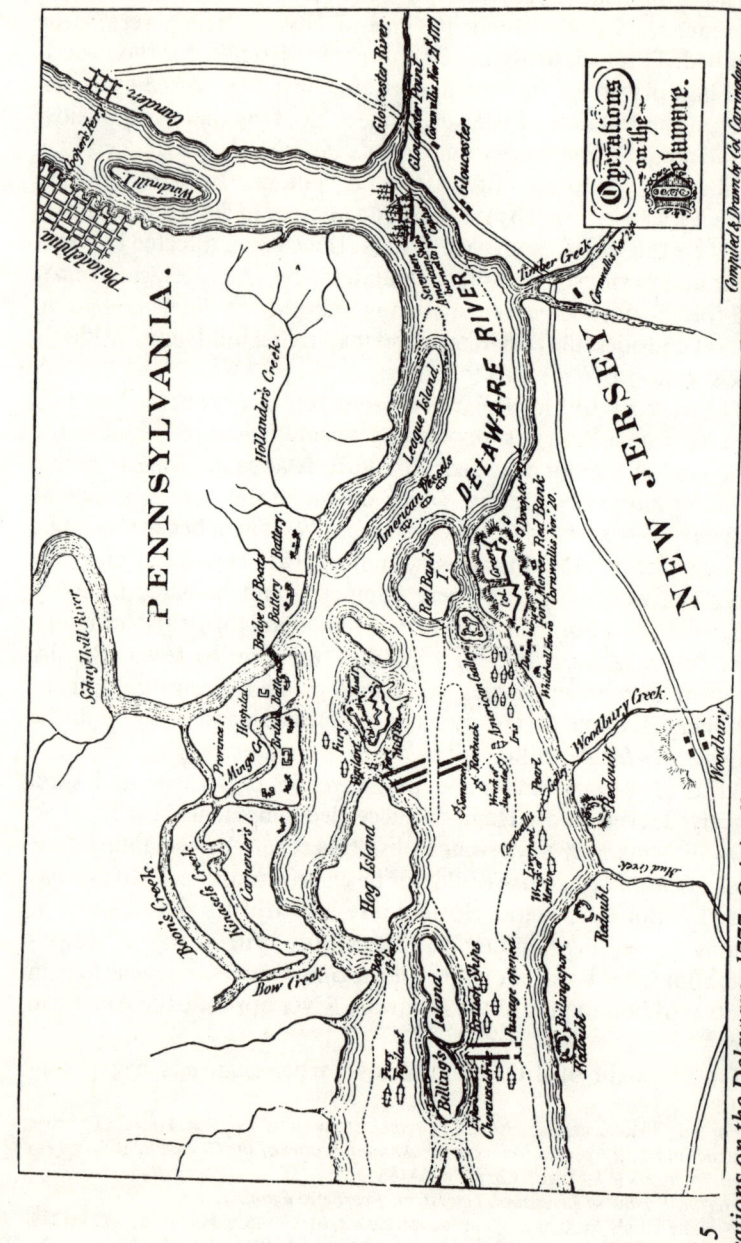

Map 5
Operations on the Delaware, 1777. Originally published in 1877 and 1881. Republished by the New York Times and Arno Press in the 1960s.

THE FAILURE OF THE BRITISH EFFORT IN AMERICA, 1777 83

structing batteries on Carpenter's and Province islands on the Pennsylvania side of the river. The work was retarded by rain and by the Americans, who not only attacked the British, but also attempted to flood the low-lying islands by destroying dykes, but on 15 October four weak batteries were completed and began to bombard Fort Mifflin.[90]

While the engineers worked on the Pennsylvania side of the Delaware, the Howes devised a plan for attacking the New Jersey side. They decided to undertake a combined ground and naval attack against Fort Mifflin and Fort Mercer at Red Bank on the New Jersey shore opposite Fort Island. The plan called for 1,600 Hessians, led by Colonel Carl Emil Kurt von Donop, a brave but impetuous officer, to storm Fort Mercer. Meanwhile, HMS *Vigilant*, a former transport of shallow draft that had been specially rebuilt to conduct shore bombardments,[91] was to proceed up the river through a narrow and shallow channel lying between Hog Island and the Pennsylvania shore and arrive at the rear of Fort Mifflin. As the Hessians and the *Vigilant* advanced, a diversion was to be created by HMS *Augusta*, a new 64-gun ship of the line, HMS *Roebuck*, HMS *Liverpool*, HMS *Pearl* and HMS *Merlin* advancing directly up the main channel towards Fort Mifflin and the lines of *chevaux-de-frise*.[92]

The attacks on Forts Mifflin and Mercer were a disaster. In the late afternoon of 22 October the Hessians, led by von Donop, assaulted Fort Mercer without scaling ladders and adequate artillery support. The attack failed and the Hessians were repulsed, with a loss of 371 men, including von Donop, who was mortally wounded and captured.[93] As the Hessians attacked Fort Mercer, the Royal Navy attempted to move simultaneously against Fort Mifflin; however, because of adverse winds, the *Vigilant* could not proceed up the channel between Hog Island and the Pennsylvania shore as planned. Nevertheless, on the floodtide and against a northerly wind, HMS *Augusta*, HMS *Roebuck*, HMS *Liverpool*, HMS *Merlin* and HMS *Pearl* proceeded up the main channel towards the *chevaux-de-frise* off Fort Mifflin in an attempt to divert American attention from the Hessian assault. Anchoring off the *chevaux-de-frise*, the five war-

[90] NYHSC, *The Montressor Journals*, pp. 463–6.
[91] David Syrett, 'HM Armed Ship *Vigilant*, 1777–1780', *Mariner's Mirror* (February 1978), vol. 64, pp. 57–62.
[92] PRO, ADM 1/488, pp. 112–14.
[93] CO 5/236, pp. 166–7; Edward L. Lowell, *The Hessians and other German Auxiliaries of Great Britain in the Revolutionary War* (New York, 1884), pp. 204–8.

ships were engaged by Fort Mifflin and a number of American galleys for several hours. With the failure of the attack on Fort Mercer and the coming of darkness and the ebb tide, the British warships then began to withdraw down-river. But in the darkness and because the current, obstructed by *chevaux-de-frise*, had changed the course of the river's channel, the *Augusta* and *Merlin* ran aground. Attempts to refloat the ships were frustrated by the northerly wind, and early the next morning the Americans discovered the plight of the British vessels. A fierce action ensued as the Americans attacked the grounded British warships with galleys, floating batteries and fire-rafts. Then, at about 11 a.m., as the British were preparing to lighten the *Augusta* to refloat her, the ship 'by some accident, not otherwise connected with the circumstances of the action but as it was probably caused by the wads of her guns . . . took fire abaft'. She was rapidly engulfed in flames and had to be abandoned by her crew. To prevent the other ships from being damaged when the *Augusta*'s magazines exploded, Lord Howe ordered that the *Merlin* be evacuated and destroyed and the *Roebuck, Liverpool* and *Pearl* withdrawn down-river. At noon the first British attempt to gain control of the Delaware ended when *Augusta* blew up with such force that the shock 'felt like an earthquake in Philadelphia'.[94]

After the failure of the attack on Fort Mercer and the loss of the *Augusta* and *Merlin*, the British concentrated their efforts on reducing Fort Mifflin. Ten heavy naval guns were emplaced on Province Island to fire on the fort from the Pennsylvania shore and, on 10 November, the British began to bombard it heavily. At the same time, navy officers were preparing to attack the fort with warships and were reconnoitring and buoying the approaches. On the morning of 15 November, with a favourable wind and a flood-tide, the British attack began. While the *Vigilant* and a hulk mounting three heavy guns inched their way through the narrow and shallow channel between Hog and Carpenter's islands towards the rear of Fort Mifflin, HMS *Somerset* and HMS *Isis* proceeded up the main channel and attacked the front of the American fortification. Simultaneously, HMS *Roebuck, Pearl* and *Liverpool* vigorously bombarded and silenced a newly constructed American battery at Manot Creek in order to prevent it from firing on the ships attacking the front of Fort Mifflin. By 9 a.m. the *Vigilant* and the hulk had

---

[94] PRO, ADM 1/488, ff. 75–6; Moomaw, '*The naval career of Captain Hamond*', pp. 153–4; NRS, *Naval Miscellany*, Vol. I, pp. 153–4.

begun to bombard the rear of Fort Mifflin, while the *Somerset* and *Isis* heavily engaged the front of the American fort. By nightfall the American fire from the rear of Fort Mifflin was silenced and the *Vigilant* had moved to within 300 feet of the fortification, ready to support with naval gunfire an amphibious assault planned for the morning. However, during the night the American forces escaped to New Jersey, so when British troops landed on Fort Island in the morning they occupied Fort Mifflin without resistance.[95]

With the loss of Fort Mifflin, the Americans gave up the fight for the Delaware River. Fort Mercer was abandoned and blown up, and most of the American galleys, gunboats and floating batteries were either captured or destroyed while attempting to escape up-river past British forces at Philadelphia. On 23 November the first British ship finally arrived at the city.[96] Fifty-nine days had elapsed between the time when the first British troops and the first British ship arrived at the city. For two months the British forces in Pennsylvania had been strategically immobilized while a protracted, costly and difficult battle was fought to secure the supply lines of the British army at Philadelphia.

The opening of the Delaware River to navigation marked the end of the Howe's campaign of 1777. The king's forces under the command of General Howe had captured Philadelphia – but it was an empty victory, for the occupation of the city would not affect the course of the war. Moreover, the campaign had involved a series of what Charles Stuart called 'incomprehensible' manoeuvres in New Jersey, a protracted sea voyage and a long battle to seize control of the Delaware River. The occupation of Philadelphia had not lessened the threat or the strength of Washington's army and was accomplished at the expense of the blockade and efforts to suppress American cruisers.

Germain's proposal to attack the American ports in which the cruisers were based had been vetoed by the Howes because it would draw ships and men away from the main offensive against Philadelphia.[97] Except for a strong squadron off the coasts of northern New England and Nova Scotia, during the summer of 1777 most of the ships of Admiral Howe's fleet were tied down in supporting the

---

[95] PRO, ADM 1/488, ff. 79–80; CO 5/236, pp. 185–6; Moomaw, '*The naval career of Captain Hamond*', pp. 369–73; G. Cornwallis-West, *The Life and Letters of Admiral Cornwallis* (London, 1927), pp. 74–80; NYHSC, *The Montressor Journals*, pp. 470–7.
[96] PRO, ADM 1/488, f. 81; Moomaw, '*The naval career of Captain Hamond*', p. 373.
[97] PRO, CO 5/236, p. 81.

operations of the army in New York and Pennsylvania,[98] thereby as Lord Howe himself admitted, making it impossible effectively to blockade America.[99] The Royal Navy in America did inflict some hard blows on the Americans during 1777. Scores of American merchant vessels were captured by Lord Howe's ships, and the thirteen large, new frigates of the Continental Navy had either been captured, destroyed or bottled up in port, while HMS *Fox*, the only warship to be captured by the Americans in 1777, was quickly retaken by Commodore Sir George Collier.[100] However, capturing American merchant ships and crippling the striking power of the Continental Navy in American waters did not prevent the flow of munitions from Europe and the West Indies, nor did it stop American cruisers from attacking British trade.

On 31 October 1777, at the height of the battle to open the Delaware navigation, news of Burgoyne's surrender reached the British in Pennsylvania.[101] The disaster at Saratoga had a shattering effect on those British in America who still believed that victory was possible, for this defeat unmasked the futility of the British effort and the realities of the war. Lord Cornwallis, with classic understatement, summed up the feelings of the majority of the British when he wrote, 'Burgoyne's disaster has greatly changed the face of affairs in this country. God only knows how this business will end'.[102]

To a few of the more perceptive among the British, those who had believed before the defeat that the war was futile, Saratoga was a grim confirmation. Commodore Marriot Arbuthnot, for example, was convinced that an 'army' could not put the American colonies 'upon a permanent footing of utility to Great Britain', while Commodore Sir George Collier, the hard-driving commander of the blockading ships in the Gulf of Maine, thought that New England could not be subdued 'during this generation'.[103] And after Saratoga, General Howe informed Whitehall that nothing could be done in America without more troops and ships, and yet he did not foresee:

> a successful termination to the war from any advantages his Majesty's troops can gain while the enemy is able to avoid, or

[98] PRO, ADM 1/487, ff. 388-9, 483-4.
[99] PRO, ADM 1/488, ff. 112-14.
[100] Allen, *op. cit.*, Vol. I, pp. 286-7, 289-90.
[101] NRS, *Naval Miscellany*, vol. I, p. 154.
[102] HMC, *Various Collections*, vol. VI, p. 316.
[103] NRS, *Sandwich Papers*, vol. I, pp. 296, 303.

unwilling to hazard, a decisive action, which might induce the leaders in Rebellion to make an overture for peace.[104]

Lord Howe in a dispatch to the Admiralty from the Delaware River, dated 10 December, flatly declared that owing to the shortage of ships and the need to support the army, the blockade of America was and would continue to be a failure. Admiral Howe wrote that the British army had not been able to subdue the Americans and was penned up in three small bridgeheads, Philadelphia, New York City and Newport, Rhode Island, which were indefensible without large-scale naval support. He further stated that he understood 'the first object of my instructions to be, cooperating with the army in the services the general is to undertake'; he carried out these instructions at the beginning of 1778 by stationing 26 warships at Rhode Island, 25 at New York, 10 in the Delaware River, 12 cruising in the Gulf of Maine or at Halifax, 5 in the entrance of Chesapeake Bay, 4 at Quebec and 6 off the coast of the Carolinas and Florida. In his dispatch Lord Howe also pointed out that the number and effectiveness of ships on blockade duty was further reduced because of the shortage of seamen; the disrepair of the ships; a lack of proper repair facilities; the need to withdraw ships, without replacement, from cruising stations in order to obtain water and provisions; and the great strain being placed on officers and men by serving constantly, even while in port, under combat conditions. As a result, until he received more ships and was freed from the need to support the army, the bulk of the ships of the Royal Navy in America would be absorbed in defensive operations instead of blockade duty.[105] Admiral Howe failed, as did most British officers in America at the end of 1777, to perceive that the war was no longer simply a matter of quelling a rebellion in America: Britain was being propelled into a world war by the indecisiveness of the British effort and the disaster at Saratoga.

In London officials were not so myopic, and by the autumn of 1777 it was painfully clear to them that Britain was slipping towards war with France, while the war in America seemed to have become a sponge that endlessly absorbed men, ships and materiel. One British army had been captured, and another was logistically dependent for supplies on the British Isles and penned up in three small bridgeheads at the edge of the continent. However, only a handful of men in

[104] CL, Sackville-Germain Papers, vol. 6, W. Howe to Germain 30 November 1777.
[105] PRO, ADM 1/488, ff. 118, 123, 128-9.

88 THE FAILURE OF THE BRITISH EFFORT IN AMERICA, 1777

London saw that the most dangerous aspect of the situation in the autumn of 1777 was not military weakness in America, but rather the Royal Navy's inability to stem the flow of munitions across the Atlantic, the failure to suppress American cruisers and the great strategic threat posed by the impending French entry into the conflict.

From the West Indies to the Irish Sea, American cruisers appeared to be capturing British merchant ships at will. Despite convoys, patrols and the capture of hundreds of American ships by the Royal Navy, the American attack on British merchant shipping did not abate. Even though the small squadron at Jamaica captured 236 American ships between 21 December 1775 and 26 February 1778,[106] rebel cruisers using French, Dutch and Danish islands as bases swarmed over the Caribbean seizing British shipping and greatly alarming the British islands.[107] Furthermore, American cruisers based in French ports roamed, apparently at will, the seas around Britain. In June 1777, for example, three Continental warships operating as a squadron captured 14 British merchant ships in the Firth of Clyde.[108] And there was a period during the summer of 1777 when, according to Germain,

> We lately had so many privateers upon our coasts and such encouragement given them by the French, that I was apprehensive a few weeks ago that we should have been obliged to have declared war.[109]

Over 300 British merchant ships were taken by American cruisers in 1777,[110] while the Royal Navy managed to capture only a mere handful of the raiders.[111] During 1777 the British were forced to suffer the humiliation of seeing the Royal Navy, the strongest navy

---

[106] PRO, ADM 1/240, ff. 496–507.
[107] PRO, ADM 1/309, ff. 563, 656.
[108] PRO, ADM 1/1434, f. 5.
[109] HMC, *Stopford–Sackville MSS.*, vol. II, p. 73.
[110] The whole subject of what number of ships were captured during a given period of time is extremely complex owing to the great number of conflicting reports and lists of captured ships, e.g. A. T. Mahan, *The Major Operations of the Navies in the War of American Independence* (New York, 1969 reprint), p. 61n, states that 331 British merchant vessels were captured in 1777. Charles Wright and C. Ernest Fayle, *A History of Lloyd's* (London, 1928), pp. 156–7, says that the British lost 340 merchant ships to enemy action; and Allen, *op. cit.*, pp. 289–90, says that the Americans captured 464 British merchant ships in 1777.
[111] Only 15 American privateers and warships are listed for the year 1777: PRO, Index to High Court of Admiralty Prize Papers, 1776–1786.

in the world and a force with a tradition of victory, unable to defeat a few rebel cruisers.

Neither the best efforts of British diplomacy nor the might of the Royal Navy could prevent the Americans, aided by neutrals, from shipping munitions across the Atlantic. The blockade of America was weak and most of the munitions were shipped on French flag vessels to the West Indies and then trans-shipped. British warships in European waters had directions from the Admiralty not to seize French vessels '*without particular orders*', for as Sandwich knew, 'bringing in a French ship upon suspicions that appear not well grounded afterwards may draw us into a war, which in our present circumstances ought by all means to be avoided'.[112] But even at the risk of precipitating a European war, the British seized French and other neutral ships in European waters on suspicion of carrying munitions to the Americans, and Whitehall was flooded with diplomatic protests.[113] Yet to seize French ships, even if they were loaded with munitions bound for the Americans, was a dangerous practice, for if it were carried out on a large enough scale to prevent sufficient arms from reaching America, war with France would be unavoidable.

The dominant concern in the Admiralty during the summer and autumn of 1777 was not American cruisers or shipments of munitions to America, but the strategic dangers of French entry into the conflict. Throughout the last months of 1777, requests arrived in London from such widely scattered places as the West Indies, the Mediterranean and India[114] for naval reinforcements to deal with the onslaught of American cruisers and to meet the impending French intervention in the conflict. But the Admiralty, confronted by the build-up of French and Spanish naval power in Europe, did not dare risk sending additional ships to reinforce overseas squadrons. At the end of August 1777 the Admiralty calculated that there were in home waters 36 ships of the line, 12 frigates and 14 sloops of war, and that these ships whose complements were 4,000 men under strength, were for the most part tied up on convoy duty or on hunts for American raiders. At the same time, the Admiralty knew that

---

[112] NRS, *Sandwich Papers*, vol. I, pp. 223, 254.
[113] E.g. PRO, ADM 1/4134, ff. 33–4, 55, 63, 68. One authority states that 158 French ships valued at 6.5 million francs were seized by the British during 1777 and the first months of 1778. NRS, *Sandwich Papers*, vol. I, p. 204. The PRO, Index to High Court of Admiralty Prize Papers, 1776–1786, is laced with the names of French ships seized during 1777.
[114] G, no. 2065; PRO, ADM 1/309, ff. 563, 658; ADM 1/386, Man to Stephens, 19 September 1777.

France and Spain had 44 ships of the line in European waters, with an additional 20 stationed overseas.[115]

During December 1777 the Admiralty, in a series of conferences and memorandums, sought to convince various members of the ministry of the grave strategic dangers posed by French and Spanish naval power and the need to concentrate on the defence of Britain. It was argued that the British were vulnerable to naval attack in the English Channel, the West Indies, India, the Mediterranean and North America; and once France decided to go to war, it would send a fleet to attack one of these places with an overpowering force. Further, since the Admiralty had no way of knowing where the blow would fall, the only true precaution was to be strong everywhere; yet the Royal Navy lacked the force required to defend these far-flung targets, simultaneously and in strength. As outlined by the Admiralty, Britain was left with a bleak choice: either send reinforcements overseas, with the possibility of 'seeing France and Spain in the channel with a superior fleet' or maintain the strongest possible force in home waters and run the risk that one or both of the Bourbon powers would gain temporary naval superiority in either the West Indies, North America, the Mediterranean or the Indian Ocean. The Admiralty advocated that the security of Britain should have first priority, 'as all our exterior efforts are derived from that centre', and that while waiting for the intentions of France and Spain to become clear, the strength of the Channel Fleet should be maintained at the expense of overseas commitments and a vigorous effort should be made to get every possible ship of the line into service.[116]

Thus as 1777 drew to a close, Britain was on the brink of a world war. The year that had opened with such high hopes of victory in America had turned out to be a cruel one, filled with frustration, humiliation and defeat. The campaign in America had not been a victory, but a disaster. A lack of foresight and strategic planning had led to the capture of Burgoyne's army at Saratoga and General Howe's futile campaign in New Jersey and Pennsylvania. By the end of 1777, America had become a quagmire for the British and the political potential of loyalism had been shattered. The British army held little more ground than that on which King George's soldiers actually stood, and it was logistically dependent on the British Isles. The Royal Navy did not have sufficient ships adequately to blockade

---

[115] NRS, *Sandwich Papers*, vol. I, pp. 242–5.
[116] ibid., pp. 327-35, 337-9.

the coast and, at the same time, support the operations of the army, maintain a two-power standard in Europe and prevent the movement of munitions across the Atlantic to the Americans; nor could it cope with the American cruiser offensive against British merchant shipping. Compounding all these frustrations and humiliations was the British conviction that their arch-enemy, France, was going to attempt to reap an advantage from their plight by entering the war.

4
ON THE DEFENSIVE IN AMERICA, 1778

The British hopes of subduing the rebellion in America were destroyed with the failure of the campaign of 1777. During the winter of 1777-78 the British stood on the defensive waiting for instructions from London, for they realized that the defeat at Saratoga had completely changed the entire nature of the war. Both of the Howes had also become disillusioned. What little remained of General Howe's military reputation vanished with the American surprise attack at Germantown, and when news of this battle reached London, a magazine quipped 'Any other general in the world than General Howe would have beaten General Washington, and any other general in the world than General Washington would have beaten General Howe'.[1] Admiral Howe thought that with the force available to him it was impossible to win the war.[2] Upon receiving news of Burgoyne's surrender, the Howes requested to be relieved of their commands. General Howe gave the reasons that the government had failed to support him properly and had not listened to his recommendations.[3] The admiral hinted in a dispatch that his health was failing, and even had his wife privately write to North requesting that he be permitted to quit the command in America.[4] But the Howes probably had other motives as well. No doubt both believed – and correctly so – that they would be blamed for the failure of the British effort and wanted to hurry to London and the House of Commons to defend themselves.

---

[1] Quoted in Maldwyn A. Jones, 'Sir William Howe: conventional strategist, 'George Athan Billias, (ed.), *George Washington's Opponents* (New York, 1969),p. 61.
[2] PRO, ADM 1/488, ff. 176-9.
[3] Jones, *op. cit.*, pp. 61-2.
[4] PRO, ADM 1/488, ff. 82-3; NRS, *Sandwich Papers*, vol. II, p. 292.

While the British army passed the winter of 1777-78 in a state of inactivity in garrisons at Philadelphia, New York City and Newport, Rhode Island, the ships of Lord Howe's command continued their coastal blockade in an attempt to suppress rebel cruisers and to prevent the importation of munitions into the colonies. Having more than ninety ships of all classes under his command, Howe nevertheless found his force inadequate to blockade effectively the coast from the Gulf of Maine to Florida while, at the same time, supporting the British army in America. Philadelphia, New York City, Newport, Halifax and Quebec all required warships for their defence and the major British positions in America – Philadelphia, New York and Rhode Island – could only contact each other by means of seaborne communications. On 9 March 1778, 44 out of 92 warships stationed in America were deployed in defence of those major points, while a further seven ships were employed carrying dispatches and escorting military convoys between various British bases. The remaining 39 ships of Howe's command were spread from Canso to St Augustine on blockade duty.[5] The ten ships stationed at the entrance of Chesapeake Bay and off the coasts of the Carolinas captured more than 80 vessels during the winter of 1777-78[6] and the commander of the British forces in East Florida even went so far as to credit the blockade of the southern colonies with preventing an American offensive against St Augustine.[7] But in a dispatch dated 23 April 1778, Howe reported to the Admiralty that while a considerable number of American vessels had been taken from the southern colonies, there was an increasing number of incidents involving neutrals, and that the blockade of the northern colonies was ineffective owing to bad weather, which damaged a number of vessels, and to an insufficient number of ships.[8] Thus during the winter of 1777-78, as in the previous years, the need to support the army, coupled with the great length of the American coast, bad weather and a general shortage of ships, conspired to render the British blockade of America ineffective.

On 21 April 1778, HMS *Andromeda* arrived at Sandy Hook with intelligence of the possibility of a war with France and dispatches ordering General Howe to return to England and the army to stand on the defensive while reinforcing Halifax and Florida and undertaking amphibious raids against New England seaports in order to

[5] PRO, ADM 1/488, ff. 190-1.
[6] Ibid., ff. 239-41.
[7] HMC, *American Manuscripts*, vol. I, p. 202.
[8] PRO, ADM 1/488, ff. 207-9.

destroy American cruisers.[9] However, before these directions could be put into effect, HMS *Porcupine* arrived in the Delaware River on 8 May with dispatches telling of the Franco-American alliance, the impending arrival of the Carlisle Commission (a British delegation that would attempt to reach a settlement with the Americans) and the possibility of French naval forces arriving in American waters. At the same time, orders were received to dispatch a force to seize St Lucia; to evacuate Philadelphia and, if necessary, New York and Rhode Island as well; to reinforce the garrisons of Halifax and the Floridas; and to return to England a battalion of marines and twenty frigates and sloops of war. Simultaneously, Admiral Howe received permission to quit the American command for reasons of ill-health and to return to England.[10] Thus, even before the open intervention of the French, the government had with one stroke radically altered the conduct of the war in America.[11]

No longer would the main British effort be directed at subduing the rebellion in the northern colonies by military conquest and blockade. Rather the government desired that positions on the flanks of America – Nova Scotia and Florida – be reinforced and that, if necessary, everything between Machias and St Augustine be abandoned. Furthermore, by ordering the return to England of twenty warships, the government gave up all hope of a successful blockade of America which, in turn, meant that the Americans would be able still to obtain from Europe the munitions required to carry on the war. In many respects this was an illogical policy when combined with the instructions and objectives of the government's peace commission. In the context of worldwide naval strategy, the evacuation of Philadelphia was arguably a price worth paying in order to gain St Lucia. But at the same time, abandoning Philadelphia and beginning a retreat that might end in Nova Scotia cut the ground out from under the peace commission before that body even reached America. Furthermore, the British were prepared to concede America by withdrawing to Halifax, if militarily necessary, but

---

[9] Ibid., f. 209; see also, PRO, CO/5/236, W. Howe to Germain, 19 April 1778.
[10] PRO, ADM 1/488, ff. 250–1; see also CL, Sackville–Germain Papers, Military Dispatches, 1775–1782, Précis of letters and instructions for Vice-Admiral Howe and notes thereon, 10 March to July 1778.
[11] As William B. Willcox notes, many historians have assumed that the order to abandon Philadelphia, and if necessary the rest of America, was the result of the threat posed by the sailing of d'Estaing's squadron when in fact those instructions were issued more than three weeks before the sailing of the squadron from Toulon: see William B. Willcox, *Portrait of a General: Sir Henry Clinton in the War of Independence* (New York, 1964), p. 224.

not to grant American independence, which was the one thing that would end the war and permit Britain to meet the French challenge freed from her American commitment. The failure of the ministry to see this contradiction meant that from 1778 until the end of the war large British military and naval forces requiring the support of a huge logistical effort would be required in a hopeless and also largely meaningless attempt to subdue the American rebellion while Britain fought for her very life against an alliance of European naval powers.

General Sir Henry Clinton arrived at Philadelphia from New York on 8 May to assume command of the army. On 18 May, in honour of the departing General Howe, the officers of the army staged 'a Regatta, Fête Champêtre, Tilts and Tournaments, Carosal, Procession through Triumphal Arches, Dancing, Exhibition of Fire works, musick and Feast'.[12] If nothing else, this spectacle, called the 'Mischianza' showed that General Howe was still popular with his officers, although it has ever since appeared a rather strange way to celebrate the relief of an unsuccessful general and the beginning of a retreat. On 25 May, General Howe sailed for England aboard HMS *Andromeda*.

Even before the departure of General Howe, the preparations were begun to evacuate Philadelphia. On the night of 6 May an amphibious expedition was sent up the Delaware River to destroy those American vessels that had escaped capture or destruction when the British first occupied the city. The British raiding force proceeded as far as Bordentown, New Jersey, and destroyed forty-two American vessels, including the frigates *Washington* and *Effingham*.[13] All through the month of May orders were issued for the collection and embarkation of army baggage, equipment and munitions[14] while, at the same time, warships and transports were collected and fitted out in order to withdraw the army by sea from Philadelphia.[15] Admiral Howe and General Clinton at first intended to dispatch the reinforcements to the Floridas and the expedition to St Lucia from Philadelphia before evacuating the rest of the army by sea to New York. But Clinton soon abandoned this plan when he discovered that there were not enough transports

---

[12] NYHSC, *Montressor Journals*, p. 492; see also [Israel Mauduit], *Strictures on the Philadelphia Mischianza or Triumph upon leaving America Unconquered* (London, 1779).
[13] PRO, ADM 1/488, ff. 282-4.
[14] E.g. NYHSC, *Kemble Papers*, vol. I, pp. 581, 584, 586.
[15] PRO, ADM 1/488, ff. 277-8.

available to carry the army, all its horses and equipment, and those Loyalists who wanted to flee the city with the British. Therefore, instead of evacuating Philadelphia by sea as instructed, Clinton decided to postpone the departure of the troops to the Floridas and St Lucia and to march the entire army overland to New York through New Jersey, while the heavy equipment, stores and the Loyalists were withdrawn by sea.[16] This was an extremely lucky decision, for although neither Howe nor Clinton knew it, if the troops bound to the Floridas and St Lucia had been dispatched directly from Philadelphia, they would be at sea as d'Estaing's squadron arrived on the American coast.

On the morning of 18 June the eight-month-long British occupation of the largest city in America ended when the last units of King George's army evacuated Philadelphia and crossed the Delaware River into New Jersey on their way to New York. At the same time, Howe's warships, escorting transports crowded with military equipment and Loyalists, dropped down the river. Owing to the lack of wind, the fleet did not clear Delaware Bay until 28 June, and the next morning off the New Jersey coast Howe met the *Grantham* packet carrying the Admiralty's dispatch of 3 May alerting him to the expected arrival in America of both d'Estaing's squadron of 11 ships of the line, one 50-gun ship and 5 frigates, and of reinforcements from England under the command of Vice-Admiral John Byron. In fact the commander of the packet informed Howe that he had encountered the French force at 30° north latitude and 48° west longitude on 6 June and had been chased by d'Estaing's squadron for three days.[17]

The news that a powerful and hostile French squadron was about to appear in America placed the British in a difficult situation. Clinton's army was in central New Jersey marching towards New York City and the ships of the Royal Navy were strung out along the American coast on blockade duty. Howe's squadron consisted mostly of small warships, and only eight British ships of the line and four 50-gun ships were in America.[18] The British positions at New

---

[16] PRO, CO 5/96, ff. 22–3 Mahan maintains, I think incorrectly, that Clinton's decision to march through New Jersey was based on fear of the arrival of the French fleet on the American coast: A.T. Mahan, *The Major Operations of the Navies in the War of American Independence* (New York, 1969 reprint), pp. 62–3.
[17] PRO, ADM 1/488, ff. 292, 294.
[18] Ships of the line, *Eagle, Nonsuch, Somerset, Raisonable, Preston, St Albans, Ardent* and *Trident*; 50-gun ships, *Renown, Centurion, Isis* and *Experiment*: PRO, ADM 1/488, ff. 190–1; the *Trident* carried the Peace Commission to America, and the *Ardent* had just arrived at New York escorting a military convoy from England.

York and Rhode Island might possibly be simultaneously attacked by the Continental Army and d'Estaing's squadron after the Royal Navy had been overpowered by sheer weight of numbers and superior firepower. However, the officers and men of the Royal Navy in America had had three years' war experience, and Admiral Howe, unlike so many other British commanders in America, could be a skilful and determined man, capable of acting quickly and effectively in adverse cirucmstances. Thus luck, French and American ineptitude, and the skill and experience of the British might possibly parry the unexpected Franco-American attack until the arrival of Byron's reinforcements.

On 29 June, Howe arrived at Sandy Hook. The next day the British army, after fighting a sharp rearguard action at Monmouth Court House, reached Navesink and then on a bridge of flat-bottomed boats crossed over to Sandy Hook whence the troops were conveyed to New York City and Long Island by the Royal Navy.[19] Immediately upon reaching New York, Howe and Clinton began defensive preparations against the unexpected Franco-American attack.[20] A dispatch was sent at once to Halifax, the supposed destination of the expected reinforcements from England, with the latest intelligence of the movements of d'Estaing's squadron.[21] Admiral James Gambier, who had been sent out to America by the admiralty as sort of a replacement for Howe, was shoved aside and made into what was in effect a port captain at New York, and Howe resolved to stay in America until the crisis passed and a suitable flag officer appeared to take command of the squadron.[22] But Howe soon found that he had very limited and weak forces with which to defend the maritime approaches to New York. There were only 15 warships at New York: seven ships of the line, two 50-gun ships, two 44-gun frigates, three frigates and an armed vessel.[23] Furthermore, the crews of these ships were sickly, and about 900 other men were ashore in the naval hospital.[24]

Howe, however, deployed the ships of his comand with great skill

---

[19] Harry Miller Lydenberg (ed.), *Archibald Robertson, Lieutenant-General Royal Engineers, His Diaries and Sketches in America, 1762–1780* (New York, 1930), pp. 178–9.
[20] CL, Clinton Papers Howe to Clinton, 1 July 1778.
[21] PRO, ADM 1/488, ff. 294–5.
[22] Ibid., f. 293; see also n.67, below.
[23] Ships of the line, *Eagle, Ardent, Trident, St Albans, Somerset, Nonsuch* and *Preston;* 50-gun ships, *Experiment* and *Isis*; 44-gun frigates, *Phoenix* and *Roebuck*; frigates, *Pearl, Venus* and *Richmond*; and armed vessel, *Vigilant*: PRO, ADM 1/488, f. 293.
[24] PRO, ADM 1/488, f. 292.

and energy to meet the unexpected French attack. A string of cruisers was stationed along the coast between New York and Chesapeake Bay to warn of the approach of d'Estaing's force.[25] On 5 July the French squadron was intercepted by Howe's cruisers off the entrance of Chesapeake Bay, and as d'Estaing proceeded northward along the coast he was constantly shadowed by British cruisers who reported to Howe every movement. On 8 July, Howe learned at 6 a.m. of the arrival of the French off Virginia, and later that same day the British commander figured out that the objective of the French force was New York City.[26] But on 10 July he also learned that units of the Continental Army were crossing the Hudson north of New York City and heading towards New England, which pointed towards an attack being made on the British at Rhode Island. Howe then planned to hold the French at Sandy Hook and to reinforce the garrison at Rhode Island before Long Island Sound could be closed by the enemy. And on the morning of 11 July, Howe received intelligence that d'Estaing was approaching Sandy Hook.[27]

As the French approached the seaward side of Sandy Hook, Howe anchored the ships of his command in a line broadside to the channel just inside of the Hook. If the French attempted to enter Lower New York Bay, each of their ships in succession would be raked by cannon fire as they passed up the channel and along the line of British ships. Lord Howe had picked an extremely strong position: the French could only enter Lower New York Bay at flood tide and with an east or southeasterly wind, and the British ships could cripple the French ships in the rigging as the enemy passed up the channel. Those French ships that were disabled would then drift into Lower New York Bay and fetch up upon the shores of either Staten Island or Brooklyn or be overpowered by British small craft. However, there were two weaknesses in the British position. According to Lord Howe's flag captain, Henry Duncan, the British ships 'in general were but very indifferently manned, owing to sickness and their being short of complement'. If when the French first approached Sandy Hook, which was then an unoccupied island, they or the Americans had seized the Hook and mounted heavy guns

---

[25] NRS, *Sandwich Papers*, vol. II, p. 285n.
[26] CL, Clinton Papers, Howe to Clinton, 1 July [1778]; PRO, ADM 1/488, f. 299. The French squadron consisted of 16 ships – ships of the line, *Languedoc, Tonnant, Cesar, Zèle, Hector, Guerrier, Marseillais, Protecteur, Vaillant, Provence* and *Fantasque*; 50-gun ship, *Sagittaires*; and frigates, *Chimère, Engageante, Aimable* and *Alcmene*: NRS, *Sandwich Papers*, vol. II, p. 286.
[27] CL, Clinton Papers, Howe to Clinton, 10 July [1778]; Howe to Clinton, Friday, p. 10 [11 July 1778].

there, the British ships could have been easily forced from their anchorage. But the British quickly saw this weakness, and on 11 July sent the 15th and 44th Regiments to occupy and dig in on Sandy Hook.[28]

On the evening of 11 July the British and French squadrons were only a mile or two apart and separated from each other by the dunes of Sandy Hook. Some of the British, such as Captain Andrew Snape Hamond, 'fully expected an attack',[29] but d'Estaing hesitated. Although on 12 July the French began to take soundings off Sandy Hook,[30] they still did not attempt to force an entry into Lower New York Bay. What deterred d'Estaing from attacking the British was a lack of information about the tides, bar and channel at Sandy Hook. d'Estaing had at hand the greatest strategic prize in America, but having already had one of his ships of the line run aground at the entrance of the Delaware, he feared that he might lose his squadron if he attempted to force his way past the British at Sandy Hook without adequate pilots. So while the French waited for pilots, the British defensive position grew stronger. By 19 July the garrison on Sandy Hook had been increased to 1,800 men, and at the request of Howe a number of cannon and howitzers were emplaced there as well.[31] HMS *Leviathan*, formerly a ship of the line that had been converted into a naval storeship, joined the squadron at the Hook after being armed with cannon drawn from the army's siege train, and a number of transports were converted into fireships. The shortage of seamen was also overcome by embarking soldiers as marines, and at the request of Howe over 1,000 seamen from the transports volunteered to serve in the king's ships on the condition that they be discharged from the Royal Navy when the admiral gave up his command.[32] As the British forces at Sandy Hook grew stronger, d'Estaing's desire to attack them grew weaker. One British officer, Commodore William Hotham, thought that the mere sight of the British 'weighed as much with the Count as the pretended difficulty of passing over the bar with his long-legged ships might do'.[33] After eleven days of being inactive for, and receiving pes-

---

[28] NRS, *The Naval Miscellany*, vol. I, p. 160; NYHSC, *Montressor Journals*, p. 504.
[29] Quote from William Hugh Moomaw, 'The naval career of Captain Hamond, 1775-1779' (unpublished PhD dissertation, University of Virginia, 1955), p. 405.
[30] NYHSC, *Montressor Journals*, p. 505.
[31] CL, Clinton Papers, Howe to Clinton, Monday 13 [July, 1778].
[32] NRS, *The Naval Miscellany*, vol. I, p. 160; NRS, *Sandwich Papers*, vol. II, pp. 304, 307; NYHSC, *Montressor Journals*, pp. 504-6; Henry Cabot Lodge (ed.), *Major André's Journal* (New York, 1930), p. 82.
[33] Quoted in Willcox, *op. cit.*, p. 239.

simistic reports on, the navigational difficulties of crossing the bar into Lower New York Bay, d'Estaing sailed from Sandy Hook on the morning of 22 July, headed south into the Atlantic and disappeared.[34]

The sudden departure of the French squadron from Sandy Hook placed the British in a strategic quandry. It was unlikely that the French would either return to Europe after such a brief appearance off New York or head for the West Indies so near the beginning of the hurricane season. On 26 July, Howe received information that d'Estaing had been sighted 30 leagues off Delaware Bay and was steering south-south-east, but the British admiral could not determine the objective of the French squadron.[35] Because of the build-up of American forces in New England, Clinton concluded by 27 July that Rhode Island was going to be attacked.[36] This was little more than an educated guess, however, for the French squadron could be going to Chesapeake Bay or some other place in the South, or d'Estaing could double back and attack either New York or Rhode Island, or possibly Halifax, which was not very well defended. The garrison of Rhode Island was weak and would probably be captured if attacked by the French squadron in conjunction with the American army. But the greatest danger to the British in America was the shortage of provisions at New York, combined with the possibility that d'Estaing's squadron would return to Sandy Hook and intercept British army victuallers as they arrived, and thereby starve the British at New York into capitulation.[37] But no matter what d'Estaing's squadron did, its mere existence in American waters posed a great threat to the British until the arrival of the expected reinforcements from England under Byron.

The speculation ended on 28 July when Howe, aided by intelligence from his cruisers, determined that d'Estaing had doubled back and was heading for Rhode Island and would arrive at that place at the beginning of August.[38] Howe decided to sail there at once with what ships he could muster in order to attempt to relieve it.[39] But unless Byron arrived or the Americans and French were incredibly

---

[34] PRO, ADM 1/488, f. 304. For d'Estaing's explanation of why he did not attempt to cross the bar at Sandy Hook see Henri Doniol, *Histoire de la Participation de la France a L'Éstablissement Des États-Unis D' Amerique* (Paris, 1888), Vol. III, pp. 448–9.
[35] CL, Clinton Papers, Howe to Clinton, 28 July 1778.
[36] HMC, *Stopford-Sackville MSS.*, vol. II, pp. 116–17
[37] Willcox, pp. 239–40.
[38] CL, Clinton Papers, Howe to Clinton, 28 July 1778.
[39] Ibid.

unlucky, Howe's efforts could not be much more than a valiant attempt, for while the British ships were more numerous, the eleven French ships of the line were greatly superior in firepower.

Before Howe could sail from New York, the badly damaged HMS *Cornwall*, one of the ships of Vice-Admiral John Byron's squadron, arrived on 30 July at Sandy Hook with the first news to reach the British in America of the fate of Byron's reinforcement. From what little information the captain of the *Cornwall* could supply, it was clear that Byron's squadron would not be of immediate assistance in the relief of Rhode Island. Byron, known throughout the service as 'Foul-weather Jack' because of his tendency to encounter bad weather, had sailed from England on 9 June. On 3 July at 48°53' north latitude and 31°16' west longitude the admiral encountered a storm that heavily damaged and scattered the ships of his command. HMS *Russell* was forced back to England. HMS *Guadaloupe* and HMS *Invincible* made it into St John's, Newfoundland, though badly damaged. HMS *Albion* reached New York in October after being refitted in Lisbon. By the end of August eight of Byron's ships had managed to stagger into New York with sick crews and with extensive damage in their masts and rigging.[40] After sighting d'Estaing's squadron on 18 August off the coast of New York, Byron headed in HMS *Princess Royal* for Halifax where he joined HMS *Culloden*. The two ships did not sail for America until 2 September.[41] Despite the tardy departure of Byron's squadron from England, the British possibly could have concentrated an overpowering naval force against d'Estaing at Rhode Island but for the ill-luck suffered by the squadron from England. However, the arrival of HMS *Cornwall* made it clear to the British at New York that they would have to counter the Franco-American attack on Rhode Island without any hope of being significantly reinforced.

Ever since the British seized Newport in 1776, Rhode Island had been a tempting target for the Americans, but as long as the Royal Navy controlled Narragansett Bay, the Americans could do little. Before the arrival of d'Estaing's squadron in America, the British restricted their main defensive effort to amphibious 'spoiling' attacks against concentrations of American small craft and supply depots at various points along the shores of Narragansett Bay.[42]

---

[40] *Cornwall, Monmouth, Royal Oak, Conqueror, Fame, Sultan, Bedford* and *Grafton*: NRS, *Sandwich Papers*, vol.II, p. 287.
[41] PRO, ADM 1/486, ff. 115–19, 126, 128; ADM 1/489, ff. 19–21; see also Robert Greenhalgh Albion, *Forests and Seapower* (Cambridge, Mass., 1926), pp. 296–300.
[42] PRO, ADM 1/488, 488, ff. 288–9.

However, with the arrival of d'Estaing off New York and the build-up of American forces in the region of Narragansett Bay, the British began to fear that their position at Rhode Island might be jointly attacked by the Americans and the French. Just before the French squadron arrived off Sandy Hook, 15 transports full of troops were dispatched on 9 July from New York up Long Island Sound to reinforce the garrison at Newport.[43] But sending additional troops to Rhode Island would not make that place secure, for the key to the defense of Newport was naval control of Narragansett Bay. Even if the Americans managed to gain a foothold on Rhode Island, the ships of the Royal Navy could cut their supply lines to the mainland. But if d'Estaing's squadron entered the bay and overpowered the British ships there while the American army attacked Newport, the British garrison would find itself in a situation similar to that of Cornwallis at Yorktown in 1781.

At 10 a.m. on 29 July, d'Estaing's squadron appeared off Newport, and the next morning two French ships of the line pushed up Narragansett Channel and anchored between the mainland and Conanicut Island, which the British then evacuated. At the same time, French frigates entered Sekonnet Passage between the mainland and the island of Rhode Island. Simultaneously, the British troops began concentrating in prepared defensive positions around the town of Newport, while Captain John Brisbane, the senior navy officer at Rhode Island, prepared to sink transports to block the approaches to Newport, stripped of guns and provisions the warships stationed at Rhode Island and formed their crews into naval battalions to fight on shore. At 4 p.m. on 8 August the French began the attack on Newport by entering the harbour with ten ships of the line and anchoring off the east side of Conanicut Island, which was occupied by French landing parties. Brisbane thereupon ordered transports to be sunk to prevent the French ships from moving closer to Newport's seaward defenses and had five warships burned to prevent them from falling into French hands. The next day several thousand Americans crossed over from the mainland to the northern end of the island of Rhode Island and began slowly to envelop the British positions at Newport.[44] By withdrawing into defensive positions around Newport and destroying their ships, the British forces at Rhode Island were preparing for a siege in order to buy time because the only thing that could save them was the prompt arrival

---

[43] NYHSC, *Montressor Journals*, pp. 504, 506.
[44] PRO, ADM 1/488, ff. 323-31. The warships destroyed at Rhode Island were *Kingsfisher* on 30 July, and on 8 August *Flora, Juno, Lark, Orpheus* and *Falcon*.

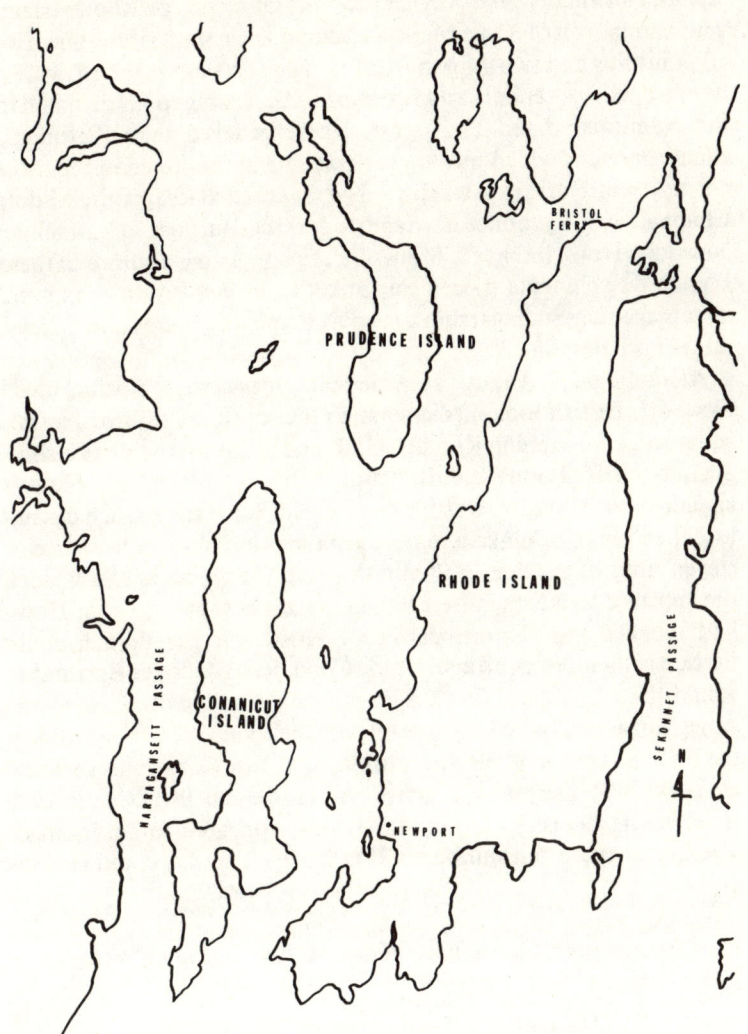

Map 6
Narragansett Bay, Rhode Island

of Howe from New York with sufficient ships either to destroy or drive the French squadron from Narragansett Bay.

Lord Howe was prevented from sailing from Sandy Hook by adverse winds and tides for several days after he had received intelligence that d'Estaing's squadron was proceeding to Rhode Island. But finally on 6 August the admiral sailed for Rhode Island with a squadron of 35 warships, including seven ships of the line, five 50-gun ships and two 44-gun frigates. The rest were regular frigates, bombs, galleys, tenders and fireships.[45] According to his dispatch to the Admiralty dated 17 August, Howe believed that d'Estaing's squadron was divided into three detachments stationed in the three entrances of Narragansett Bay – Narragansett Passage, the Middle Channel and Sakonnet Passage – for the purpose of attacking Newport. Howe intended, if possible, to attack one or more of these French detachments piecemeal, in order to employ to maximum advantage the small warships, such as bombs, fireships and galleys, under his command.[46]

At noon on 9 August as American troops were closing in on Newport, British lookouts saw far to the south the sails of Howe's squadron approaching Rhode Island, and at 7 p.m. the British ships anchored off Point Judith.[47] But with the arrival of Howe's squadron the situation was far from saved, for if the French did not lose their nerve or make a major mistake they could with a force of eleven ships of the line, a 50-gun ship and four frigates easily block the entrance to Narragansett Bay in much the same way that Howe had blocked the channel at Sandy Hook. Or the French could barricade themselves up against the Conanicut Island, as Barrington would do at St Lucia. With a little thought and skill aided by the American army, there is no reason why the French could not subject the British garrison at Newport to the same fate Cornwallis suffered at Yorktown. Despite the arrival of Howe, on the evening of 9 August, the British garrison at Newport appeared to be doomed. The Continentals outnumbered King George's soldiers, and Howe's

---

[45] Ships of the line, *Eagle, Trident, Cornwall, Nonsuch, Raisonable, Somerset, St Albans* and *Ardent*; 50-gun ships, *Experiment, Isis* and *Renown*; 44-gun frigates, *Phoenix* and *Roebuck*; frigates, *Venus, Richmond, Pearl, Apollo* and *Sphinx*; armed vessel, *Vigilant*; sloop, *Nautilus*; fireships, *Stromboli, Sulphur* and *Volcano*; bombs, *Thunder* and *Carcass*; galleys, *Philadelphia, Hussar, Ferret* and *Cornwallis*; plus two tenders: PRO, ADM 1/488, f. 319.
[46] Ibid., f. 314.
[47] *Diary of Frederick Mackenzie: Giving a Daily Narrative of His Military Service as an Officer of the Regiment of Royal Welch Fusiliers during the years 1775–1781 in Massachusetts, Rhode Island, and New York* (Cambridge, Mass., 1930), vol. II, p. 341; NRS, *The Naval Miscellany*, vol. I, p. 161.

squadron, if not shot to bits, could be very roughly handled by the French while attempting to relieve Newport. All the French and the Americans had to do was to maintain their present positions in the face of inferior British forces, and the British at Newport would in the end be forced to surrender.

But d'Estaing did not desire to fight a defensive battle in the confined waters of Narragansett Bay: if any of his ships were damaged, he feared they would be forced by the prevailing southerly winds on to the shores of British-held Rhode Island.[48] Therefore, on the morning of 10 August when a northeasterly wind developed, d'Estaing sailed from Narragansett Bay with the apparent intention of either fighting a decisive battle with Howe's squadron, or at least driving the British naval force away from Rhode Island. When Howe saw the French squadron leaving the bay, he detached HMS *Sphinx* to escort to New York the squadron's tenders, bombs and galleys. With his main force, including three fireships, formed into a line of battle, Howe retreated before the wind on a southerly course with d'Estaing in pursuit. Howe was in a difficult situation, for his squadron did not have the firepower to stand up to the French ships of the line in a regular ship-to-ship engagement, as long as the wind remained northerly, which is unusual for the coast of New England during the summer, d'Estaing had the weather gauge and could, if he overtook the British, force Howe to fight at a disadvantage. Howe nevertheless hoped that the wind would swing around to a prevailing south or southwesterly direction later in the day, so that he would then have the weather gauge and could turn on the French and attack them with his fireships and frigates.[49]

The wind did not shift around to the south. On the morning of 11 August it was east–north-east and the French squadron was hull down and directly to the windward of the British. Howe then began a series of manoeuvres in order to gain the weather gauge, so that he could engage d'Estaing's force. Both the British and the French squadrons assumed line-astern formations sailing before the wind, with the lead French ship following the rearmost British ship. At 8 a.m., Howe began gradually to change the course of the British line

---

[48] Doniol, *op cit.*, Vol. III, p. 452.
[49] Howe in his dispatch to the Admiralty does not mention his intention of attacking the French with fireships, but only that he has kept three of them with him: PRO, ADM 1/488, ff. 314-15; but Duncan believed that Howe kept the fireships with the squadron in order to attack d'Estaing with them if the wind changed direction: NRS, *The Naval Miscellany*, vol. I, p. 161. See also [Thomas O'Beirne], *A Candid and Impartial Narrative of the Transactions of the Fleet under the Command of Lord Howe* (London, 2nd edn, n.d.), p. 30.

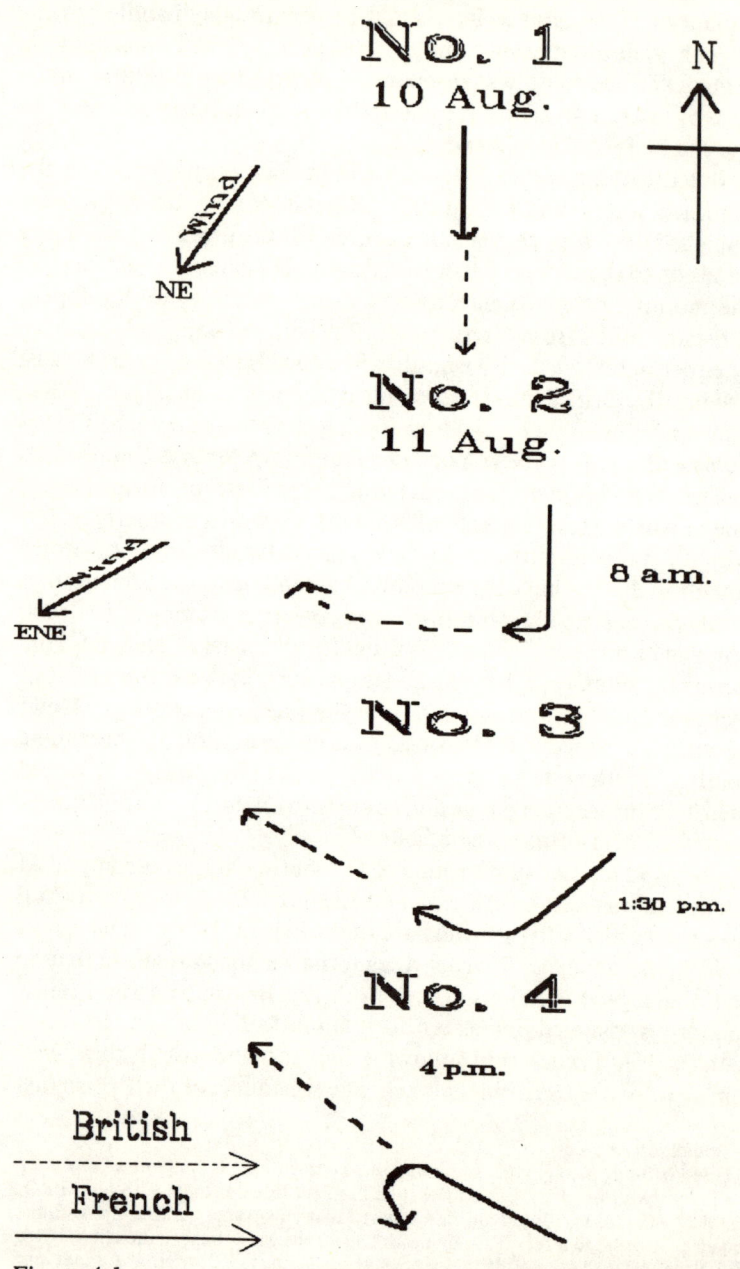

Figure 4.1
Howe and D'Estaing, 10–11 August 1778

towards a westerly heading and then towards a more northerly one. These changes in course were performed by the British line in succession from the van; that is, the lead British ship would change its course and then the manoeuvre would be repeated, in turn, by each British ship. The French squadron followed in the wake of the British with d'Estaing not countering Howe's actions, but only adjusting his course to match the British changes in direction. The result of these manoeuvres was that by 1.30 p.m. Howe's squadron, still in line-astern formation, had made almost a complete about-face and was steering north-west with the line of French ships still astern on the same course.

In the middle of the afternoon Howe shifted his flag to the frigate *Apollo*, so that he would be in a better position to supervise the movements of his ships. By 4 p.m. the French squadron had been manoeuvred into a position so far leeward of the British that if he had attacked, Howe could have weathered d'Estaing's squadron and gained the weather gauge. But before Howe could execute this manoeuvre, the French squadron, which was now south-south-east of the British, turned away to the southward because of the lateness of the day and the increasingly foul weather.[50]

In the evening of 11 August the weather turned bad with heavy seas and gale-force winds. Both Howe's and d'Estaing's squadrons were scattered and suffered heavy damage in the masts and rigging before the storm blew itself out on 13 August. Because of the bad weather, Howe could not return to his flagship from the *Apollo*, which had been reduced by the storm to little more than a wreck, until the afternoon of 13 August.[51] By then the only ships that still remained in company with Howe were one 50-gun ship, four frigates and an armed ship. The rest of the British squadron was limping back to Sandy Hook with broken masts and shattered rigging.[52] The French ships of the line *Languedoc* and *Marseillais* lost all their masts, except for the latter's mainmast, in the storm, and during the evening of 13 August these two disabled French ships were attacked by HMS *Renown* and HMS *Preston*. But because of heavy seas and darkness, the captains of the two British 50-gun ships did not press their attacks during the night, and the British ships were driven away from the *Languedoc* and *Marseillais* the next morning when six

---

[50] PRO, ADM 1/488, ff. 315–16; NRS, *The Naval Miscellany*, vol. I, pp. 161–2.
[51] For an account of the condition of the *Apollo* after the storm and Howe's difficulty in leaving that ship see Moomaw, *op. cit.*, pp. 409–11.
[52] The ships remaining with Howe on 13 August were the *Centurion*, *Apollo*, *Richmond*, *Roebuck*, *Phoenix* and *Vigilant*: PRO, AD, 1/488, ff. 315–17, 332–3.

enemy ships of the line appeared. Three days later, on 16 August, HMS *Isis*, some 20 leagues from Sandy Hook, engaged the 74-gun *Cesar* in an hour-and-a-half running battle, during which the rigging of both ships were badly shot up. But despite such chance engagements, both the French and British squadrons were for some time virtually disbanded as organized fighting formations by the storm.

After shifting his flag to HMS *Centurion*, Howe, with the remnants of his squadron, proceeded south along the coast in quest of d'Estaing. On the morning of 15 August, after hearing gunfire in the distance, Howe located a number of French warships laying at anchor about 20 leagues east of Cape May. Leaving a ship to shadow the French force, the British admiral sailed for Sandy Hook where he arrived on 18 August to find most of the missing ships of his squadron anchored with varying degrees of damage in their masts and rigging.[53]

The danger to the British garrison at Rhode Island had not passed with the departure of d'Estaing's squadron. The American army, in the absence of the French ships, had been laying siege to Newport, and if the French returned, the situation at Newport would be exactly the same as it was before 10 August when d'Estaing had sailed forth in pursuit of Howe's squadron. The danger seemed imminent when, on 22 August, Howe learned from HMS *Galatea*, which had sighted nine French ships of the line off Block Island, that d'Estaing was returning to Rhode Island, apparently with the intention of renewing the siege of Newport in conjunction with the American army.[54] During the next two days Howe learned from other frigates that all of d'Estaing's ships, including the dismasted *Languedoc* and *Marseillais* had returned to Rhode Island. On 24 August, after having passed through the French squadron at night in a small boat, Lieutenant John Stanhope, RN, arrived at Sandy Hook from Newport with information that the British garrison at Rhode Island was still capable of continued resistance. Howe thereupon planned to sail as soon as possible from Sandy Hook for Rhode Island with what ships he could muster in order either to drive or again draw d'Estaing's force away from Newport. Meanwhile Clinton would ready transports and troops at the western end of Long Island Sound in order to reinforce Newport quickly as soon as the French squadron left the region.[55]

[53] PRO, ADM 1/488, f. 316.
[54] CL, Clinton Papers, Howe to Clinton, 22 August 1778.
[55] Ibid., Howe to Clinton, 24 August 1778; Clinton to Howe, 24 August 1778; PRO, ADM 1/488, f. 336.

On 25 August Howe, whose ships had been quickly repaired, sailed from Sandy Hook for Rhode Island. Just after leaving the Hook, however, the British admiral received intelligence that d'Estaing's entire squadron before daylight on 22 August had left Rhode Island and was apparently proceeding to Boston.[56] The departure of d'Estaing for Boston enraged the rebels at Rhode Island, for they believed that if the French squadron had remained a short time longer off Newport, the British garrison there would have been forced to surrender. But the French ships had been greatly damaged in the storm of 11 August; Howe at New York was obviously preparing to return to Rhode Island to attack the French squadron; and the brief encounter with Byron's flagship HMS *Princess Royal* on 18 August, off the coast of Long Island, indicated to the French that the British in America were being reinforced. d'Estaing explained to his allies that he was bound by his instructions not to risk his force in an engagement against a superior enemy squadron and that, after dismasting of the *Languedoc* and *Marseillais* and the shooting up of the *Cesar*, his squadron had been greatly weakened and the British were now superior.[57] To the French, America was a sideshow that tied down British forces: the West Indies and the English Channel were the important theatres of operations. Most likely, d'Estaing's main – if unstated – reason for withdrawing from Rhode Island was not the supposed superiority of the British, but rather the need to preserve and repair his damaged ships, so that his squadron would at the end of the hurricane season be ready to undertake operations in the West Indies.[58]

Upon learning that d'Estaing had left Rhode Island, Howe decided to attempt to intercept the French before they could reach the safety of Boston Harbor. Howe believed that the French squadron because of the dismasted condition of the *Languedoc* and *Marseillais* would have to pass to the eastward of George's Bank; if he acted quickly and proceeded directly towards Boston through the Muskeget Channel between Martha's Vineyard and Nantucket, passing to the westward of George's Bank, he had a good chance of intercepting d'Estaing either off Cape Cod or in Massachusetts Bay.[59] Arguably, however, Howe should not have pursued d'Estaing's squadron, but rather sailed directly for Rhode Island, then

---

[56] PRO, ADM 1/488, f. 338.
[57] Otis G. Hammond (ed.), *Letters and Papers of Major-General John Sullivan, Continental Army* (Concord, NH, 1931), Vol. II, pp. 237–8.
[58] Cf. E.H. Jenkins, *A History of the French Navy* (London, 1973), p. 153.
[59] CL, Clinton Papers, Howe to Clinton, 25 August 1778; PRO, ADM 1/488, f. 338.

proceeded up Narragansett Bay as far as Bristol Ferry in order to trap the Continental Army besieging Newport.[60] Clinton intended to send a 4,000-man reinforcement down Long Island Sound and land the force on Bristol Neck before the Americans could get off Rhode Island. But because of calms and other delays, the Americans were warned of the approach of the transports carrying the troops from New York and evacuated Rhode Island on 30 August just as the force reached Newport.[61] If he had gone to Rhode Island instead of Massachusetts Bay, Howe could have cut off the rebel army on that island, for the admiral's squadron would have approached Newport without warning by a route that was out of sight of land. There had been ample time, for on 30 August, the day the Americans evacuated Rhode Island, Howe was already off Boston. The possibility, however, of trapping and destroying an American army apparently never entered Howe's head: the British admiral considered d'Estaing's squadron to be his major objective.

Howe, after intercepting and capturing while en route for Boston the Continental armed brig *Resistance*, entered Boston Bay on 30 August and found that d'Estaing had already reached the safety of Boston Harbor. Hamond in HMS *Roebuck* stood in near to the shore to reconnoitre the French position, and reported to Howe that d'Estaing's squadron could be successfully attacked if it were done at once. However, it was almost dark and Howe decided to withdraw from the entrance of Boston Harbor and reconnoitre the French position further the next day. But during the night of 30–31 August HMS *St Albans* ran aground near the end of Cape Cod and by the time the ship had been refloated and the British squadron had re-crossed Massachusetts Bay, it was the evening of 1 September, and in the meantime the French had moved their ships deeper into Boston Harbor and fortified the approaches to that port. Howe then concluded that the French position at Boston was too strong to attack and that d'Estaing intended to remain there for some time, so on 2 September the British sailed for Rhode Island.[62]

Howe's squadron arrived off Rhode Island on 4 September and remained there for the next five days while British amphibious forces raided New Bedford, the shores of Buzzard's Bay and Martha's Vineyard, seizing provisions and cattle and destroying ships and

---

[60] See e.g. Willcox, *op. cit.*, p. 250.
[61] William B. Willcox (ed.), *The American Rebellion: Sir Henry Clinton's Narrative of His Campaigns, 1775–1782, with an appendix of original documents* (New Haven, Conn., 1954), pp. 102–3.
[62] PRO, ADM 1/488, ff. 340–1; Moomaw, *op. cit.*, p. 412.

buildings. During this period Clinton urged over and over again that the admiral return to Boston accompanied by 6,000 troops under the general's command to attack and destroy d'Estaing's squadron in port before it could be refitted for further service. But this scheme received a cool reception from Howe who, according to Clinton, was determined now that d'Estaing was safely in Boston and the naval crisis in America had passed, to give up his command to Byron and to return to England as soon as possible.[63] Whether or not Clinton's plan for destroying the French squadron at Boston by an amphibious attack would have been successful will never be known. But Howe's failure seriously to consider the general's scheme is one of the many opportunities to strike a heavy blow at their enemies in America that the British passed lightly over.

On 9 September the wind swung around to the eastward, signalling the onset of bad weather. Thereupon, Howe withdrew from the coast of southern New England and sailed for New York where he arrived on 11 September to find at anchor six ships of Byron's squadron under command of Rear-Admiral Hyde Parker, Sr, which had reached Sandy Hook on 28 August.[64] Howe then informed Clinton that he was turning over command of the ships at New York to Gambier and would leave for England as soon as possible.[65] On 24 September, in HMS *Eagle*, Howe left New York to go to Rhode Island in order to transfer command of the squadron in America to Byron, who was at Newport. Two days later Howe sailed for England, and after being chased by two French ships of the line off the Scilly Islands, reached St Helens on 25 October.[66]

By September 1778, when Howe sailed for England, the whole conduct of the war in America was being changed. No longer was it British policy to crush American resistance in the northern colonies by means of blockade and military conquest. The army at New York was to be reduced in strength in order to supply troops for operations in the West Indies and the American South. For all practical purposes, the blockade of America was abandoned with the arrival of d'Estaing's squadron in the Western hemisphere, for the ships of the Royal Navy were not deployed on blockade duty, but rather to defend New York, Newport and Halifax, and to counter French naval power in America. On 11 September, for example, of the 85

---

[63] Willcox, *The American Rebellion*, p. 104.
[64] *Royal Oak, Fame, Grafton, Bedford, Sultan* and *Conqueror*: CL, Clinton Papers, Howe to Clinton, 11 September 1778; PRO ADM 1/489, f. 21.
[65] CL, Clinton Papers, Howe to Clinton, 12 September 1778.
[66] PRO, ADM 1/488, ff. 372-3

warships of all classes under Howe's command, four were in the St Lawrence River, two were at St Augustine with orders to sail to New York, and the remaining 79 were deployed either near or at New York, Rhode Island or Halifax. Not one ship of the Royal Navy was stationed along the American coast between New York and St Augustine. Delaware Bay, Chesapeake Bay and the coasts of the Carolinas were unguarded: the blockade had ceased to exist.[67]

The blockade was abandoned because of the strategic requirement to concentrate British naval power in the face of the threat posed by the arrival of d'Estaing's squadron in America, but also by a conscious change in British strategy. To Sandwich and other officials at the Admiralty the great threat to Britain was French naval power; operations in America were considered secondary. Thus the major objective set forth in Byron's instructions, unlike those issued to Howe in 1776, was not subduing the rebellion in America, but rather pursuing and destroying d'Estaing's squadron.[68] So when the French squadron at Boston left America, Byron would sail in pursuit of it and thereby reduce British naval forces in America to a mere shadow of their former strength.

At the same time, Germain and others in the American secretary of state's office realized that the blockade of America had been a paradoxical failure. While alone in the eleven months between October 1777 and September 1778 those ships of Howe's command operating north of Chesapeake Bay had captured 218 American vessels,[69] the rebels continued to be able to import munitions, and the American cruiser offensive against British seaborne trade steadily grew in intensity.[70] Therefore, in an attempt to make up for

---

[67] Ibid., ff. 419-20.
[68] NRS, *Sandwich Papers*, vol. II, pp. 374-6.
[69] PRO, ADM 1/488, ff. 484-90.
[70] An indication of the strength and growth of the American attack on British merchant shipping can be gained by studying the rate at which privateer commissions were issued. During the war the Continental Congress issued letters of marque at the following rates:

1776 - 34	1780 - 300
1777 - 69	1781 - 566
1778 - 163	1782 - 397
1779 - 209	1783 - 22

These 1,760 letters of marque do not include privateers comissioned by the various state governments, nor warships commissioned either by the state or continental authorities: Charles Henry Lincoln (comp.), *Naval Records of the American Revolution* (Washington, DC, 1906).

the failures of the blockade, Germain introduced a new policy that would, if successful, make a blockade unnecessary. On 10 February 1778, Germain issued orders for the British forces in America to undertake large-scale and systematic amphibious raids against New England seaports with the objective of destroying not only American cruisers and blockade runners in port, but their bases as well.[71] Clinton was right when he described this policy as war by 'conflagration', for by Germain's orders the blockade would be replaced by a policy of burning every American seaport to the ground.

Many British commanders in America rejected on humanitarian grounds the policy of destroying American seaports as a means of preventing the Americans from waging war. The Howes, despite many injunctions from London, flatly refused to put into effect a scorched-earth policy. Clinton was less than enthusiastic about the idea of bringing fire and sword to American seaports and only halfheartedly carried out Germain's raiding policy. A number of British, however, were enthusiastic about burning American towns. William Knox, an under-secretary of state, thought that the destruction of New Bedford alone did more to subdue the Americans than any other action taken by Lord Howe.[72] On 24 October 1778 a young Scots officer wrote from New York:

> We have been a little employed of late in burning and destroying and are in hopes that the fashion may take root, which perhaps might prove as speedy a means of finishing the Rebellion as what has been hitherto adopted.[73]

Charles Stuart, in a remarkable letter to his father, Lord Bute, was one of the few among the British who asked and then answered the most basic of all questions about the raiding policy, namely: was it in the best interests of Britain and would it work? Stuart's answer was a flat 'no', for he thought that a 'war of destruction' was beyond the capabilities of the British. In order to destroy American ability to continue the war the king's forces would have to destroy everything in a 10-mile-wide strip running along the coast from New Hampshire to Georgia, and clearly 'this scheme could not be effectually executed'. Moreover, even if the British could wreak so much destruction that the rebels stopped fighting, it would be bad policy, for as Stuart pointed out:

---

[71] CL, Sackville–Germain Papers, p. 406.
[72] HMC, *Various Collections*, vol. VI, p. 153.
[73] Eric Robson (ed.), *Letters from America* (New York, 1950), p. 61.

There are some who argue that in case . . . the Country is left, rigorous measures should be adopted in order to prevent a rapid growth of an Empire in order to prevent a rapid growth of an Empire; this would be rational if one could be sure of injuring them sufficiently, but it is rash to incure their determined enmity forever. In political language, we must weigh their Friendship and their Hatred, and decide accordingly.[74]

Nevertheless, beginning with the burning of New Bedford, numerous American towns would be attacked and destroyed in a futile attempt to break American resistance.

As soon as d'Estaing's squadron entered Boston, the British at New York prepared to dispatch troops both to the West Indies to seize the island of St Lucia and to the Floridas to undertake an invasion of Georgia as called for in the government's instructions of 21 and 22 March 1778.[75] Meanwhile the shattered and sickly ships of Byron's command were being repaired, refitted and remanned. Every one of the ships that had left England with Byron and had managed to reach New York was damaged en route, while the six ships that arrived at New York on 5 September under the command of Rear-Admiral Parker had some 1,200 sick crewmen. Because of a general shortage of naval stores, masts, slops and seamen in America, Byron's force of ships of the line did not get to sea again until 19 October.[76]

Even after the departure of Howe, Clinton did not drop the idea of destroying d'Estaing's squadron at Boston by means of an amphibious *coup de main*. Nothing could be done, however, without Byron, and owing to adverse weather, the admiral did not reach New York until the beginning of October. But with Byron's arrival, Clinton grew more cautious and quickly gave up the idea of attacking Boston. Many years after the war, the general wrote: 'Though I would have attempted it with Lord Howe, I could not [be] so pressing with Byron, whom I did not know and who knew nothing of Boston.'[77] Byron thereupon lost all interest in attacking Boston, if he ever had any, and instead planned to intercept d'Estaing's squadron as it left Boston Bay. The concept of cruising with a squadron of ships of the line within Massachusetts Bay during the late autumn was rash because of the great danger of the ships being

[74] E. Stuart Wortley (ed.), *A Prime Minister and His Son* (London, 1925), pp. 132–3.
[75] See above, pp. 93–4.
[76] PRO, ADM 1/486, ff. 129–30; NRS, *Sandwich Papers*, vol. II, p. 309.
[77] Quoted in Willcox, *Portrait of a General*, p. 253.

driven to leeward and ashore on Cape Cod in the event of a northerly gale. However, this danger did not deter Byron, who always encountered bad weather. The admiral, thinking that the French were about to sail from Boston, sent four ships[78] to cruise the Massachusetts Bay and, on 19 October, Byron himself with his whole force of ships of the line sailed for Boston Bay with the intention of intercepting d'Estaing. Before reaching Boston Bay, Byron on 1 November encountered fogs and gales of wind that scattered, damaged and drove his squadron offshore. On 6 November, as the unlucky British admiral was proceeding to the safety of Rhode Island, he captured two small French ships whose men told him that d'Estaing had left Boston, but they did not know the destination of the French squadron.[79]

It would have been madness knowingly to dispatch three troop convoys while d'Estaing's squadron was at sea. But Clinton did not receive Byron's warning in time. On 3 November, the same day that d'Estaing left Boston for Martinique, Commodore William Hotham, with a squadron of seven warships escorting 59 transports carrying over 5,000 troops, sailed from Sandy Hook for the West Indies to attack St Lucia.[80] At the same time, transports carrying 1,000 troops left New York for Pensacola. Four days later an additional 2,000 men sailed from New York for St Augustine in order to begin an invasion of Georgia from East Florida.[81] And on 11 December after patching up his ships and learning that d'Estaing's destination was the West Indies, Byron sailed in pursuit from Rhode Island with ten ships of the line and several smaller warships for Antigua. Needless to say, Byron again encountered bad weather.[82]

With the departure of Byron's squadron for the West Indies, the northern colonies in America became a military backwater and a strategic liability. Clinton's army was reduced to 13,000 rank and file. With the departure of the troops sent to the West Indies and the

---

[78] *Diamond, Ariel, Savage* and *Diligent*: PRO, ADM 1/486, f. 129.

[79] *Princess Royal, Royal Oak, Sultan, Cornwall, Raisonable, Trident, Renown, Conqueror, Bedford, Fame, Culloden, Albion, Somerset, Grafton* and *Stromboli*: PRO ADM 1/486, ff. 129, 132-4; NRS, *Barrington Papers*, vol. II, pp. 121-2.

[80] This expedition consisted of the *Preston, Nonsuch, St Albans, Centurion, Isis, Venus* and *Carcass* bomb, and the 4th, 5th, 15th, 27th, 28th, 35th, 40th, 49th and 53rd Regiments of infantry, plus attached units of artillery and engineers: PRO, ADM 1/310, f. 29; NRS, *Barrington Papers*, vol II, pp. 97-8.

[81] NYHSC, *Kemble Papers*, vol. I, pp. 164-5.

[82] *Princess Royal, Royal Oak, Albion, Cornwall, Grafton, Sultan, Monmouth, Trident, Pearl, Star, Carysfort, Conqueror, Fame* and *Diamond*: NRS, *Barrington Papers*, vol. II, p. 210.

Floridas, Clinton's army was not strong enough to conduct any meaningful offensive operations. The Royal Navy was in no better condition: owing to detaching ships to the West Indies, losses and the wear and tear of continual employment, it was so weakened that it had barely enough ships to defend the British enclaves at New York and Rhode Island and to cover the army's amphibious raiding expeditions. The seeming unimportance of the squadron in America was quickly perceived at the Admiralty: New York became a dumping ground for unwanted and incompetent admirals who, for the most part, distinguished themselves by quarrelling with Clinton.[83] From the end of 1778 when the centre of the war shifted from New York until the advent of the catastrophic Yorktown campaign, the British forces remaining in the northern colonies were in many respects nothing more than just another logistical burden.

---

[83] See William B. Willcox, 'Arbuthnot, Gambier, and Graves: "old women" of the navy', in George Athan Billias, (ed.), *George Washington's Opponents* (New York, 1969), pp. 260–90.

5
AMERICAN COASTAL WATERS: TOWARDS YORKTOWN, 1779-80

By the beginning of 1779, British authorities both in London and America should have had enough experience in waging war in America to have learned a number of political and strategic facts about the conflict. The failure to end the fighting by the Carlisle Commission in 1778 should have made it clear that the government in London totally misunderstood the political realities of the situation, for no concessions that the British were willing to make could stop the American rebels from continuing the war until they either gained complete political independence or were totally crushed. The British were in a trap: they would not grant the rebels independence, yet they were unable to muster either the political or military strength to solve successfully the American problem.

The American winter campaign of 1776-77 in New Jersey had forced the British to concentrate their forces in a few enclaves, such as New York City and Newport, Rhode Island, and had shown that the British forces could not overrun and then hold large areas of the countryside where they could build a political base and from which they could draw supplies such as firewood. The loss of Burgoyne's army at Saratoga in 1777 demonstrated the great dangers confronting a British force cut off from maritime communications and attempting to operate deep in the American hinterland. In 1778 the Franco-American attempt to capture Newport, Rhode Island, showed that the safety of British enclaves on the American continent depended completely on the British maintaining naval superiority in American coastal waters. The failure to learn these lessons would result in a series of near-disasters and then defeats in American coastal waters at the hands of the Americans, French and Spanish; and by 1782 not only would Britain's military power in America be crippled, but its political will and ability to continue the war for America would be destroyed.

The dispatching of 3,000 troops to the Floridas in November 1778 marked the beginning of a major change in British strategy in America. On 3 November 1778, 1,000 troops sailed from New York City to reinforce the garrison of Pensacola. Four days later an additional 2,000 troops were detached from the main army at New York and sent to St Augustine in order to invade Georgia from East Florida.[1] From the onset of the fighting around Boston in 1775, and until 1778, British strategy, for the most part, had been one of concentrating the bulk of their forces in Canada and the northern colonies in an attempt to crush the rebellion by defeating Washington's army and occupying and holding major American cities such as New York. At the end of the 1778 campaign British forces in America abandoned the policy of concentration of force and in its place adopted a strategy of dispersal.

At the beginning of 1779, the centre of the war was moving away from the northern colonies. With the dispatch of 5,000 troops to the West Indies and 3,000 more to the Floridas, General Sir Henry Clinton, commander-in-chief in America, saw his main force reduced to only 13,830 effectives, including the garrison of Newport, Rhode Island, which had 5,071.[2] Clinton believed a force of this size was far too small to mount any major offensive operations.[3] Nevertheless, from the beginning of 1779 until the end of the war, British forces would occupy at various times a series of posts and enclaves that stretched along the coast from the banks of the Mississippi River to Halifax, Nova Scotia. From its enclaves in the South, British forces would attempt to destroy rebel military forces and set up royal governments in a bid to regain political control of such colonies as Georgia and the Carolinas. What the planners in London and the commanders in America failed to see, despite the Franco-American attack on Newport in 1778, was that the security of these enclaves depended absolutely on naval superiority in American coastal waters. In a series of attacks from 1779 onwards, the enemy would gain local naval superiority and then deploy land forces to attack and attempt to destroy British posts and enclaves.

[1] NYHSC, *Kemble Papers*, vol. I, pp. 164–5.
[2] PRO, CO 5/97, f. 69.
[3] William B. Willcox (ed.), *The American Rebellion: Sir Henry Clinton's Narratives of His Campaign, 1775–1782, with an appendix of original documents* (New Haven, Conn., 1954), pp. 118–19)

The first victims of the policy of dispersal were the British bases along the Gulf of Mexico and on the Mississippi River. In 1779 Spanish forces based in Louisiana and Cuba began an offensive from west to east against British posts on the Gulf of Mexico, which ended with the capture of New Providence in the Bahamas in 1782 by an American-Spanish taskforce. An attempt was made by the Americans and French in 1779 to capture the British enclaves at Castine, Maine, and Savannah, Georgia; and in 1781 they succeeded in overpowering a British army at Yorktown. Almost no one among the British saw the inherent contradictions of a strategy that made the security of its army dependent upon naval power at a time when the Royal Navy was stretched to the limit in a war against the combined naval forces of America, France and Spain.

At the beginning of 1779 the Royal Navy in America was confronted with horrendous problems, and it had neither the ships nor the leadership to deal with them. Rear-Admiral James Gambier was in command of the Royal Navy at New York, a command that he had held since late 1778. The Admiralty never intended that Gambier should command anything; in fact he had been sent to New York to serve as second in command under Admiral Lord Howe as a way of getting him to resign as commissioner of the Portsmouth dockyard, so that Captain Samuel Hood could take control of that important establishment when the French entered the war. Although Gambier was ill-suited for the job of commissioner of a major naval dockyard, he could not simply be removed from that position because he was related to the Pitt family and his brother-in-law was Charles Middleton, Controller of the Navy. Further, there were few precedents for dismissing a dockyard commissioner, and this position still had almost the status of property, which just could not be taken away without offering an equivalent appointment. So Gambier was sent to New York as second in command, and Howe used him as a port admiral.[4] When Howe gave up command of the American station, it was thought in London that he would be replaced by Vice-Admiral John Byron. But within a few weeks of his arrival in North American waters, Byron sailed for the West Indies in pursuit of the French squadron under Admiral d'Estaing, which left Gambier in command of the Royal Navy in North America.

As early as April 1778, Lord North, the first lord of the treasury, had pointed out to Lord Sandwich, the first lord of the admiralty, that Gambier was unfit for any major command;[5] nevertheless, the

[4] NRS, *Sandwich Papers*, vol. II, p. 289.
[5] Ibid., pp. 39–40.

admiral was sent to New York. When Gambier arrived at New York in the summer of 1778, he was looked upon and treated as a lightweight. Colonel Charles Stuart, for example, declared in a letter to his father that Gambier was 'an idiot'.[6] During his brief command Gambier proved so incapable of commanding anything that his departure from New York in the spring of 1779, according to one observer caused, 'universal joy of all ranks and conditions. I believe no person was ever more generally detested by the navy, army, and citizens than this penurious old reptile.'[7] In fairness to Gambier, it should be pointed out that while the admiral did not have very many ships to command, he did have great responsibilities. A number of warships and transports had been lost during the 1778 campaign, the squadron at New York had been stripped of seamen to man Byron's squadron before it sailed for the West Indies, and yet warships and transports had to be provided to convey troops to the west Indies and the Floridas. With greatly reduced forces, Gambier had to guard the British enclaves at New York and Rhode Island and, at the same time, supply the required number of ships to support the operations of the army. Moreover, Clinton was demanding that enough transports be held in readiness to embark 24,000 troops.[8] When confronted with such enormous responsibilities and so few resources, Gambier collapsed into nervous inactivity during the first months of 1779.[9]

The authorities in London saw at the beginning of 1779 that Gambier was unfit to command the squadron in America, and also that the squadron had to be reinforced if any major military operations were to be carried out in the northern colonies.[10] The Cabinet decided to send to New York four ships of the line and ten frigates and other small warships,[11] and on 23 January 1779 the Admiralty decided to replace Gambier at New York with Admiral Marriot Arbuthnot.[12] The commander of the squadron in North America would need ability and tact. Tact was required in order to work with Clinton, who was notorious for fighting with his naval opposite number; and superior ability was essential, for in 1778 the

---

[6] E. Stuart-Wortley (ed.), *A Prime Minister and His Son* (London, 1925), p. 132.
[7] William B. Willcox, 'Arbuthnot, Gambier and Graves: "old women" of the navy', George Athan Billias, (ed.), *George Washington's Opponents* (New York, 1969), pp. 264-6; the quotation is on page 266.
[8] PRO, ADM 1/489, ff. 199-20; NRS, *Sandwich Papers*, vol. II, pp. 322-5.
[9] CL, Sackville-Germain Papers, vol. 9, Germain to North, 11 January 1779.
[10] NMM, SAN/T/6, Cabinet minutes, 16 January 1779.
[11] PRO, ADM 2/373, pp. 263-5.
[12] PRO, ADM 3/86, 23 January 1779.

North American command had taxed even Howe, and one false step could cost Britain an army and perhaps the war. Arbuthnot, throughout a long and undistinguished career, had shown no great ability and even less tact. If the lords of the Admiralty had gone through the navy list looking for a flag officer who should not be sent to New York, they could not have come up with a better choice than Arbuthnot.

Gambier having left and Arbuthnot not yet arrived, Commodore Sir George Collier became, on 4 April 1779, the acting commander-in-chief of the Royal Navy's squadron in North America. Collier was a man of action who thought offensively and was prepared to act immediately even with a command that was 'extremely reduced in Number'.[13] The acting commander-in-chief had spent most of the first three and a half years of the war on blockade duty off the coast of New England, during which time he came to the conclusion that the place to attack the Americans was Chesapeake Bay.[14] There were some officials in London who simply wanted to let the war wind down, sending the bulk of Clinton's army to the West Indies rather than continue major operations in America.[15] Instead the British commitment was going to be increased by the deployment of the king's forces along the entire length of the American coast from Maine to Florida.

On 7 November 1778, 2,000 troops were sent to St Augustine to invade Georgia; simultaneously, an invasion of eastern Maine was undertaken by troops from Nova Scotia. As early as March 1777, the British military in Nova Scotia wanted to gain control of the coasts of New Brunswick and Maine by setting up a post in the region of Penobscot Bay. Germain approved and ordered the occupation of Castine, Maine, because he thought it would hinder the American rebels in obtaining naval stores and also serve as a base from which attacks could be made against the coast of northern New England.[16] Thus, on 26 June 1779, on orders from London, troops from Nova Scotia began to occupy and fortify Castine at the head of Penobscot Bay.[17]

Clinton disagreed with the plan to occupy Castine. He did not think that the war in America would be won by setting up outposts on the Maine coast. Clinton believed that the army at New York

---

[13] PRO, CO 5/97, ff. 94–5; NMM, HIS/7, p. 114.
[14] HMC, *Stopford-Sackville MSS.*, vol. II, pp. 125–6.
[15] NRS, *Sandwich Papers*, vol. I, p. 365.
[16] PRO, CO 5/97, f. 148.
[17] *American Rebellion*, p. 135.

should be reinforced by some 30,000 troops, otherwise the war in the northern colonies should be abandoned. The commander-in-chief of the British army in America thought that the authorities in London either should give him the troops required to attack up the Hudson, capture the Hudson Highlands and destroy Washington's army in battle, or decide to end the attempt to suppress the rebellion in the northern colonies by means of military force.[18] Only when he was told that he was not going to receive massive reinforcements did Clinton embrace a programme of coastal raiding and a limited drive up the Hudson River to King's Ferry.[19]

There was no British overall plan for the conduct of the war in America in 1779; instead there were almost as many schemes, plans and notions as there were planners and commanders. Germain felt that he had to approve or try 'every means and occasion' offensive in nature to end the war with the American rebels because 'the powers Great Britain has to contend with in Europe are so potent as to require her utmost efforts to withstand them'.[20] What neither officals in London nor officers in America saw was that the British were undertaking, with weak naval forces in American waters, operations which would spread the British army the length of the American coast in an ever increasing number of enclaves vulnerable to destruction by any enemy who gained local naval superiority. Lord Cornwallis, second in command of the British forces in America, did not know how close he was to the truth when he wrote on 5 May 1779, 'I am now returning to America, not with views of conquest and ambition, nothing brilliant can be expected in that quarter'.[21]

Clinton and Collier began the campaign of 1779 with a large-scale raid on the Chesapeake Bay region of Virginia, but they had very different motives for it. Believing that Washington's army drew the bulk of its supplies and exported its goods, such as tobacco, in exchange for military stores from the region around Chesapeake Bay, Collier was also convinced that an effective blockade of the bay 'would probably answer very considerable purposes, if not of itself *sufficient* to end the War, would drive the Rebels to infinite Inconveniencies and Difficulties, especially as Washington's Army was

---

[18] William B. Willcox, *Portrait of a General: Sir William Clinton in the War of Independence* (New York, 1964), p. 256.
[19] *American Rebellion*, pp. 122–3.
[20] PRO, CO 5/96, f. 25; CO 5/97, ff. 13–14, 95, 144; CO 5/98, ff. 86–7; CO 5/130, f. 91; CL, Sackville–Germain Papers, vol. 4, pp. 48–9; HMC, *Stopford–Sackville MSS.*, vol. II, p. 136.
[21] HMC, *Various Collections*, vol. 6, p. 319.

constantly supplied with Salted Provisions sent by Water through the Chesapeake.'[22] Clinton, however, looked upon the raid as a means both of tying down rebel forces in Virginia and destroying military supplies and, most important, of diverting attention from New York City while he was preparing for an attack up the Hudson River to King's Ferry.[23] On 5 May 1779, six warships escorting 28 transports carrying 1,800 British, Loyalist and German troops under the command of Brigadier Edward Mathew sailed from Sandy Hook for Chesapeake Bay.[24] On 10 May the king's troops landed on the shore of the Elizabeth River near Fort Nelson, and meeting almost no opposition, began a reign of destruction. Ships and vessels of various kinds, scores of warehouses, thousands of tons of provisions, ordnance, naval stores, and tobacco and other produce were destroyed by the British forces around the Elizabeth River. Before the king's troops re-embarked on 24 May, Fort Nelson was destroyed, and that evening the

> Night appeared grand beyond Discription, tho' the light was a melancholy one: Five Thousand Loads of fine seasoned Oak Knees for ship building, an infinite Quantity of Plank, Masts, Cordage, & numbers of beautiful Ships of War on the Stocks were all the Time in a blaze, & all totally consumed, not a vestage remaining, but the Iron Work, that such things *had* been.

For fourteen days British forces in the Elizabeth River had smashed and burned American stores, produce and vessels, but Collier did not want to stop there. He wanted to set up a post at Portsmouth, Virginia, to be used as a base to bring fire and the sword to every corner of the Chesapeake Bay, but Mathew would not co-operate in this scheme because his orders from Clinton directed that the troops be re-embarked by 24 May and returned to New York. So the expedition left Virginia, reaching New York on 29 May. The worth of the American goods in Virginia that they had destroyed was estimated at over a 'Million Sterling'.[25] If the amount of enemy property destroyed was a measure of success in the war in America, then the Collier-Mathew raid on Virginia was very successful indeed: it was the most destructive British raid yet undertaken in the war.

[22] NMM, HIS/7, pp. 117-18.
[23] *American Rebellion*, p. 122.
[24] *Raisonable, Rainbow, Otter, Diligent, Haerlem* sloop and *Cornwallis* galley: NMM, HIS/7, pp. 119-20.
[25] NMM, HIS/7, pp. 121-31; PRO, CO 5/97, ff. 241, 311-14, 319-20.

Collier was very disappointed when he could not occupy Portsmouth, Virginia, and use it as a base. The commodore thought it a 'place whose importance and utility stood higher in my opinion than almost any other in America'. He blamed Mathew for insisting on following his instructions from Clinton to the letter and for not garrisoning Portsmouth and continuing raiding the shores of Chesapeake Bay.[26] Although Collier was a great combat commander, he either did not understand or think through the strategic consequences of his scheme to occupy Portsmouth. He had a force of only six warships, of which four were small, and 1,800 troops. What he intended to do was set up a lightly held base that could not be reinforced quickly in hostile territory and then conduct a series of raids that would most likely have goaded the American rebels into attacking it. The great danger inherent in Collier's scheme would soon be demonstrated at Stony Point.

The day after Collier and Mathew returned to New York City, Clinton began his drive up the Hudson River towards King's Ferry in order to capture and hold the American posts at Stony and Verplancks points. The occupation of the two places would prevent the rebels from using King's Ferry for north–south communications, adding 60 miles to the trip because the Americans would be forced to use crossings of the Hudson River much farther north in the mountains of the Hudson Highlands for north–south movements. Also Stony Point and Verplancks points were located on opposite sides of the Hudson River about 12 miles from West Point, which Washington considered the 'key to the Continent', and could serve as bases or jumping-off points for an attack on the Hudson Highlands if Clinton ever obtained a sufficient number of troops. With the ships and troops from Virginia, Collier joined Clinton's force in the drive up the Hudson. On 1 June, having landed under the guns of Collier's warships on the east and west banks of the river with almost no opposition, British troops captured and began to fortify Stony and Verplancks points.

After this success, Collier and the bulk of his ships sailed down the Hudson River to carry out a series of punitive raids against coastal towns in Connecticut. The intent of this operation was to draw Washington's army away from the Hudson Highlands, prevent the Connecticut militia from assembling and end the raids from Connecticut by rebels who used small craft, such as whaleboats, against the British in Long Island Sound, Queens County, and the East River.

---

[26] HMC, *Stopford–Sackville MSS.*, vol. II, pp. 128–9.

On 5 July, with Major General William Tryon commanding the troops, Collier attacked, occupied and looted New Haven.

On 8 July, Fairfield was attacked and then burned to the ground. The next day Green Farms was destroyed and, on 11 July, Norwalk was captured and destroyed. After the destruction of Norwalk, the expedition sailed to Huntington Bay on Long Island to obtain a resupply of ammunition from New York City. Collier and Clinton met at Great Neck, where they decided that the destruction of New London would be the next objective. But before the British force sailed again, the attack against New London was called off when news arrived that the Americans had captured Stony Point.

Stony Point is a hill some 150 feet high about 12 miles south of West Point and connected to the west bank of the Hudson River by tidal marshes. It is little more than a huge rock jutting out into the Hudson. After Stony Point's occupation by the British on 1 June 1779, the position, which was naturally very strong, was fortified and garrisoned by the 17th Regiment and attached supporting units. On the night of 15-16 July 1779 about 1,300 American light infantry led by Brigadier General 'Mad' Anthony Wayne passed through the marshes in two columns and assaulted the northern and southern flanks of the British position at Stony Point with unloaded muskets and fixed bayonets. Because of the strength, speed and unexpected nature of the attack, the Americans achieved total surprise. They overpowered the British outposts, entered the British fortifications before the king's troops could organize any type of defence and, in a wild 10 or 15 minutes of hand-to-hand fighting with bayonets, swords and spontoons, killed or captured the entire garrison. The American assault on Stony Point was over before most of the British garrison knew what was happening. The British lost 624 officers and men killed, wounded, missing or captured.

When news of this battle reached Clinton and Collier at Throgs Neck, the two British commanders reacted quickly. Collier's squadron, with Tryon's troops on board transports, left Long Island Sound, passed through Hell Gate and the Harlem River, and then proceeded up the Hudson River to Stony Point. As they approached, however, Washington issued orders to destroy Stony Point's fortifications and to withdraw the American troops. When the king's troops had reoccupied Stony Point, Collier sailed for New York City with the bulk of his squadron. To Clinton, the American capture of Stony Point was 'a very great affront'. It should also have been a warning to every British commander in America, for it showed the great dangers inherent in the British strategy of dispersal. An

American light infantry brigade had appeared out of nowhere and captured by a *coup de main* a British force that was isolated from the main British army yet held a fortified strong point on what, from a topographical point of view, can only be described as a miniature Gibraltar. Although garrisoned with a reinforced regiment, Stony Point still had been taken by surprise by a unit of Washington's army.[27] In the future, what could prevent the Americans from unexpectedly picking off a British brigade, division or even a whole field army that had become isolated from the main British force?

Upon his arrival at New York City, Collier was informed that the British post at Castine, Maine, was under attack by superior American forces. After the British from Nova Scotia had placed a garrison at Castine to prevent the Americans from gaining supplies of timber from Maine, the government of the Commonwelath of Massachusetts mounted an expedition to retake the town from the king's forces. But the British commanders at Castine would not give it up without a fight.[28]

At 4 p.m. on 24 July 1779 the British at Castine sighted an American fleet proceeding up Penobscot Bay towards them. The American fleet, under the command of Commodore Dudley Saltonstall, was comprised of some 17 major warships[29] and 19 transports, carrying some 1,000 Massachusetts militia commanded by Brigadier General Solomon Lovell of the Massachusetts service. Lovell and Saltonstall lacked the drive, skill and experience for an operation of the size and type that they were undertaking against Castine; for if the Americans, who greatly outnumbered the British, had made a determined, skilful and speedy assault, the town could have been taken easily.

The American attack began at 3 p.m. on 25 July when nine American warships attempted to force the entrance of Castine Harbor in much the same way that d'Estaing attacked Barrington's squadron at St Lucia. The American ships anchored off three British sloops of war,[30] and there was an ineffectual exchange of cannon

---

[27] *American Rebellion*, pp. 131-3, 411, 415; HMC, *American Manuscripts*, vol. I, p. 481; NMM, HIS/7, pp. 147-54; Henry Philps Johnston, *The Storming of Stony Point on the Hudson, Midnight, July 15, 1779: Its Importance in the Light of Unpublished Documents* (New York, 1900).

[28] *American Rebellion*, p. 135; HMC, *American Manuscripts*, vol. I, p. 463; NMM, HIS/7, p. 162; John Calef (ed), *The Siege of Penobscot* (New York, 1971 reprint), pp. 122, 15-17, 46.

[29] *Warren, Sally, Putnam, Hector, Revenge, Vengeance, Black Prince, Sky Rocket, Hazard, Active, Tyrannicide, Defence, Diligence, Pallas, Providence, Hunter, Hampden.*

[30] *Albany, North and Nautilus.*

fire for two hours before the engagement ended. While the British and American warships were firing at each other, the Americans made an attempt to land at Dice Head near Castine, only to be driven back to their boats by British infantry. On 26 July, American troops captured Nautilus Island opposite Castine and began to mount cannon to fire on the three British sloops of war. Captain Henry Mowat, RN, countered this move by withdrawing farther into Castine Harbor out of range of the American guns and by using the three armed transports as warships to strengthen and lengthen his line of ships. Two days later the Americans made a successful landing near the British fortifications at Castine. For the next 16 days Lovell and Saltonstall played a game of cat and mouse with the British, while American troops undertook elaborate and slow siege operations against the weak fortifications.

At 5 p.m. on 13 August both the Americans and the British saw strange sails on the horizon heading up Penobscot Bay towards Castine. That night the Americans embarked their troops, and the next morning Collier's squadron[31] was in sight of the American vessels. The wind was 'very faint, tho' it blew directly into the Bay', from the south. At first, given the movements of the American ships, the stillness of the sea and the lightness of the wind, Collier thought that the Americans might attempt to board his warships and overpower their crews with troops. However, with the exception of two warships the American fleet turned northward and headed towards the mouth of the Penobscot River. Collier, upon seeing what he called the 'ignomimious Flight' of the American fleet, made the signal for action and a general chase. Two American warships, the *Defence* and *Hunter*, attempted to escape down the passage between Long Island and the western shore of Penobscot Bay; Collier, in HMS *Raisonable*, captured the *Hunter* and destroyed the *Defence*. The remainder of the American force, chased by the ships of Collier's squadron, fled in panic towards the mouth of the Penobscot River. As night fell the American ships sailed up the Penobscot River while Collier and his ships, lacking pilots, anchored for the night at the river's mouth. Throughout the night the men of Collier's squadron saw great fires and heard frequent explosions as the Americans beached their ships and set them on fire before soldiers and seamen alike fled into the woods to make their way on foot back to the settlements in southern Maine.

The next day, as British warships went up the Penobscot River,

[31] *Raisonable, Blonde, Virginia, Greyhound, Camilla, Galatea and Otter.*

'the scene was awful'; its banks were lined with the shells of still-burning and burnt-out ships and abandoned military and naval equipment of all kinds. Other than the *Hunter*, only the 22-gun ship *Hampden*, which had been captured before she could enter the Penobscot River, escaped destruction. Collier's victory was complete: out of 37 American warships and transports, two warships were captured and the remaining 35 vessels destroyed. The ships' crews and Lovell's soldiers had scattered into the Maine woods in complete and utter panic.[32]

In the battle for Castine, Collier's squadron inflicted the largest naval defeat of the whole war on the Americans when he destroyed completely one of the biggest naval and military expeditions ever undertaken by the Commonwealth of Massachusetts. But it was a very near-run thing, for the Americans were about to storm the British positions at Castine at the very moment Collier's squadron arrived in Penobscot Bay. Although Castine very nearly became a naval Stony Point or a miniature Yorktown, the Americans lost because of the skill of Captain Henry Mowat, RN, and Brigadier Allan MacLean, the commander of the troops at Castine; and because of the speed with which Collier reacted to the news of the American attack and the lack of skill and the slowness with which Lovell and Saltonstall conducted the American operations. While the British victory was total, all was not amicable among the victors. Mowat became enraged at Collier for not sending him to England with the dispatches telling of the victory;[33] and Collier, when he returned to New York, must have been less than pleased to find that Arbuthnot had arrived from England to take command of the squadron in America. On 30 October 1779, Collier sailed for England from New York aboard HMS *Daphne* after serving three and a half years in America.[34]

Vice-Admiral Marriot Arbuthnot had finally arrived at New York on 25 August 1779 after a voyage protracted by adverse winds and

---

[32] *The Siege of Penobscot*, NMM, HIS/7, pp. 164–71; ADM/L/A/66, 14–15 August 1779; ADM/L/N/137, 14–15 August 1779; ADM/L/R/25, 14–15 August 1779; ADM/L/B/115, 14–15 August 1779; ADM/L/G/1, 15–16 August 1779; ADM/L/G/192, 14–16 August 1779; ADM/L/C/25, 14–16 August 1779; ADM/L/V/83, 15–16 August 1779; Public Archives of Nova Scotia, MacLean to Germain, 26 August 1779 and Collier to Stephens, 20 August 1779; Wiliam M. Fowler, Jr, *Rebels under Sail: The American Navy during the Revolution* (New York, 1976), pp. 122–18; Gardener W. Allen, *A Naval History of the American Revolution* (Williamstown, Mass., 1970 reprint), vol. II, pp. 419–38.

[33] *The Siege of Penobscot*, pp. 53–4.

[34] NMM, HIS/7, 173–4.

the involvement of his force in operations in the English Channel.[35] Arbuthnot brought with him four ships of the line and several thousand troops to reinforce Clinton's army. To Clinton, Arbuthnot's arrival was just one more of many frustrations; for the 3,800 troops that arrived with the admiral were sick with 'a malignant jail fever', which infected and sent to the hospital 6,000 of Clinton's troops.[36] Clinton felt his 'spirits . . . worn out by struggling against the consequences of many adverse incidents' such as the American capture of Stony Point and the near-loss of the British base at Castine. To make matters worse, the army under Clinton's command 'at present or that will be during this campaign is not equal to the services expected from it'.[37]

Clinton had been promised 6,600 troops from Europe and the West Indies. As early as May, he had been informed that he would not receive any troops from the West Indies; and Arbuthnot's convoy had brought only 3,800 soldiers from Europe.[38] On 21 August, before Arbuthnot arrived at New York, Clinton wrote to Germain:

> Your Lordship will no doubt have been aware that the delay of our expected reinforcements, the waste of the season, and the operations of the enemy in that important interval, must naturally have so influenced circumstances as to render utterly unsuitable to the present hour that plan to which the past movements of this campaign have been merely preparatory.[39]

In the middle of September dispatches arrived at New York saying that the island of Jamaica was about to be invaded and requesting immediate reinforcements. Clinton and Arbuthnot ordered three ships of the line and 4,000 troops to be sent to Jamaica. The force was recalled, however, when intelligence reached New York that a powerful French squadron under the command of d'Estaing was on the coast of Georgia.[40]

The news of the arrival of d'Estaing's squadron in American waters threw Arbuthnot into a panic. The British at New York

---

[35] NRS, *Sandwich Papers*, vol. III, pp. 128–9.
[36] *American Rebellion*, pp. 140–1.
[37] PRO, CO 5/98, ff. 201–2.
[38] Ibid., ff. 113–14.
[39] Ibid., f. 206.
[40] Ibid., f. 276; NRS, *Sandwich Papers*, vol. III, p. 134.

thought that d'Estaing's objective was one of three places: New York City, Newport, Rhode Island, or Halifax. Arbuthnot stationed his ships at Sandy Hook in much the same way as Howe had done in 1778, when d'Estaing had appeared off New York. Although Arbuthnot adopted the same method that Howe had used the year before to defend New York Harbor, the admiral believed the French squadron so superior to his own that d'Estaing could fight his way into Upper New York Bay. On 4 October Arbuthnot wrote to Clinton saying that the naval defence of New York Harbor was very weak, and that if d'Estaing got into the harbour, it would be up to Clinton and the army to save the British position at New York.[41]

Arbuthnot did not believe Newport, Rhode Island, was of much use as a naval base, although it was occupied for that purpose in 1776. He believed as well that Newport could not be reinforced or defended if a joint attack were made on it by d'Estaing's squadron and Washington's army. For these reasons, Arbuthnot proposed to Clinton that Rhode Island be evacuated and its garrison moved to New York. Clinton accepted Arbuthnot's suggestion, and on 7 October issued orders for the evacuation of Rhode Island; the garrison from Rhode Island arrived at New York on 27 October 1779.[42] Arbuthnot, upon learning that the British had discovered on a Spanish packet some papers indicating that Halifax was one of d'Estaing's objectives, wanted to reinforce the garrison there.[43] Fifteen hundred troops were embarked at New York to reinforce Halifax but never sailed because adverse weather conditions and the approach of winter greatly reduced the probability of a French attack on Halifax.[44]

At this time, Clinton decided to withdraw the British forces at Stony Point and Verplancks Point in order to concentrate his army at New York City, so that he would have enough troops to defend that city while undertaking offensive operations in the South.[45] Also Arbuthnot received intelligence that the Americans at Boston were secretly preparing another attack on Castine. In response to this threat, HMS *Roebuck* and HMS *Romulus* were sent to Penobscot Bay.[46] By the time the threat posed by the presence of d'Esta-

---

[41] *American Rebellion*, p. 145.
[42] PRO, CO 5/98, ff. 278, 280, 320, 324, 326–32, 336.
[43] HMC, *Various Collections*, vol. 6, p. 322.
[44] NRS, *Sandwich Papers*, vol. III, p. 138.
[45] *American Rebellion*, p. 147.
[46] HMC, *Stopford-Sackville MSS.*, vol. 2, p. 147.

ing's squadron on the American coast had passed, British forces had been withdrawn from Rhode Island and from the southern edge of the Hudson Highlands and had concentrated at New York City.

D'Estaing's objective was not New York or Rhode Island, or even Halifax, but the British force occupying Savannah, Georgia. He suddenly appeared off the coast of Georgia in September with 33 warships and transports carrying 4,000 troops. The French squadron's arrival off the coast of Georgia was so unexpected that the 50-gun-ship HMS *Experiment*, the frigate HMS *Ariel* and two storeships were surprised and captured. Among the booty was a £30,000 payroll for the British forces at Savannah.[47]

On 9 September the French began landing troops and equipment near Savannah; and on 16 September French forces approached the city and demanded that it be surrendered 'to the arms of the King of France'. That night the French were joined outside Savannah by some 1,500 American troops under the command of Major-General Benjamin Lincoln. On the night of 23 September the American and French forces began a regular siege of the 2,400 British troops who were dug in around Savannah under the command of Lieutenant-Colonel Archibald Campbell. The siege went slower than d'Estaing had intended, and he was under mounting pressure from the captains of his warships to leave America because they feared the appearance of a British naval force, their men were dying of scurvy at the rate of 35 a day and the hurricane season was approaching. Therefore, on the night of 8 October, d'Estaing ordered that Savannah be stormed at dawn the following day. The main attack was to be made on the British works at Spring Hill by two American and three French columns across roughly 500 yards of open ground.

The 9 October attack consisted of a mad, unco-ordinated rush towards the British fortifications. The French columns were beaten back by British grapeshot and small-arms fire, but the Americans managed to plant the flag of the 2nd South Carolina Continentals on the parapet of the British works. The British then counterattacked and in fierce hand-to-hand fighting drove the Americans back. D'Estaing, who led the French attack, was wounded and Brigadier-General Casimir Pulaski was mortally wounded in a foolhardy cavalry charge against the British fortifications. The unsuccessful assault on Spring Hill cost some 800 American and French lives, while the British lost only sixteen killed. After that fiasco, the French

---

[47] *American Rebellion*, p. 149.

although strongly urged by Lincoln to remain and continue the siege, re-embarked on 10 October and sailed for Europe, and the Americans were forced to retreat into South Carolina. D'Estaing had failed the Americans again as he had done in 1778 at New York and Newport, Rhode Island.[48]

While American, British and French forces were fighting along the Atlantic coast, the Spanish at New Orleans and Havana began a campaign against British posts in the Floridas and the Bahama Islands with the objective of removing the British threat to Spanish communications in the Gulf of Mexico and the Straits of Florida. All Spanish seaborne commerce between Old Spain, Cuba, Mexico and Central America passed through the Gulf of Mexico and the Straits of Florida. When Britian was ceded the Floridas at the end of the Seven Years War, it gained bases, such as Pensacola and St Augustine, from which attacks could be undertaken against Spain's most important maritime trade route. With the beginning of fighting between Spain and England in 1779, Spanish colonial authorities at New Orleans and Havana decided to use Britain's troubles as an opportunity to remove this threat.

In 1779, Governor Bernardo de Galves of Spanish Louisiana learned of the outbreak of war between Britian and Spain before the British authorities in West Florida and seized the opportunity to attack the British posts at Manchac, Baton Rouge and Natchez and forced them to surrender on 21 September. Several months later, Galves landed at Chocta Point in Mobile Bay with a force of some 2,000 troops from Cuba and Louisiana and laid siege to the British post at Mobile. On 1 March 1780 the Spanish demanded that the British surrender but were refused. However, after several more days of siege and bombardment, on 12 March the British surrendered Mobile to the Spanish. With the fall of Mobile to the Spanish, all that remained of British West Florida was the weak post at Pensacola. The British at Pensacola were isolated from other British forces in North America and had to depend on Jamaica for supplies and naval support. The British position in West Florida was further weakened after the loss of the posts along the Mississippi and of Mobile because the Choctaw Indians began to waver in their loyalty to Britain and became at best neutral in the conflict between Britain

---

[48] Ibid., pp. 432–4; Alexander A. Lawrence, *Storm over Savannah: The Story of Count d'Estaing and the Siege of the Town in 1779* (Athens, Ga, 1951); Charles C. Jones, Jr (ed.), *The Siege of Savannah by the Fleet of Count d'Estaing in 1779* (New York, 1968).

and Spain along the Gulf Coast.⁴⁹ It was only a question of time before the Spanish would attack and capture Pensacola, thus removing the British from West Florida forever.

During 1779, with the exception of the amphibious raids in Chesapeake Bay and along the coast of Connecticut, the push up the Hudson to the southern edge of the Highlands, and the invasion of Georgia from East Florida, the British for the most part only reacted to American, French and Spanish actions. And the Spanish at New Orleans had opened up a new theatre of operations in America by capturing Mobile and the British posts along the Mississippi River. It was against this strategic background that the British decided to begin major operations in South Carolina with an invasion by a force from New York.

The capture of Charleston, South Carolina, as a base had been considered on many occasions since the failure of the Clinton-Parker expedition against that city in 1776. General Howe had planned an attack against Charleston to take place in the winter of 1777–78. Germain had suggested an attack on Charleston in the spring of 1779. Clinton, independent of Germain, decided in the summer of 1779 to attack and capture Charleston.⁵⁰ On 21 August 1779, Clinton wrote to Germain saying that Washington's army was out of reach in the Highlands of the Hudson and without a great reinforcement of troops nothing could be done in the region around New York City. Clinton informed Germain that he was going to strengthen the fortifications around New York City and undertake a winter campaign in South Carolina. Clinton decided to attack South Carolina because of the supposedly large number of Loyalists in the province and because 'if we do not conquer South Carolina, everything is to be apprehended for Georgia'.⁵¹ Clinton also was thinking of establishing a post in Chesapeake Bay to be used as a base for raiding operations to draw American attention away from South Carolina and to hinder the rebels' north–south communications. The establishment of a base in Chesapeake Bay had been suggested many times by various people since the British had been forced to withdraw from Virginia in 1776.

Germain was in total agreement with Clinton's intention to invade South Carolina; on 27 September 1779 he wrote to Clinton, 'the

---

⁴⁹ *American Rebellion*, p. 154; Juan Manuel Zapatero, *La Guerra del Carribe en el Siglo XVIII* (San Juan, Puerto Rico, 1964 reprint), pp. 229–44; Peter Joseph Hamilton, *Colonial Mobile* (Boston, Mass., 1943), pp. 213, 215–16.
⁵⁰ *American Rebellion*, p. 151.
⁵¹ PRO, CO 5/98, ff. 106–208.

possession of Charles Town would, therefore, I flatter myself, be attended with recovery of the whole of that province, and probably North Carolina would soon follow'. However, the Chesapeake and South Carolina operations were postponed when the news reached New York that d'Estaing's squadron was on the American coast.[52] When further intelligence reached New York that several French warships were going to spend the winter in Chesapeake Bay, Arbuthnot, the commander of the squadron in North America, wanted to attack these ships and destroy them. Clinton would not agree to this plan because it would hinder what he thought to be the main operation, which was the invasion of South Carolina. The general then decided to postpone establishing a post in the Chesapeake Bay region and to attack Charleston as soon as d'Estaing's squadron left American waters.[53] But Clinton did not adandon the idea of undertaking operations in Chesapeake Bay; he wrote to Germain from South Carolina on 9 March 1780 that 'should no superior fleet threaten this coast, I still hope my projected operations in Chesapeake bay may take place'.[54] Clinton's strategic thinking was turning more and more towards a campaign that in the end would scatter British forces up and down the length of the American coast, a strategy which would lead to Yorktown and defeat.

After weeks of waiting, intelligence finally reached New York that d'Estaing had been repulsed at Savannah and that the French had sailed for Europe. On 26 December 1779, Arbuthnot and Clinton sailed from Sandy Hook for South Carolina with 7,594 troops.[55] Two days out from New York the convoy encountered bad weather and its transports began to scatter. The transport *Ann* with Hessian troops on board was dismasted after running afoul of another transport, bore away and fetched up in St Ives, Cornwall, while an ordnance transport ended up in Bermuda.[56] Captain Johann Hinrichs of the Jägers wrote in his diary on 3 January 1780,

> It may be safely said that the most strenuous campaign cannot be as trying as such a voyage; for (1) one cannot prepare a decent meal; (2) one takes every morsel with the greatest difficulty and discomfort; (3) one enjoys not a moment of sleep because of the

[52] Ibid., ff. 85, 176–7, 354.
[53] *American Rebellion*, p. 153.
[54] PRO, CO 5/99, f. 51.
[55] Ibid., ff. 15, 29, 50.
[56] Harry Miller Lydenburg (ed.), *Archibald Robertson, Lieutenant General Royal Engineers. His Diaries and Sketches in America, 1762–1780* (New York, 1930), pp. 207, 221; PRO CO /99, f. 31.

fearful rolling and noise, which is worse in the cabin than in any other place in the ship.[57]

After a rough voyage, Clinton's and Arbuthnot's force arrived at Tybee Island at the mouth of the Savannah River.[58]
Clinton's attack on Charleston in 1780, unlike the Howes' assault on New York City in 1776, was not designed to push the rebel forces out of the city, but rather to use to the fullest extent possible British naval and amphibious capabilities to envelop and trap the American forces there. The environs of Charleston are a maze of islands, marshes and waterways, and the entrance to Charleston Harbor was narrow, filled with obstacles to navigation, such as sand-bars, and guarded by a number of forts. In 1776, when a squadron under the command of Commodore Sir Peter Parker attacked Fort Moultrie at the entrance of Charleston Harbor, the Royal Navy suffered heavy casualties and Clinton could not attack the landward site of the American fort because his approach was blocked by an unfordable waterway. Clearly, in the past few years Clinton must have given considerable thought to the problem of how to conduct an attack on Charleston. The obvious approach to Charleston for an invader from the sea was to attempt to overcome the fortifications guarding the entrance to Charleston Harbor before attacking the city itself. This type of strategy had been followed in 1776 and had failed. Arbuthnot wanted to land Clinton's army on John's Island from the Stono Inlet just a few miles south of the entrance of Charleston Harbor. Clinton, however, overruled this idea and demanded that the admiral land his 5,000 troops at North Edisto Inlet on Simmons Island, some 20 miles south of the city of Charleston. Although the admiral gave into Clinton's wishes as to where the army was to be put ashore, it showed that Arbuthnot and Clinton were at odds almost from the beginning of their first joint operation. Over the next months the disagreements and quarrels between the admiral and the general would become so bitter that operations would grind to a halt.[59]

On 11 February 1780, 5,000 men of Clinton's army began landing on Simmons Island. Assisted by naval small craft and a detachment of naval personnel under the command of Captain George Keith

[57] Bernard Alexander Uhlendorf (ed. and tr.) *The Siege of Charleston with an Account of the Province of South Carolina: Diaries and Letters of Hessian Officers from the von Jungkenn Papers in the William L. Clements Library* (Ann Arbor, Mich., 1938), p. 119
[58] NRS, *Keith Papers*, vol. I, p. 135.
[59] *American Rebellion*, p. 160n.

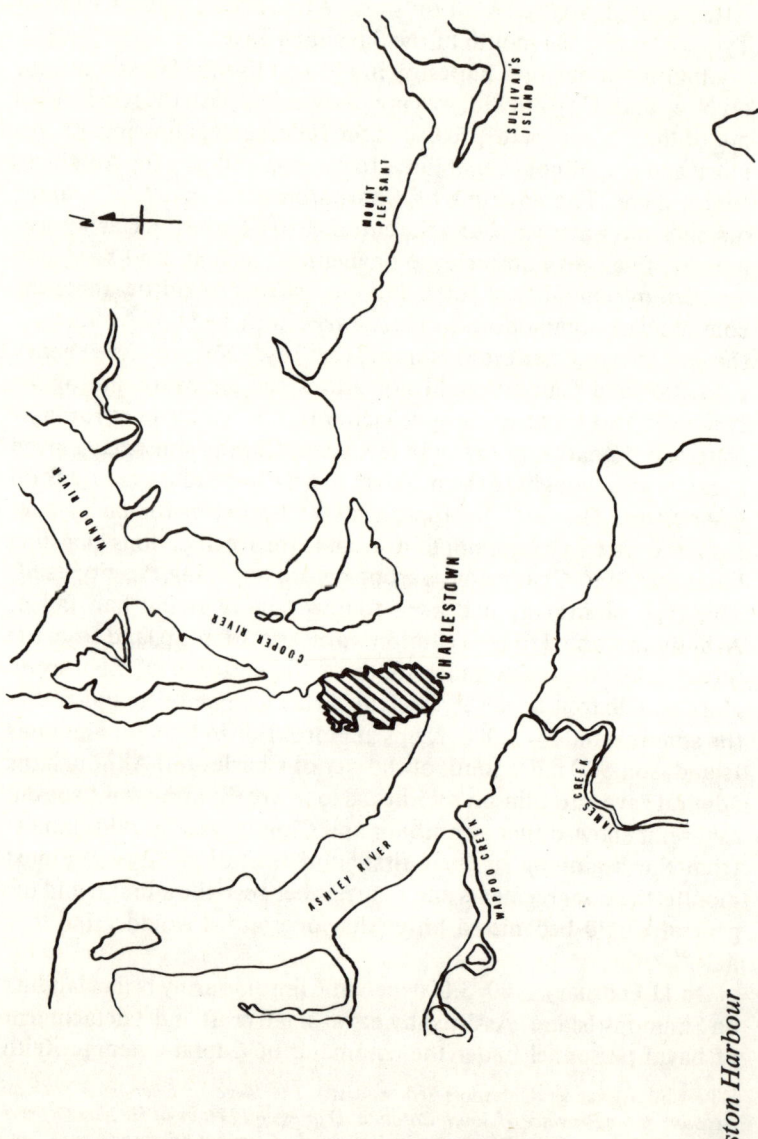

*Map 7
Charleston Harbour*

Elphinstone, RN, Clinton's troops advanced slowly northward from Simmons Island using back roads and crossing marshes and waterways, until by the middle of March 1780 the whole southern side of Charleston Harbor had been overrun by the king's troops. Fort Johnson, Lighthouse Island and other rebel works on the south side of Charleston Harbor were occupied and fortified by Clinton's troops and a bridge between James Island and the mainland was captured.[60]

It is clear that the American commander at Charleston, Major-General Benjamin Lincoln, did not comprehend the dangers confronting the American forces at Charleston, and more and more rebel troops were moved into the city, which is located on a peninsula between the Ashley and Cooper rivers. If British forces occupied Charleston Neck, controlled the landward approaches to the city and moved warships into Charleston Harbor, then the American troops at Charleston would be trapped and forced to surrender: either they would run out of supplies or the city would be reduced to rubble by heavy British guns and carried by assault. Perhaps Lincoln was overconfident, for Charleston had withstood a British assault in 1776. Maybe the extreme slowness with which Clinton's troops advanced on Charleston from the south was thought by the Americans to be a sign of weakness or hesitation on the part of the British. Evidently, Lincoln did not understand, as did Washington, that American forces should never be placed in a position, such as on a peninsuala, where they could be trapped and overpowered by British amphibious forces.

On 20 March, Arbuthnot, with his flag in HMS *Roebuck* and accompanied by HMS *Renown* and HMS *Romulus*, passed safely over the bar at Charleston Harbor and entered Five Fathom Hole.[61] When British warships entered the outer approaches of Charleston Harbor, the Americans immediately withdrew their warships into the Cooper River and sank five of them along with several merchant ships to block the entrances of the river on both sides of the island of Shute's Folly.[62] The remaining American and French armed ships in the Cooper River were to be used as floating batteries on the right flank of the American defences of Charleston. On 29 March, Clinton was reinforced by 1,400 troops from Georgia. Meanwhile the Royal Navy moved under cover of darkness 75 flat-bottomed

---

[60] *Ibid.*, pp. 160–2; *Keith Papers*, vol. I, pp. 145–50.
[61] NRS, *Keith Papers*, vol. I, pp. 140–6.
[62] The American rebels sunk in the Cooper River of the ships *Bricole, Queens of France, Truite, Notre Dame* and *General Moultrie*: NRS, *Keith Papers*, vol. I. p. 174.

boats with muffled oars up the south side of Charleston Harbor, into the Ashley River, and passed undetected the place where the Americans thought Clinton would cross the river. On the night of 29 March several élite assault units of Clinton's army crossed in flat-bottomed boats without opposition to the north bank of the Ashley River about 15 miles north of Charleston at Drayton Hall. The next morning the remainder of the army crossed the Ashley River, and Clinton, encountering almost no opposition, advanced towards Charleston's fortifications. On 1 April, within 800 years of Charleston's outer fortification and with the flanks of the British army reaching across the peninsula from the Ashley River to the Cooper River, Clinton's troops began to undertake siege operations against the American works. Arbuthnot had assigned a number of seamen and 22 boats in addition to flat-bottomed boats (under the command of Elphinstone) to assist the army in the siege of Charleston and to maintain communications between the fleet and the army by water along the south side of the Ashley River and Charleston Harbor. Also, after some wrangling with Clinton, Arbuthnot supplied the army, which had lost the storeship carrying its siege train on the voyage from New York, with heavy naval cannon, shot and powder for the bombardment of the city. Although Charleston was not completely cut off because the British did not yet control the northern side of Charleston Harbor, the Americans had been outmanoeuvred and boxed up in the city in much the same way as the British were at Boston in 1775.[63]

When the siege operations had begun, the British next moved to gain control of the northern approaches of the city completely to isolate it from any outside assistance. Clinton, after investing Charleston, dispatched troops under Colonel James Webster to cut American communications with the city from the north-west by occupying Strawberry Ferry at the forks of the Cooper River. Lieutenant Colonel Banastre Tarleton's and Major Patrick Ferguson's corps were deployed north and east of the Cooper River. With the arrival of five more regiments[64] from New York, some 1,800 additional troops were sent under the command of Cornwallis across the Cooper River further to block American communications with Charleston.[65]

---

[63] *American Rebellion*, pp. 162–3, 438–9; NRS, *Keith Papers*, vol. I pp. 136, 152–4; Stuart-Wortley, *A Prime Minister*, p. 168.
[64] 42nd Foot, Queens' Rangers, Prince of Wales Volunteers, Volunteers of Ireland and the Hessian Dittfurth Regiment.
[65] *American Rebellion*, pp. 164–8.

Next Arbuthnot, with seven warships,[66] broke into the inner harbour of Charleston by forcing his way past American guns at Fort Moultrie and Mount Pleasant on the north side of the harbour and came to anchor off James Island. The Royal Navy lost the transport *Aeolus*, which ran aground in range of Fort Moultrie's guns and had to be abandoned and destroyed. Twenty-seven seamen were either killed or wounded in this operation. Next Arbuthnot attempted to enter the Cooper River but found that his way was blocked by ships the Americans had sunk as obstructions. The admiral then decided to reduce the American positions along the north shore of Charleston Harbor. At daybreak on 29 April a force of 500 seamen and marines was landed before the American works at Mount Pleasant, which was occupied without resistance. Then the British marines and seamen marched west to attack the American works at Hobcaw Point, but upon the approach of the British seamen and marines, as well as a force under Ferguson, the American garrison escaped to Charleston, not having time enough to destroy their works and guns. Arbuthnot next turned his attention to Fort Moultrie, the last American fortification remaining on the north side of Charleston Harbor. On the night of 4 May, 300 marines and seamen seized without opposition the eastern end of Sullivan's Island, on which Fort Moultrie stood. Another force of some 300 marines and seamen landed on the landward side of Sullivan's Island at the rear of Fort Moultrie, and soon afterwards the fort surrendered to Arbuthnot's marines and seamen without a fight.[67] The capture of the American works along the north shore of Charleston Harbor and the operations of British troops north and east of the Cooper River had cut the last remaining approaches to Charleston.

While the British were gaining control of Charleston Harbor and cutting the enemy's lines of communication to the north and east of the city, the siege operations under the direction of Major James Moncrieff of the Engineers, which had begun on 1 April, were being carried out with great dispatch. By the first week in May, British approaches were near enough to Charleston's fortifications for British heavy guns to blast the American works; and by the night of 11 May, Clinton's troops had gained a lodgement within about 30 paces of the fortifications. The next morning British artillery began firing hot shot into Charleston. Lincoln had twice refused British demands that the city be surrendered, and Clinton was coming to the

[66] *Roebuck, Richmond, Romulus, Blonde, Virginia, Raleigh* and *Sandwich* armed ship.
[67] NRS, *Keith Papers*, vol. I, pp. 140–1.

conclusion that the Americans 'will be blockheads enough to wait the assault. *Je m'en lave les mains*.'[68] But on 12 May, just as the British were preparing to carry Charleston by assault, the Americans surrendered. According to Clinton's count, the British captured seven general officers, about 6,000 troops of various kinds, the rebel Lieutenant-Governor of South Carolina with a number of other rebel civil officials, 400 guns, 5,000 stand of small arms, a large quantity of gunpowder and a number of warships.[69] The British lost 268 soldiers and 51 seamen were killed or wounded during the siege.[70]

The capture of Charleston was the greatest defeat inflicted upon the Americans during the revolutionary war. The number of soldiers surrendered would not be equalled until 1862, when 10,700 Union troops were surrendered to Stonewall Jackson at Harper's Ferry, and it was a defeat by a foreign enemy that would not be surpassed until Bataan. But the British had little time to rejoice over the surrender of Charleston, for at 2 p.m. on 12 May, as American troops were being disarmed, there was a huge explosion, the result of British troops carelessly throwing loaded muskets taken from Americans into a warehouse containing gunpowder. The explosion destroyed several buildings and sent muskets, ramrods and bayonets flying in every direction. For the next several hours, small arms continued discharging at random. Several thousand stand of arms were lost and more artillerymen were killed during this explosion than during the entire siege.[71]

As units of King George's army fanned out across South Carolina after the surrender of Charleston, rebel authority appeared to collapse throughout the province. On 4 July 1780, Cornwallis wrote to his brother from Charleston that 'the province of South Carolina has totally submitted, and American affairs wear a better aspect than they have done for some time'.[72] Cornwallis was being overoptimistic: while his lordship might not have been able to foresee that the British effort in the American South would be engulfed in guerrilla warfare, he was aware that two days before the surrender of Charleston, Clinton had received intelligence from London dated 15 March 1780, saying that the French were sending an expeditionary

---

[68] *American Rebellion*, p. 170n.
[69] The French ship *L'Aventure*, the Continental Navy's ships *Providence, Boston Ranger* and several vessels in the South Carolina service: NRS, *Keith Papers*, vol. I, p. 174.
[70] *American Rebellion*, pp. 169-71; NRS, *Keith Papers*, vol. I, p. 142.
[71] Uhlendorf, *Siege*, pp. 297-8.
[72] HMC, *Various Collections*, vol. 6, p. 325.

force to North America consisting of an unknown number of troops and 12 ships of the line.[73] So even though rebel resistance appeared to be collapsing in the American South, this intelligence forced Clinton and Arbuthnot to change their plans. Clinton again put off his intention of sending a force to establish a post in the Chesapeake Bay region.[74] And on 31 May, Arbuthnot wrote a dispatch to London saying that his squadron was in no condition to handle 12 enemy ships of the line. Of the admiral's large warships at Charleston, only HMS *Europe* was in good condition. The crews of HMS *Russell* and HMS *Robust* were sickly, and these ships had been sent north in order that their crews might regain their health. HMS *Raisonable* and HMS *Renown* were 'very foul and out of repair'. On 8 June, Arbuthnot and Clinton sailed for New York with the bulk of the British squadron at Charleston and transports carrying some 4,500 troops.

When he arrived at New York at the beginning of July, Clinton learned from Major-General Benedict Arnold of the Continental Army, who was secretly in league with the British, that the destination of the French force was Rhode Island. Arbuthnot, perhaps because he was not aware of its source, was very sceptical about this information.[75] Several days later Clinton received intelligence from London dated 3 May, that the French force consisted of seven ships of the line, a 64-gun ship with her lower tier of guns removed, two frigates, and transports carrying 5,200 troops. It was thought in London that this force was proceeding to Canada. At the same time, Clinton was informed of a second French squadron made up of two ships of the line, some frigates and an unknown number of troops thought to be proceeding either to the Chesapeake or Delaware bays.[76] For unknown reasons, Clinton placed great weight on this intelligence, as opposed to the information he had received from Arnold, and proposed to Arbuthnot that a joint attack should be undertaken in Chesapeake and Delaware bays before the French arrived. Arbuthnot turned down Clinton's proposal, saying that he needed more information before he could act.[77] Clinton, from the information supplied by Arnold, actually had better intelligence of French intentions in North America than did the authorities in London.

---

[73] *American Rebellion*, pp. 17n, 439–40.
[74] HMC, *Stopford-Sackville MSS.*, vol. 2, pp. 166–7.
[75] *American Rebellion*, pp. 191–6.
[76] PRO, CO 5/99, f. 60.
[77] *American Rebellion*, pp. 195–6.

The government in London knew as early as 6 March 1780 that the French were going to dispatch an expedition to North America under the command of Chevalier de Ternay d'Arsac.[78] The next day the Cabinet decided on the basis of intelligence from France that six ships of the line should be made ready 'with the utmost Expedition to be sent to North America'.[79] By 11 March, Germain having concluded that the French were going to attack Halifax and Quebec, suggested to Sandwich that the reinforcement to be sent to North America should be increased from six to eight ships of the line.[80] Two days later, on 14 March, the Cabinet agreed with that suggestion,[81] and on 16 March the Admiralty began to issue the necessary orders to carry it out. Rear-Admiral Thomas Graves was appointed to be second in command in New York and to command the ships being sent to North America. Why Graves, who did not have a distinguished naval career, was given this command is not known.[82] Without realizing it, the Admiralty had appointed Graves to be commander-in-chief of the squadron at New York during the greatest crisis of the war in America. At the same time that Graves was appointed to command the ships going to North America, the Admiralty sent Arbuthnot the dispatch informing him of the expected arrival of French reinforcements in North America. To counter that suspected action, the Admiralty was going to send to New York a squadron of eight ships of the line and a frigate under the command of Graves.[83]

The British were following a strategy of 'detachments', which by its very nature forced the Royal Navy to react to the enemy instead of placing the enemy in the position of having to react to it. When the authorities on London learned from intelligence sources that the French were fitting out an overseas expedition, they attempted to counter the expected enemy move by drawing ships from the Channel squadron and dispatching them to race the French force to their supposed objective in order to prevent the French and the Spanish from gaining local naval superiority in North America or the West Indies. This strategy did not work in 1778 when Byron was sent to America, and it would not work with Graves's squadron in

[78] NRS, Sandwich Papers, vol. III, p. 243.
[79] G, no. 2968.
[80] NRS, *Sandwich Papers*, vol. III, pp. 244-5.
[81] G, no. 2968.
[82] French Ensor Chadwick (ed.), *The Graves Papers and Other Documents Relating to the Naval Operations of the Yorktown Campaign, July to October 1781* (New York, 1968 reprint), pp. lxxv-lxxvii, 1-3.
[83] PRO, 30 20/12, Admiralty to Arbuthnot, 16 March 1780.

1780. If a policy of countering enemy moves by detachments from the Channel squadron was going to be successful, then the government not only had to know the enemy's objectives, but also have the necessary ships fitted out and able to sail immediately.

On 15 March, the day before the Admiralty issued the order setting up Graves's command to reinforce the squadron in North America, Germain's office concluded that there were three possible French objectives: Halifax, Quebec or Newfoundland.[84] In fact none of those places were to be attacked by the French in 1780; moreover, Graves's squadron could not sail at once because the ships were not fitted or manned for immediate service.[85] The strategy of 'detachments' has been attacked as one of the main reasons for British failures during the American war, but it was a method born of necessity: open to attack in Europe, the East and West Indies and North America, the British simply had more strategic commitments than they had ships and men to defend them.

On 25 March 1780, Graves was ordered by the Admiralty to sail from Spithead for North America. Bad weather and the need to provision and water his ships held Graves in port until 8 April when the admiral signalled the ships of his squadron to weigh anchor. But the crews of HMS *America*, HMS *Shrewsbury* and HMS *Invincible* mutinied, refusing to weigh anchor, locking themselves up between decks and shutting all the hatches and ports. The seamen refused to put to sea because their pay had been withheld contrary to the Act of Parliament known as 'Grenville's Act' (after George Grenville, the then Treasurer of the Navy). This Act called for sailors to receive two months' pay before proceeding to sea. In the case of Grave's ships, the commissioner of Portsmouth Dockyard could not pay the seamen, for in a number of cases the men had been drafted from ship to ship faster than the necessary paperwork could be completed: so while they were entitled to pay, the records did not show this. Remembering that HMS *Resolution*'s crew had mutinied over pay in December, Graves had warned the Admiralty on 7 April that there might be trouble, but to no avail.

Graves put down the mutiny by prying open the aft ports and hatches on the ships and then forcing the seamen up on deck by using marines who had orders 'to mark those by wounds who stood in their way as they proceeded from aft to Bow opening the Ports as they went on – and if any man ventured to oppose by violence to put him

[84] PRO, CO 5/99, ff. 31–2.
[85] NRS, *Sandwich Papers*, vol. III, p. 245.

to Death'. Once the seamen were up on deck, those with bayonet or gunshot wounds would be noted for possible court martial. When all the seamen were assembled on deck and guarded by armed officers and marines, each man was ordered by name to take his station, and if he refused he would be court-martialled. Using measures of this type, Graves and the commander at Portsmouth, Admiral Sir Thomas Pye, quelled the mutiny. But Graves's ships were still short of stores and provisions.[86]

The ships of Graves's squadron made their way down the Channel in ones and twos to Plymouth, in order to embark further stores and provisions. On 22 April the Cabinet decided to send two of Graves's ships of the line to the West Indies, the remaining six ships of the line and the frigate lay windbound at Plymouth until 17 May, when they sailed for New York by the southern great circle route and after a fast passage arrived off Sandy Hook on 13 July.[87] Even with the delayed departure of Graves's squadron for New York, the authorities in London did not know the objective of the French force under de Ternay. On 8 April, for instance, intelligence reached London that the French objective was Delaware Bay; but in six days another report said it was New York City.[88] Until 30 June, London did not learn that the objective of the French expedition was Rhode Island.[89]

On 8 July 1780, Arbuthnot received news that the previous day his cruisers had intercepted de Ternay's squadron, which was on a course for Rhode Island. The French were off Point Judith on 10 July, and the next day the French warships and transports anchored in Newport Harbor. On 13 July, Graves arrived off Sandy Hook with his squadron.[90] The arrival of seven ships of the line and a small French field army at Rhode Island was not a surprise either to Clinton or Arbuthnot.[91] Strategically a French army of some 5,000 men based at Newport was not a great danger, for the French troops could not move five feet without the British at New York quickly learning of it. But seven French ships of the line based in Newport and supported by a French land force posed grave strategic dangers.[92] Newport was an ice-free harbour which was extremely

---

[86] G, no. 2989; NRS, *Sandwich Papers*, vol. III, pp. 238–9, 246–7; *Graves Papers*, pp. 3–11.
[87] Graves's squadron consisted of the *London, Resolution, Bedford, Royal Oak, Prudent, America* and the frigate *Amphitrite*: G no. 3002; NRS, *Sandwich Papers*, vol. III, pp. 239, 246–7; *Graves Papers*, pp. 12–3; PRO, CO 5/99, f. 69.
[88] PRO, CO 5/99, ff. 49, 51, 55.
[89] PRO, ADM 1/4142, f. 64.
[90] PRO, CO 5/100, ff. 67–8
[91] E.g. HMC, *Stopford-Sackville MSS*, vol. 2, p. 169.

difficult to blockade. Using it as a base, the French squadron could not only threaten British maritime communications to New York, but attack British ships proceeding between New York and either Halifax or the British Isles, as well as the supply lines between New York and the British forces operating in the South. As the war expanded into Virginia in 1780 and 1781, the French at Newport were also in a position to attack British forces operating Chesapeake Bay. Thus strategically it was imperative for the British to attack and destroy, or at the very least, cripple or drive away, the French at Newport.

The only possible way for the British at New York successfully to attack the French would be to mount a major amphibious operation in which both the French army and navy at Newport would be trapped and destroyed. The British in America had the ships and the troops to undertake an operation of this type; additionally, and perhaps more important, the British had all the special skills and equipment required for large-scale amphibious operations, as they had proved during the Seven Years War and the first five years of the American war.[93] The capture of Charleston at the beginning of 1780 by Arbuthnot and Clinton had been a major amphibious operation. But by the time the French arrived at Newport on 11 July 1780, the numerous and increasingly bitter disputes between Clinton and Arbuthnot had paralysed the army and the navy and rendered them incapable of mounting the type of operation required to remove that strategic threat. During the attack on Charleston there had been some disagreements, such as whether to land the army on Simmon's Island or on John's Island, but Clinton and Arbuthnot managed to keep their heads clear enough, so that operations were not greatly affected. After the surrender of Charleston, however, a dispute broke out between the army and the navy over the division of booty from the campaign, and as more and more prizes were captured, intensified to such a degree that even the government in London could not stop it. Major-General Alexander Leslie was so exasperated by the wrangling over booty that he was driven to exclaim, in May 1781, 'I wish to God all prizes were immediately destroyed'.[94]

On 15 July, Clinton wrote to Arbuthnot saying that no time should be lost in mounting an amphibious attack against the French

---

[92] For an account of the make-up and strength of the French force at Newport see Lee Kennett, *The French Forces in America, 1780-1783* (Westport, Conn., 1977), pp. 20-33.
[93] E.g. David Syrett, 'The methodology of British amphibious operations during the Seven Years War and The American war, *Mariner's Mirror* (August 1972), vol. 58, pp. 269-80.
[94] CL, Clinton Papers, Leslie to Clinton, 29 May 1781.

at Rhode Island. In 1778, when d'Estaing and the Americans were besieging the British at Newport, Clinton had suggested that the American troops on Rhode Island be trapped by British amphibious forces enveloping the Americans by occupying Bristol Neck.[95] In 1780, Clinton was again thinking in terms of amphibious envelopment; he suggested to Arbuthnot a plan in which the admiral's ships of the line would blockade the French warships in Newport Harbor while 5,000 British troops covered by a force of frigates would proceed up the Sakonnet Passage, land on the east side of Rhode Island and then defeat the French army at Newport before they could fortify the place. The French warships could then be subjected to cannon fire from the land and would either be destroyed or forced out of Newport Harbor, in which case they would have had to fight Arbuthnot's squadron. Clinton thought that these plans could be carried out 'with little risk' and that the destruction of the French force at Newport would 'probably' end the war. In case Arbuthnot did not want to undertake a combined expedition against Newport, Clinton proposed another plan: he would ask the admiral to supply enough warships to cover large-scale raids against the Connecticut River and New London, Connecticut.[96] The British had the necessary ships and the troops, but the effectiveness of these plans depended on Arbuthnot's and Clinton's co-operation, and that was an impossibility. They could not even agree upon a joint plan of action.

On 16 July, Arbuthnot wrote Clinton from Sandy Hook that if his squadron was superior in strength to the French warships at Newport, then the French could not 'escape' and 'their whole force must submit'. The admiral ended his letter by stating that he had no ships to be employed for raiding operations in Long Island Sound. The next day Clinton, not understanding Arbuthnot's letter, sent Captain Thomas Murray to Sandy Hook to explain to the admiral the two plans for attacking the French at Newport. On 18 July, Arbuthnot wrote to Clinton that he was proceeding to Rhode Island at once and would inform the general immediately if it were possible to carry either plan into effect. Clinton then asked Captain Thomas Tonken, the senior agent for transports, to begin embarking troops on the transports that Clinton had requested be made available several weeks earlier, only to be informed by Tonken that most of the transports were employed carrying water to Arbuthnot's squad-

---

[95] Willcox, *Portrait*, p. 127
[96] *American Rebellion*, pp. 198–9, 443–4.

ron at Sandy Hook. By the time that Arbuthnot's squadron finished using the transports, according to Clinton, the navy 'had torn them to pieces'. Until 27 July, Clinton was unable to assemble 6,700 effectives on board transports in Huntington Bay on the north shore of Long Island with orders to proceed to Rhode Island and attack the French. In the meantime Murray returned to Clinton's headquarters on 22 July with a letter from Arbuthnot saying that the admiral's frigates 'perceived' that there were eleven French ships of the line at Newport, which Clinton did not believe. Arbuthnot's letter ended, according to Clinton, with the promise that if Clinton attacked the east side of the island of Rhode Island, 'nothing but a hurricane could oblige him [Arbuthnot] to quit the coast and abandon me [Clinton], should I go in the Sakonnet as proposed'.[97]

By 22 July, Clinton had surmised that the French had been at Newport long enough to have fortified the town and therefore a surprise attack undertaken from the east side of Rhode Island did not have much chance of success. Clinton then sent Captain Henry Savage and some Rhode Island Loyalists to Arbuthnot's squadron off Rhode Island to reconnoitre the French position at Newport. Savage carried with him a letter from Clinton to Arbuthnot stating that while a *coup de main* was probably impossible, Clinton was still prepared to attack the French in any way that the admiral could suggest. Arbuthnot responded on 23 July off Newport that there were seven French ships of the line and four frigates at Newport and that the French were fortifying the place; however, if Clinton still wanted to attack the town, he would prevent the French warships from leaving harbour and supply frigates to cover a landing. On 27 July, Savage met with Arbuthnot on the admiral's flagship, HMS *Europe*, off Block Island. Savage later reported to Clinton that at this meeting '*the Admiral expressed his wishes that he could stop your [Clinton's] intentions of proceeding*' because the French had fortified Newport and had been reinforced by a large number of Americans; if, however, Clinton wanted to attack the French at Newport, Arbuthnot was prepared to land the army and to prevent the French warships from leaving Newport Harbor, but Clinton could expect nothing more from the navy. Arbuthnot told Savage that the army would not even be permitted to borrow or use naval guns or ammunition. After the meeting with Arbuthnot, Savage, accompanied by Captain Charles Hudson of HMS *Richmond*, reconnoitred the seaward approaches of the French positions at

[97] Ibid., pp. 191–201, 444.

Newport, and then proceeded to Huntington Bay to report to Clinton.

After hearing Savage's report on conditions at Rhode Island, Clinton wrote to Arbuthnot on 30 July that the French force at Newport was an objective of such strategic importance that an attack on it must be made if at all possible, and he requested a meeting to discuss the problem. Several days later Clinton received a letter from Arbuthnot dated 3 August off Block Island:

> I never was here before and am totally ignorant of the situation of the place. As to the conversation between Captain Savage and myself, *I said no more than*, if upon his report you judge your force insufficient to warrant an attempt upon the enemy, I thought it better not to come. Far was my idea from pretending officially to know their strength. For I pledge myself, if I had, you should certainly have received an earlier information of it. *It is sixteen days since I have been about this place, in anxious expectation of hearing from you. The fleet being in a very critical situation with upward of 900 sick, and short of complement.* I shall for a few days repair to Gardiners Island to water and put the sick on shore.

The confusion between Arbuthnot and Clinton was heightened by the fact that their letters kept crossing each other. On 13 August, Clinton received a letter from Arbuthnot at Gardiner's Island, dated 8 August, requesting a meeting with Clinton and telling him to prepare army units for immediate deployment. On 11 August, Clinton had written Arbuthnot a fairly full letter, summing up the reasons why in his opinion the British had been unable to attack and destroy the French at Newport. When Clinton received Arbuthnot's letter of 8 August, he wrote to the admiral that he had ordered the troops and transports at Huntington Bay to be ready to sail at a moment's notice and that he was setting out overland to meet Arbuthnot at Gardiner's Island. Before beginning the journey to the east end of Long Island, Clinton ordered that Generals William Dalrymple and Edward Mathew proceed to Arbuthnot's squadron by sea. On 15 August, Clinton began his overland journey from New York City to Gardiner's Island in the heat of summer. When he arrived at Moriches, he sent ahead a party of light dragoons with a note to Arbuthnot saying he would arrive the next day; but when Clinton reached East Hampton on 18 August, he discovered that Arbuthnot had put to sea. Arbuthnot left a note for Clinton saying:

I am this moment honoured with Your Excellency's letter of yesterday. And, as I am preparing to weigh to cruise for the enemy between Montauk Point and the southward of Nantucket Shoals, I do not think it proper to delay a moment.

After writing an angry letter to Arbuthnot, Clinton made his way back the length of Long Island to New York City. Being stood up by Arbuthnot at Gardiner's Island marked the end of the last serious attempt by Clinton to formulate a joint plan to attack and destroy the French at Newport.[98]

Why could not Arbuthnot and Clinton agree on a plan to attack the French at Newport? Several years after the event, Clinton was 'unwilling to ascribe the failure of this enterprise to any particular cause'.[99] Certainly, in the cold light of history, Arbuthnot's actions appear inexplicable, even irrational. Perhaps the answer lies in Arbuthnot's fifty-four years of undistinguished service in the Royal Navy.[100] With the arrival of Graves's six ships of the line at Sandy Hook on 13 July, Arbuthnot had ten ships of the line with which to fight de Ternay's seven. Perhaps Arbuthnot thought that the French squadron would come out of Newport Harbor and he could end his long career with a smashing victory over the French, a victory he did not want to share with the army. All this is speculation, but in his letter to Clinton on 16 July, Arbuthnot makes it very clear that he expected to fight and beat the French squadron.[101] However, the French squadron did not leave Newport, and with each day that passed Newport's defences became stronger. Also Clinton was continually pressing Arbuthnot for an amphibious assault on Newport; but amphibious operations of the type Clinton wanted can be risky, and perhaps Arbuthnot did not want to end his career with a defeat in an operation thought up by the army? On 19 August, Arbuthnot told Dalrymple and Mathew, 'nothing could be done after the first day of their [the French] *arrival*'.[102] And on 20 August, in a letter to Sandwich, Arbuthnot blamed Clinton for the failure to attack Newport, saying:

> Sir Henry Clinton's amusing me with his situation at Huntington Bay, with his troops in transports and aid-de-camps dancing backwards and forwards with reports of intelligence with respect

[98] Ibid., pp. 201–8, 444–51.
[99] Ibid., p. 207.
[100] NRS, *Sandwich Papers*, vol. III, p. 268.
[101] *American Rebellion*, p. 444.
[102] Ibid., p. 452.

to the enemy, kept me in constant hope of an éclaircissement one way or other, till time slipped from under my feet and obliged me at last to retire to Gardiner's Island Bay . . . after loitering away my time 19 days to no purpose.[103]

That Clinton and Arbuthnot were unable to agree on a plan for attacking Newport is not surprising because Clinton wanted a truly joint operation against the French, in which the British could exploit their amphibious capabilities to the greatest extent possible, while Arbuthnot would very reluctantly commit himself only to putting Clinton's troops ashore at the place of the general's choosing and while blockading the French warships in Newport Harbor. Beyond this, Arbuthnot would not go, no matter how hard Clinton pushed him. And what better way to put Clinton off than to write noncommittal letters and avoid meeting him by simply putting to sea when Clinton seemed likely to appear? After Arbuthnot and Clinton failed to reach an agreement on a plan to attack the French at Rhode Island, Arbuthnot, using Gardiner's Island as a base, continued cruising with nine ships of the line and a 50-gun ship off Rhode Island and the eastern end of Long Island in order to be in position to intercept the French if they should leave Newport.[104]

Shortly after his futile trip to the eastern end of Long Island in quest of Arbuthnot, Clinton sent his quartermaster general, William Dalrymple, to London with an ultimatum demanding that Arbuthnot be removed from command of the squadron in North America, that all transports and other vessels employed in support of the army be put under Clinton's command, that at least 10,000 additional troops be sent to America and that he be made the sole commissioner for restoring peace in America. If these requests were not complied with, Clinton threatened to resign as commander-in-chief of the army in America. Clinton then turned his back on Arbuthnot and the French at Rhode Island, even though he believed that the arrival of the French in America produced a 'new epoch in the war'. Unable to work with Arbuthnot and convinced of the 'utter impossibility of prosecuting the war in this country without reinforcement',[105] Clinton considered the need for additional troops self-evident, for all one had to do was 'glance upon the returns of the army divided into garrisons and reduced by casualties on the one part, with consideration of the task yet before us on the other . . . we are by

[103] NRS, *Sandwich Papers*, vol III, p. 249.
[104] PRO, 30 20/12, Arbuthnot to Rodney, 20 September 1780
[105] Willcox, *Portrait*, p. 355.

some thousands too weak to subdue this formidable rebellion'. If reinforced by 6,000 troops and given naval superiority, Clinton thought that he could capture and hold the peninsula between Chesapeake and Delaware bays, where the inhabitants were thought to be Loyalists.[106] But by the beginning of September, Clinton was again considering attacking the Chesapeake Bay region and perhaps setting up a 'small post there' in order 'to call a part of the enemy's attention from Carolina'.[107] Clinton probably reasoned that without considerable reinforcements the war in America could not be won unless the rebels made a major mistake or the entire direction of the conflict was changed by some fluke or chance.

Clinton was working on producing a fluke himself which, if carried off and then exploited correctly, could possibly have changed the direction of the war. For some months, Major John André, Clinton's adjutant general – and before André, Captain George Beckwith, an aide-de-camp to General Wilhelm Knyphausen – had been conducting a secret correspondence with Major-General Benedict Arnold of the Continental Army with the objective of obtaining the surrender, without a fight, of West Point with its guns, garrison and outposts. If West Point and its outposts could be gained by Arnold's treason, then the British could seize the Hudson Highlands.[108]

While Clinton and Arnold conspired over West Point, the balance of naval power in America shifted dramatically with the arrival of Admiral Sir George Rodney from the West Indies. On 14 September 1780, Admiral Rodney anchored without any warning with ten ships of the line off Sandy Hook.[109] Rodney, the commander-in-chief of the Royal Navy in the Lesser Antilles, had received intelligence that a French squadron was thought to be sailing from the West Indies to America in order to reinforce the French squadron at Rhode Island. Rodney's squadron sailed for the Carolinas and then northward along the coast towards New York. Rodney left the West Indies to avoid the hurricane season and to prevent any French squadron from the West Indies gaining naval superiority in American waters, as d'Estaing had done in 1779 at Savannah. Immediately upon reaching Sandy Hook, Rodney sent five ships of the line to reinforce

[106] PRO, CO 5/100, ff. 88–9.
[107] Ibid., f. 159.
[108] Willard M. Wallace, *Traitorous Hero: The Life and Fortunes of Benedict Arnold* (New York, 1954).
[109] *Sandwich, Russell, Centaur, Triumph, Culloden, Alcide, Terrible, Shrewsbury, Torbay, Suffolk, Intrepid* and *Yarmouth*; frigates, *Fortune, Boreas* and *Greyhound*: *Graves Papers*, p. 15.

Arbuthnot's squadron off Newport and informed the Admiralty that he was going to consult Clinton about attacking and destroying the French at Rhode Island.[110]

The unexpected appearance of Rodney with ten ships of the line gave the British total naval superiority in American waters. The question was, could three men of such different and difficult personalities as Arbuthnot, Clinton and Rodney exploit this naval superiority in such a way as to inflict a major defeat on the rebels or the French forces at Newport, or both? On the day that he arrived at Sandy Hook, Rodney wrote to Clinton that he would come to New York City as soon as possible to ascertain 'in what manner I can best second your efforts towards the Reduction of His Majesty's Rebellious Subjects – the Sole motive for my coming to this Coast'.[111] There were three possible offensive actions, or combinations of them, that the British could undertake at the time of Rodney's arrival at New York. Having naval superiority, the British could attack the French at Rhode Island or they could attempt by means of Arnold's treason to gain control of West Point and the Hudson Highlands or they could undertake amphibious operations against the Americans in Chesapeake Bay.

On 17 September, and on the following morning, Clinton and Rodney met at New York City to discuss a joint action. Rodney wanted to attack Rhode Island, but Clinton was already locked into the Hudson Highlands operation with Arnold, and the ill-fated mission for which André left New York City on 20 September.[112] On the afternoon of 18 September, after their meeting was ended, Clinton wrote Rodney a long letter explaining his position on the conduct of the war, omitting for security reasons any mention of Arnold and the Hudson Highlands. Clinton thought Rodney's arrival had thrown the Americans and the French completely on the defensive, forestalling any attempt to attack the British at New York. Clinton also enclosed copies of all his correspondence with Arbuthnot about Rhode Island. The general then stated that when the French had first landed at Rhode Island, he was prepared to attack them with 6,000 troops. But now, since the French had fortified Rhode Island and Washington 'might assemble the whole force in America' to protect the Franco-American position there, Clinton did not have the troops required to attack it. However, if

---

[110] NYHSC, *Letter-Books and Order-Book of George, Lord Rodney, Admiral of the White Squadron, 1780–1782*, vol. I, pp. 8–11.
[111] CL, Clinton Papers, Rodney to Clinton, 14 September 1780.
[112] Wallace, *Traitorous Hero*, p. 232.

Rodney was bound and determined to attack Rhode Island, then Clinton would give the admiral 'every possible secondary assistance of the army for with about 3,000 men all I can *now* spare from this important post I cannot undertake a siege, against an Army of 10,000 men'. Clinton's letter ended with an oblique request for the admiral's support of the Arnold and Hudson Highlands operation, while stressing the 'necessity and importance' of sending an expedition to Chesapeake Bay.[113] Clinton avoided flatly turning down Rodney's proposal for a joint attack on the French at Rhode Island by consenting to the operation while offering an insufficient number of troops for such an attack.

For Rodney, the meetings with Clinton on 17 and 18 September must have been the first signs that something was wrong with the command of the British forces in America. A quick reading of the Arbuthnot-Clinton correspondence about the French at Newport must have shown that Arbuthnot and Clinton could not work together? To base all operations conducted by the British who had total naval superiority on a scheme to capture a group of fortifications, which were many miles inland and assisted by a defecting rebel major-general - although Rodney does not mention it in his next dispatch to the Admiralty[114] - should have appeared to the admiral as something less than the proper strategic utilization of the men and ships available. No doubt, Rodney understood Clinton's wanting to send an expedition to Chesapeake Bay, but the refusal by Clinton to consider seriously an attack on the French at Rhode Island must have appeared odd, if not irrational. The French squadron and troops at Newport were an objective that could be obtained with naval power and amphibious operations, while Arnold and the West Point project were at best strategically problematic. The French ships at Newport could be captured or destroyed - either of which would have been a British victory of importance - but what would happen if Clinton managed to occupy West Point? Could the British hold the place, or would it suffer the same fate as Stony Point? Assuming that Clinton captured and was able to hold West Point, what then would be the next strategic step? Its capture, like the capture of any other geographical point in America, might very well be meaningless unless Washington's army was destroyed. Questions of this nature must have occupied Rodney's thoughts during the last days of September, especially after the Arnold conspiracy collapsed

---

[113] CL, Clinton Papers, Clinton to Rodney, 18 September 1780.
[114] NYHSC, *Rodney Letter-Books*. vol. I, pp. 28-31.

with the capture of André on 23 September.[115] Rodney, if he had a philosophical turn of mind, probably would have agreed with the official in London who wrote on 29 September, 'I fear the golden dreams we had after taking Charleston are all over. There was a period of French history under their kings who they call *Les Fainéants*. The whole war in America had been conducted by such generals'.[116] Perhaps this is giving Rodney too much strategic insight. But it is very difficult to tell what he thought about Clinton's conduct of the war, for his relations with Clinton were good-natured, although some of the admiral's personal letters to London were very critical of the way the war was being conducted in America.

Almost from the minute he appeared at Sandy Hook, Rodney was in conflict with Arbuthnot. Upon his arrival at New York, Rodney, because he was senior to Arbuthnot, claimed to be now the commander-in chief of all the ships and vessels of the Royal Navy in American waters. Arbuthnot, however, did not acknowledge Rodney's authority and attempted to play the kind of games with Rodney that he had with Clinton during the preceding summer over the problem of Rhode Island. Arbuthnot should have understood what was going on, for Rodney had a long history, known throughout the service, for usurping authority and grasping every penny that came near him. Further, Rodney was not Clinton: if Rodney was senior, then his commands would be obeyed and he would enjoy all the rights of seniority and rank. Arbuthnot would find it very difficult to prevent the strong-willed Rodney from taking control of naval affairs at New York.

Heated disputes between Arbuthnot and Rodney arose over the question of prize money and the deployment of warships. On his voyage northward along the American coast, Rodney had not encountered one British warship. One of his first acts at New York was to order the deployment of a number of ships along the coast southward of New York to hunt down enemy cruisers and blockade-runners and to protect British shipping. On 16 October, Arbuthnot wrote to Rodney:

> Your partial interference in the conduct of the American war, is certainly unaccountable upon principles of reason and precedents of service. The frigates attendant on a cruizing squadron you have

---

[115] Wallace, *Traitorous Hero*, p. 244–59.
[116] HMC, *Various Collections*, vol. 6, p. 172.

taken upon you to counter order, a due representation which, I shall certainly make, where it will have every possible effect.[117]

Arbuthnot's complaint about 'interference' went unheeded, for Rodney would not tolerate that kind of letter or threat from an officer of inferior rank. On 19 October, Rodney bluntly informed Arbuthnot:

> Your anger at my partial interfering (as you term it) with the American War not a little surprizes me. I came to Interfere in the American War, to Command by Sea in it, and to do my best Endeavours towards putting an End thereto.
> I knew the Dignity of my own Rank, and the power invested in me by the Commission . . . intitled me to take the supreme Command, which I ever shall do on every station where his Majesty's and the Public Service may make it necessary for me to go, unless I meet a Superior Officer, in which Case it will be my Duty to Obey his orders.

Rodney's letter goes on for eight more paragraphs, taking to task Arbuthnot for such things as not obeying legally constituted orders and noting that Arbuthnot's conduct 'is . . . unprecedented in the annals of the British Navy. My Duty will oblige me to report it to the Lords Commissioners of the Admiralty.'[118]

Both Arbuthnot and Rodney had already written letters to Sandwich complaining about each other. On 5 October, Arbuthnot complained to the first lord about the ill-effects of Rodney's taking command at New York; five days later Rodney wrote a letter to Sandwich implying that it was Arbuthnot's incompetence that had prevented the British from attacking and destroying the French force at Newport that summer.[119] Rodney clearly thought that Arbuthnot was at best incompetent; the division of prize money between the two admirals was also an issue. The commanding officer of a squadron was entitled to one-eighth of the value of every prize taken by any ship under his command. On 2 October, at Gardiner's Island, Arbuthnot had his secretary draw up a circular that was sent to every prize agent in New York City claiming the commander-in-chief's share of the value of any prizes taken by the forty-four warships that were stationed in North America before Rodney's arrival. Arbuth-

---
[117] PRO, 30 20/9, p. 11.
[118] NYHSC, *Rodney Letter-Books*, vol. I, pp. 43–6.
[119] NRS, *Sandwich Papers*, vol. III, p. 252–4.

not claimed these ships were not under Rodney's command, but rather under his own, by reason of his being 'Stationary Commander in Chief in North America'. This document was bound to cause a fight, for to Rodney money was as important as rank, honour and respect.

On 28 October, Rodney hit back at Arbuthnot by sending a long letter to the Admiralty explaining all the steps he had taken since arriving at New York to put the affairs of the Royal Navy in North America in order and detailing Arbuthnot's every error and failure to obey commands of a superior officer. In a letter filled with bile, Rodney's harshest criticism of Arbuthnot was the accusation that 'I am asham'd to mention what appears to me the real cause and from whence Mr. Arbuthnot's Chagrene proceeds, but the Proofs are so plain, that Prize Money is the Occasion, that I am under the necessity to transmit them'. Arbuthnot, Rodney continued, had threatened him with 'litigous Suits' over the question of prize money. Rodney enclosed copies of all the letters and orders he had written and issued to Arbuthnot, of all Arbuthnot's letters to him and of Arbuthnot's circular of 2 October to the New York prize agents.[120]

Rodney was going to have his share of prize money and Arbuthnot was going, albeit with considerable ill-grace, to obey Rodney's orders. The war between the two admirals continued until Rodney left New York for the West Indies. Arbuthnot should have known that – if push came to shove – Rodney would win. Victory in a dispute over prize money with a man such as Arbuthnot really did not amount to much and, in many respects, Rodney's stay at New York was a waste of time. The presence of Rodney's squadron at New York gave the British total naval superiority in American waters, but this superiority was not used to any purpose. Rodney's role in the war in America was mostly that of a spectator from the deck of his flagship HMS *Sandwich*, which for most of the admiral's stay at New York was anchored in the North River between New York City and Paulus Hook.

Back when Rodney first appeared upon the coast of the Carolinas, he received intelligence that on 16 August Cornwallis had fought and won the Battle of Camden.[121] Cornwallis followed this victory by invading North Carolina but was checked when a large detachment of Loyalist militia, under the command of Major Patrick Ferguson, was destroyed on 7 October at King's Mountain by a force of

---

[120] NYHSC, *Rodney Letter-Books*, vol. I., pp. 22–3.
[121] Ibid., vol. I, p. 10.

frontier rebel militia known as the 'Over the Mountain Men'. At the same time, Georgia and the Carolinas became alive with rebel guerilla bands led by men such as Thomas Sumter and Francis Marion. After receiving at New York the news of King's Mountain and not knowing the strength or intentions of Cornwallis, Clinton decided that an operation must be undertaken to attempt to take some of the pressure off King George's forces in the South. The commander-in-chief of the British army in America thought that the best way to hinder American operations not only in the American South, but also in the middle colonies, was to dispatch an expedition to Chesapeake Bay.

At the beginning of the war, there had been fighting in coastal waters off Virginia and, in the summer of 1779, the British had carried out a large amphibious raid along the shores of Chesapeake Bay; at various times the British had also wanted to set up a base in Virginia. The Chesapeake Bay region with its many rivers, which are navigable almost to the edge of the Appalachian Mountains, appeared to a number of British commanders and officials to be the ideal area in which to attack the Americans by using amphibious forces to strike at north-south communications as well as what was thought to be the logistical base of rebel armies both in the South and around New York City. Now with Rodney's squadron at New York, a British raid on Chesapeake Bay could be undertaken without fear of losing naval control of the waters off Virginia.

On 12 October 1780, Major-General Alexander Leslie was ordered to proceed to Chesapeake Bay with a force of 2,500 troops to attack and destroy American supply depots at Petersburg, Richmond and other places in Virginia and then 'to establish a post on Elizabeth River'. Leslie also was directed 'to follow all such orders' as he might receive from Cornwallis.[122] Clinton, it is clear, really did not think out the consequences of his orders to Leslie, for the commander-in-chief was gambling with this expedition to Chesapeake Bay. There were just too many unknowns. For example, what would happen after Rodney's squadron left New York and the British then lost control of Virginia coastal waters? In such an event would not a British base on a peninsula in Virginia become a trap? Also Clinton virtually had turned the command of Leslie's forces over to Cornwallis, when neither the location of the earl nor his intentions and objectives was known.

Leslie arrived in Chesapeake Bay on 20 October only to find a

---

[122] *American Rebellion*, pp. 228-467.

hostile population and no intelligence of Cornwallis. On 4 November, Leslie wrote to Clinton that he was going to establish a base at Portsmouth before undertaking raiding operations up the James River.[123]

Shortly after reaching Chesapeake Bay, Leslie received orders that he was to move his force to Cape Fear, North Carolina, to support Cornwallis in North Carolina. However, in order to strengthen the British position in South Carolina, Cornwallis ordered Leslie to Charleston, where the forces from New York arrived on 14 December.[124] As Leslie's force made its way southward along the coast, nothing was accomplished other than reinforcing the British army in the South for no offensive operations were undertaken either in Chesapeake Bay or at Cape Fear.

While British and American armies clashed in the South and British naval superiority was squandered, at New York Rodney mostly attended to the strategic problems of the West Indies and to naval administrative affairs. The major strategic problem confronting Rodney was the possibility that the seven ships of the line under de Ternay could escape from Rhode Island without being intercepted by Arbuthnot's blockading squadron. On 8 October, Rodney wrote to Arbuthnot, 'As the season is so far advanced I believe there is little probability of a French squadron of any considerable force arriving on this coast'.

But at the same time, Rodney warned Arbuthnot that the French ships at Rhode Island might attempt to escape to the West Indies.[125] Arbuthnot was directed, should the French ships at Newport leave American waters without being intercepted and destroyed, that Graves should be detached 'with Eight or Ten Copper Bottom'd Ships of the Line and two Frigates, without one moments loss of time, push'd for Martinique and Station'd himself in such a manner to Windward of that Island so as to enable him to bring Monsr. Ternay to Action on his Approach'.[126]

The prisoners of war held by the Royal Navy at New York were one of the problems that required Rodney's attention. When Rodney arrived at New York, he found about 400 naval prisoners on two prison ships with nobody in charge of them because, as he informed the Commissioners of Sick and Hurt Seamen, Arbuthnot's secretary had taken away David Sproat's warrant to act as commissary of

[123] Ibid., pp. 472–3.
[124] Ibid., pp. 230–1, 471–3.
[125] PRO, 30 20/9, p. 6.
[126] NYHSC, *Rodney Letter-Books*, vol. I., pp. 29–30.

prisoners and Arbuthnot had not returned the warrant or appointed anyone in Sproat's place. Rodney issued a new warrant to Sproat and ordered both that the hospital ship *Jersey* be converted to a prison ship and that all French prisoners held by the Royal Navy at New York be sent to France on a cartel ship for exchange. By 28 October, Rodney's ships had taken in American waters eleven rebel privateers and warships, yielding some 1,400 American naval prisoners. These prisoners were placed in the newly converted prison ship *Jersey*, which by the end of the war would be infamous for the high death rate among prisoners aboard her, and were held there until either the war ended or they were exchanged on a one-to-one basis for British naval prisoners. Because it was thought that the Americans were having trouble finding seamen to man their cruisers, these prisoners were held as long as possible as a means of reducing American naval and privateer operations.[127]

While at New York, Rodney dealt with a wide range of administrative problems,[128] but the admiral was merely marking time until he could return to the West Indies; he hated both the climate at New York and Arbuthnot, and surely saw that there was little more that he could do at New York than to push papers. Just before he left New York on 12 November, Rodney wrote to George Jackson, the Judge Advocate of the navy, that 'The war is carried on here in a manner I do not like, there is a slugishness in every operation as if they did not desire it should end'.[129] While waiting at Sandy Hook for a fair wind, Rodney wrote a last letter to Clinton in which he said: 'God bless you and send me from this Cold Country, and from such men as Arbuthnot.'[130] Finally, the wind turned favorable and, on 16 November, Rodney sailed from Sandy Hook for the West Indies with a squadron of fifteen ships and vessels.[131]

During the summer and autumn of 1780 the commanders of the British forces at New York had been at odds with each other and unable to agree on anything. Clinton and Arbuthnot could not, or would not, work together, and when Rodney arrived at New York, he also found that he could not work with Arbuthnot. During Rodney's stay in New York, Clinton proposed that the North American and West Indian naval command be combined, with

[127] Ibid., vol. I, pp. 55–6, 63–4.
[128] Ibid., vol. I, pp. 8–79.
[129] PRO, 30 20/10, Rodney to Jackson, 12 November 1780.
[130] CL, Clinton Papers, Rodney to Clinton, 13 November 1780.
[131] *Sandwich, Shrewsbury, Resolution, Triumph, Terrible, Alcide, Torbay, Intrepid, Cyclops, Boreas, Triton, Shark, Pacahunta, Lizard* schooner and *St Lucia* brig: NYHSC, *Rodney Letter-Books*, vol. I, p. 90.

Rodney in sole command in both North America and the West Indies. Rodney, though, was thinking along the lines of transferring troops back and forth between the West Indies and North America depending upon the season of the year.[132] Needless to say, nothing came of these ideas, for Clinton would not lend several thousand troops to Rodney to take to the West Indies. Ironically it would be the French, not the British, who in 1781 managed to move troops and warships back and forth between the West Indies and North America. The size and scope of any naval command, and to whom it would be given, was only to be decided in London, so Clinton's idea of a joint North American/West Indian naval command was never taken seriously, if the scheme ever reached the Cabinet.

On 11 October 1780 the Cabinet met at Germain's house to attempt to straighten out the problems at New York caused by Arbuthnot's and Clinton's many disagreements. At this meeting it was agreed to recall Admiral Sir Peter Parker, commander-in-chief at Jamaica, to send Arbuthnot to replace him, and to replace Arbuthnot at New York with a flag officer from England. In addition, if the removal of Arbuthnot from New York to Jamaica did not prevent Clinton from resigning, this being the only one of Clinton's demands they complied with, then Cornwallis would be named commander-in-chief of the British army in America.[133] It is not known why the Cabinet simply did not recall Arbuthnot or why he was offered the command at Jamaica at the expense of Parker. On 16 October, Sandwich wrote to both Arbuthnot and Parker informing them of the decision of the Cabinet. Parker, in a letter dated 17 February 1781, acquiesced to the plan, for he thought it his duty 'to serve my Royal Master in any situation that he may be most agreeable to my Sovereign'. Arbuthnot, who was now in a state of ill-health, requested on 16 December 1780 and on 20 February 1781, and again on 15 April 1781, to be recalled for reasons of health and turned down the command at Jamaica.[134]

The Cabinet had decided at an earlier meeting, on 14 September 1780, to send 'peremptory orders' to Arbuthnot, even if the seven French ships of the line were still at Newport, to send at least five ships of the line under the command of Graves to the West Indies 'when the winter season sets in, and ships of the line can no longer act

---

[132] Cl, Clinton papers, Clinton to Rodney, 10 November 1780, and Rodney to Clinton, 4 November 1780.
[133] G, no. 3160.
[134] NRS, *Sandwich Papers*, vol. III, pp. 255-8, 264-8.

upon the American coast'.[135] The Cabinet's decision to weaken the squadron at New York appears to have been based on the assumption that the whole weight of naval war in America would shift to the West Indies with the onset of winter in America. However, on 11 October 1780, on the basis of additional intelligence that showed that the French were preparing to strengthen their forces in North America, the Cabinet decided to 'revoke the *peremptory* orders' to Arbuthnot and to leave it to the admiral's discretion whether or not to detach ships to the West Indies.[136] These two orders are an example of the difficulties and dangers of trying to conduct a war in the age of sail from a distance of 3,000 miles – by the time the original orders reached Arbuthnot at New York, events had rendered them useless.

When Arbuthnot informed Clinton on 9 December of his orders to send at least five ships of the line to the West Indies, the general was dismayed. In a series of letters Clinton pointed out to Arbuthnot that if the ships were sent to the West Indies as ordered by London, the British would lose naval control of American coastal waters; in that event, the British position at New York and also in the South would be open to attack. Moreover, lack of naval superiority would prevent the British forces from undertaking any offensive action at the very time when Cornwallis's army needed any support that could be rendered. Clinton asked that instead Arbuthnot continue to blockade the French at Newport, and with supply frigates and other vessels, to support the army in 'conjunct operations'. For once, Arbuthnot saw the logic of Clinton's request; and on 13 December he informed the general that no ships would be sent to the West Indies and that he would support another expedition to Chesapeake Bay.[137]

The next day, Clinton issued orders to Brigadier Benedict Arnold (now in the British army) to proceed with a force of about 1,800 troops to Chesapeake Bay. In many respects, Arnold's orders were similar to those issued to Leslie. Arnold was directed to conduct raids up the James River with the objective of destroying supplies en route to the American army in the South and also establish a post at Portsmouth on the Elizabeth River to be used for future raiding operations.[138] The dispatch of Arnold's force in the Chesapeake at the end of 1780 was the first step in the complex set of movements

---

[135] Ibid., vol. III, p. 251.
[136] Ibid., p. 255.
[137] *American Rebellion*, pp. 479–81.
[138] Ibid., pp. 235, 482–3.

and manoeuvres that would lead to the British defeat at Yorktown. The British were dividing their army in America into three major groups: one force at New York, another in South Carolina and Georgia and another in the Chesapeake Bay region. The safety of these three armies depended absolutely upon British naval superiority in American coastal waters; however, Rodney's powerful squadron had sailed for the West Indies on 16 November, leaving the French squadron at Newport blockaded by Arbuthnot. What would be the fate of any one of these British field armies if the French at Newport, or a French squadron from the West Indies, gained local naval superiority and then the American and French armies concentrated against one force of the British army that was cut off from support of the Royal Navy? The choice of Arnold, a traitor to the American cause, also seemed to be tempting fate, for Arnold was more hated by the rebels than any other officer in the British forces. Would not his mere presence at the head of a British raiding force in the Chesapeake goad the Americans into strongly reacting to British operations in Virginia?

On 20 December, Arnold sailed from Sandy Hook and arrived at Hampton Roads on 30 December. On the voyage from New York his expedition encountered a storm that forced several transports to part company with the main force. The stragglers did not reach Chesapeake Bay until 19 January 1781. Arnold was an extremely gifted battlefield commander who understood combat. After landing his force at Westover on 4 January 1781, Arnold moved with great speed and, at 1 p.m. on 6 January, his troops entered Richmond. Arnold offered to spare Richmond from destruction if Governor Thomas Jefferson of Virginia would permit the British to carry off, without molestation, the tobacco stored there. Jefferson refused, and the British thereupon destroyed most of Richmond along with the cannon foundry and munition depots at Westhand and the clothing-stores at Chesterfield. Arnold's troops then fell slowly back, with almost no opposition, to Portsmouth, destroying everything of value in their path. Once at Portsmouth, Arnold began, as called for in his orders, to fortify the place.[139]

To the Americans, December 1780 and January 1781 must have been one of the most difficult and despairing periods of the entire war. The British seemed to control Georgia and South Carolina, North Carolina was threatened with invasion, Arnold's raiders were running amok in Virginia, the Pennsylvania and New Jersey Continental lines within Washington's army mutinied and the French at

[139] Ibid., pp. 236-7; Wallace, *Traitorous Hero*, pp. 274-5.

Newport appeared sunk in inactivity. The whole American effort seemed about to collapse from its own weight.

On the other side, however, the British were perhaps checkmated and surely baffled. Clinton could not figure out how to take advantage of the mutinies in Washington's army.[140] The British army in the South suffered a major setback when Lieutenant-Colonel Banastre Tarleton was defeated on 17 January 1781 by Major General Daniel Morgan at an obscure place in north-western South Carolina called Cowpens. Under Morgan, Tarleton was not only out-thought, but also out-fought, by the Americans. The British lost 812 men killed or captured out of a total strength of 1,100.[141] Further, Arnold wrote to Clinton on 23 January 1781 that to hold Portsmouth 2,000 additional troops would be required because intelligence pointed to about 4,000–5,000 American militia gathering to attack the British in Virginia. Arnold, if he received the reinforcement that he requested, intended to garrison Portsmouth with 2,000 troops while embarking another 1,000 troops in specially constructed boats to run the Americans off their feet by raiding the length and breadth of the Chesapeake and the banks of the numerous rivers that flow into that bay. If the reinforcements were not sent and Clinton intended that the British in the Chesapeake stand on the defensive, then Arnold requested to be assigned to the army at New York.[142]

The greatest danger to Arnold's force at Portsmouth was not the militia of Virginia but the Continental Army and the French squadron at Newport. On 21 January, Arbuthnot informed Clinton that the French ship of the line *Eveille* and two frigates had escaped from Newport and were most likely heading for the Chesapeake. When Graves, who was then in command of the squadron blockading Rhode Island, sent three ships of the line in pursuit of the French, they encountered bad weather. HMS *Culloden* was driven ashore on Long Island and lost, HMS *Bedford* lost all her masts and standing rigging and HMS *America* was badly damaged.[143] When the three French warships appeared off Portsmouth, Arnold moved his transports and small craft up the Elizabeth River and out of reach of the French man-of-war. The French, after capturing a few British merchant ships as well as HMS *Romulus*, returned to Rhode

---

[140] CL, CLinton to Arnold, 5 February 1781.
[141] Don Higginbotham, *Daniel Morgan, Revolutionary Rifleman* (Chapel Hill, NC, 1961), pp. 135–42.
[142] CL, Clinton Papers, Arnold to Clinton, 23 January 1781.
[143] Ibid., Arbuthnot to Clinton, 21 and 29 January 1781.

Island.[144] This French sally from Newport accomplished almost nothing, except to show that the British forces in Virginia were open to attack from the sea. But the French at Newport were not the only ones who thought Arnold's isolated position at Portsmouth vulnerable to attack. On 19 February, Washington ordered Major-General Marquis de Lafayette to proceed to Virginia with 1,200 Continentals who were, for the most part, élite light infantry drawn from the New England Continental regiments. The next day, Lafayette's troops crossed the Hudson River en route for Virginia, and by 3 March the force had reached the head of the Elk River.[145]

As Lafayette's troops marched towards Virginia and Chesapeake Bay, Clinton and Arbuthnot exchanged letters in an attempt to formulate some kind of strategy for the conduct of the war. Upon learning of Arnold's raid on Richmond, Arbuthnot wrote to Lieutenant-General James Robertson that the British forces in the Chesapeake should be reinforced because 'the moment is arrived in which our enemies may recieve a mortal blow and put an end to this business, if we follow it up with spirit'.[146] Robertson showed this letter to Clinton, who did not understand what Arbuthnot thought would be a 'mortal blow' and therefore sent his deputy quartermaster general to Gardiner's Island to speak with Arbuthnot.[147] On 21 February, Arbuthnot wrote to Clinton that he intended to reinforce Arnold from New York, so that the British force in the Chesapeake could link up with Cornwallis's army in North Carolina, and the British would then be able to cut American north–south communications in Virginia. If this strategy were followed, according to Arbuthnot, then the Americans could not obtain 'any decisive advantage from a Co-operation with the French at Rhode Island'. The admiral continued, 'Therefore [I] propose to your Excellency if it accords with your ideas the expediency of an immediate embarkation of your Troops, which I will escort with my whole force to the Chesapeake'. Without waiting for Clinton's reply, Arbuthnot ordered the senior navy officer at New York City to make available the necessary transport tonnage required by Clinton to send troops to Virginia.[148]

---

[144] PRO, CO 5/101, ff. 224–5.
[145] Louis Reichenthal Gottschalk, *Lafayette and the Close of the American Revolution* (Chicago, 1942), pp. 188–95.
[146] CL, Clinton Papers, Arbuthnot to Robertson, 13 February 1781.
[147] Ibid., Clinton to Arbuthnot, 17 February 1781, and Arbuthnot to Russell, 21 February 1781.
[148] Ibid., Arbuthnot to Clinton, 21 February 1781, and Arbuthnot to Russell, 21 February 1781.

As usual, Clinton and Arbuthnot were working at cross-purposes. On 23 February, Clinton wrote to Arbuthnot that he had 1,300 troops prepared for immediate embarkation, and that from the contents of the admiral's letter of 21 February, he assumed that Arbuthnot intended to escort these troops to Virginia with his entire squadron, although the French squadron remained at Newport. Clinton's assumption was not without justification, for the admiral had used the phrase 'escort with my whole force to the Chesapeake' without any mention of what steps he was going to take to check the activities of the French squadron at Newport. Clinton informed Arbuthnot that if his whole squadron went to Chesapeake Bay while the French squadron remained at Newport, the French then would be able to gain control of Long Island Sound and the maritime approaches to New York at a time when supply convoys were expected from Europe.[149]

On 25 February, Arbuthnot wrote back to Clinton that the general had misunderstood his last letter, for 'I cannot stop from pursuing the French, in case they do sail, for any unimportant consideration and that I must govern myself by their movements'. Arbuthnot also informed Clinton that the reason he had requested the embarkation of the troops was for 'saving time', and that he had good intelligence that the French squadron at Newport was about to sail to Chesapeake Bay.[150] Clinton at New York City still did not understand Arbuthnot's intentions because the admiral's letter of 25 February did not state what they were.

Clinton had written Arbuthnot on 25 February that the admiral's letter of the 21st had been 'miss conceived'. He went on to say that he was not sure that the objective of the French squadron at Newport was Chesapeake Bay, but if the French squadron did sail, then perhaps it would be best for Arbuthnot's squadron to chase the French 'unincumbered' with transports; as soon as Arbuthnot had cornered the French squadron, Clinton then would send troops to assist the admiral in his attack. If, however, the objective of the French at Newport was indeed Chesapeake Bay, most likely they would head for Yorktown because, according to Clinton, they did not have the necessary force to attack Arnold at Portsmouth. Clinton also told Arbuthnot that if the French remained at Newport and Washington sent units of the Continental Army to Virginia, then Arnold would be reinforced with troops from New York City.[151]

---

[149] Ibid., Clinton to Arbuthnot, 23 February 1781.
[150] Ibid., Arbuthnot to Clinton, 25 February 1781.
[151] Ibid., Clinton to Arbuthnot, 25 February 1781.

Learning on 1 March that a detachment from Washington's army was marching south, Clinton thought its objective was probably Portsmouth and Arnold. He wrote at once to Arbuthnot, requesting that warships be sent to Chesapeake Bay to prevent the French from gaining control of that body of water. Clinton also requested that Arbuthnot come to New York City, so that some sort of joint strategy could be worked out for the defence of the British position in the Chesapeake. Clinton would not risk sending reinforcements to the Chesapeake until the location and intentions of the French squadron were known in New York City. Although he understood that without naval superiority in American coastal waters, 'any enterprize depending on water movements must certainly run great risk', Clinton was nevertheless fairly optimistic about the overall strategic situation. On 2 March he wrote to Cornwallis that 'there seems little wanting to give a mortal stab to Rebellion, but a proper reinforcement, and permanent Superiority at Sea for the next Campaign.'[152]

On 2 March, Arbuthnot wrote from Gardiner's Island to both Clinton and Robertson that he had intelligence that the French at Newport had embarked 1,000 troops and that their objective was the base at Portsmouth.[153] On 4 March, Arbuthnot received Clinton's letter telling of Washington's sending troops to Virginia and responded that he was sending a frigate to reconnoitre the French squadron at Newport and that his actions would depend upon the state and location of the French warships. He told Clinton that Captain Charles Hudson, the senior navy officer at New York City, was ordered, with HMS *Richmond*, HMS *Orpheus* and HMS *Savage*, to escort transports carrying any troops that Clinton might want to send to Cheaspeake Bay.[154] Clinton had already taken steps to send troops to Virginia; for Hudson, at Clinton's suggestion, was anchored in the North River with his three warships and the transports with troops on board. Two days later, the convoy moved down to Sandy Hook;[155] Clinton, however, would not allow the convoy to sail until he had certain intelligence that there were no French warships in Chesapeake Bay.[156]

---

[152] Ibid., Clinton to Arbuthnot, 1 March 1781, and Clinton to Cornwallis, 2 March 1781.
[153] Ibid., Arbuthnot to Clinton, 2 March 1781, and Arbuthnot to Robertson, 2 March 1781.
[154] Ibid., Arbuthnot to Clinton, 4 March 1781, and Arbuthnot to Hudson, 4 March 1781.
[155] Ibid., Hudson to Clinton, 4 March 1781, Clinton to [Hudson], 4 March 1781; Clinton to [Hudson], 6 March 1781.
[156] Ibid., Hudson to Clinton, 11 March 1781.

On 8 March, five days after Lafayette's troops reached the head of the Elk River, the French squadron at Newport sailed, carrying 1,120 troops. Captain Destouches, who succeeded to the command of the French squadron when de Ternay died of a fever on 15 December 1780, attempted to avoid being intercepted on the coast by the British by sailing a 100 miles due east before setting course for Chesapeake Bay. The French found that a number of their ships had become very slow sailers because they were not coppered and their hulls were greatly fouled by months of inactivity in Newport Harbor.[157] On 9 March, Arbuthnot sent HMS *Pearl* and HMS *Iris* to look into Newport Harbor, and on the morning of 10 March the admiral was informed that the French squadron was no longer at Newport. Within hours of this news reaching Arbuthnot, he sailed from Gardiner's Bay with his entire squadron for Chesapeake Bay, which he assumed to be the objective of the French[158] and, on 12 March, Arbuthnot learned that the French squadron had been sighted at 31°30′ north latitude and was steering south west.[159]

On the day that Arbuthnot learned the location and course of the French, Clinton received intelligence at New York from the master of a vessel in the service of the quartermaster general's department that there were no French warships in the Chesapeake. Thereupon the general told Hudson to sail with the troops to reinforce Arnold; however, the convoy was delayed by the need to resupply some recently arrived warships and by contrary winds. It was not until 20 March that the convoy sailed, escorted by eight warships[160] and carrying over 2,000 troops under the command of Major-General William Phillips; seven days later it arrived safely in Chesapeake Bay.[161]

At about 6 a.m. on 16 March, HMS *Iris* of Arbuthnot's squadron made the signal for sighting six French warships bearing north-east and astern of the British force. The weather was hazy, there was a fairly heavy sea running, and Arbuthnot's squadron was about five or six leagues from Cape Charles at the entrance of Chesapeake Bay when they sighted the convoy. The British reported that the wind was out of the west; Destouches stated that it was from the south-west. Arbuthnot immediately went about and made the signal to steer for the French squadron. At 7 a.m. the British admiral made the signal

---

[157] Kennett, *French Forces* p. 99.
[158] CL, Clinton Papers, Arbuthnot to Clinton, 11 March 1781.
[159] Ibid., Arbuthnot to Clinton, 12 March 1781.
[160] *Richmond, Orpheus, Chatham, Roebuck, Bonetta, Savage, Halifax* and *Vulcan*.
[161] *American Rebellion*, pp. 254–5; CL, Clinton Papers, Clinton to Hudson, 12 March 1781; Hudson to Clinton, 12, 15 and 17 March 1781.

for more sail and to form a line of battle. The French squadron consisted of seven ships of the line, a 44-gun ship, one ship of the line armed *en flute*, and several small warships. Arbuthnot's squadron was made up of seven ships of the line, a 50-gun ship and several smaller warships.[162] When the French were sighted, it seemed that because of the superior sailing qualities of his copper-bottomed ships, Arbuthnot could force a pell-mell fight on the French in which the superiority of British gunnery would settle the issue. However, the weather continued hazy and rainy and the wind was shifting to the north-east. Both squadrons spent the morning manoeuvring to gain the weather gauge. At about 1 p.m., both squadrons were steering, in line-ahead formation, east–south-east with the British to leeward and gaining on the French line. At about 2 p.m., as HMS *Robust*, the lead British ship, was about to overhaul the sternmost French ship, the French wore their ships and made a hairpin turn, placing themselves on a course approximately west–northwest. According to Arbuthnot, the *Robust* immediately turned on to the same course as the French, and at about 2.15 p.m. began to engage the lead enemy ship. The action taken by the captain of the *Robust* forced the rest of the British line to steer west–north-west. Arbuthnot later wrote that he had 'to form under the fire of the enemy's line; and as the van was by this means put into confusion, I was single in bearing down to connect the line, exposed to the fire of the (French) admiral and his seconds'. The French, being to leeward, could open their lower-deck gun ports, while the British being to windward could not, which gave each French ship greater firepower than the British also a greater proportion of the fire of the French ships was directed at the upper works and rigging of the British ships. Because of the confusion among the British, the weight of the French fell first on the three leading ships of the British line. Destouches then ordered the ships at the head of the French line to change on to the other tack, steering a course of east–south-east while the rest of the French line was ordered to tack in succession on to the same course and to throw their broadsides into the three damaged ships of the British van as they passed them. Arbuthnot wanted to turn on a east–south-east course and pursue the French, but three of his ships were so badly shot up in their upper works, standing rigging and masts that he was prevented from giving chase. In this action the

---

[162] British ships of the line, *London, Royal Oak, Bedford, Robust, Europe, America, Prudent*, and the 50-gun ship *Adamant*; French ships of the line, *Duc de Bourgogne, Neptune, Conquérant, Eveille, Jason, Ardent, Fantasque* (armed *en flute*), and the 44-gun *Romulus*: PRO, CO 5/101, f. 238; ADM 5/238, 16 March 1781.

British lost 30 men killed and 73 wounded, and the French casualties were 72 dead and 112 wounded. Arbuthnot's battered squadron entered Lynnehaven Bay in the Chesapeake on 14 March, and the French sailed for Rhode Island, reaching Newport on 26 May.[163]

During the 16 March battle off the Virginia capes, the French outmanoeuvred and outfought the British. Destouches took advantage of his superior control over his ships and the prompt obeying of signals by their captains to outmanoeuvre Arbuthnot completely. He then lost the battle by breaking off the engagement without attempting to enter Chesapeake Bay. If Destouches had exploited his tactical advantage, he probably would have gained control of the bay but he did not have the resolve or understanding of his tactical advantage to gain a strategic victory. It was Arbuthnot who won a strategic victory on 16 March off Cape Henry by preventing the French from gaining control of Chesapeake Bay, thus saving Arnold's force from being trapped by the French and the Americans. Arbuthnot's contemporaries, however, thought, and rightly so, that Arbuthnot had been a poor tactician, for the British admiral had not exploited the chance in the morning to force free-for-all action on the French, and when he did engage the enemy, he never hoisted the signal for close action, nor did he pull down the signal for maintaining the line of battle, thereby not allowing a general chase. In some respects, his strategic victory was a matter of luck, for if, after all the tacking, wearing and changes of direction of the British and French lines of battle on the afternoon of 16 March, the French had ended the battle on a westerly course, they would have been inside Chesapeake Bay. But it was Destouches, not Arbuthnot, who made the decision to break off the battle and steer east–south-east out to sea. Once again, the French navy had failed to achieve anything in American coastal waters.

On 6 April, Arbuthnot's damaged squadron arrived at New York from Chesapeake Bay, but there was very little there in the way of naval stores with which to repair them. Nevertheless, Arbuthnot thought that his squadron would be ready for sea by 25 April. The admiral intended to resume the blockade of the French at Rhode Island and to intercept any French reinforcements proceeding to Newport.[164]

At the beginning of April, Clinton wrote to Germain that the

---

[163] NMM, MS 70/132, pp. 1239–40; PRO, ADM 51/48, 16–17 March 1781; ADM 51/552, 16–17 March 1781; Kennett, *French Forces*, pp. 99–100; NRS, Sandwich Papers, vol. IV, pp. 167–9; Alfred Thayer Mahan, *Major Operations of the Navies in the War of American Indepence* (New York, 1969 reprint), pp. 170–3.
[164] NRS, *Sandwich Papers*, vol. IV, p. 171.

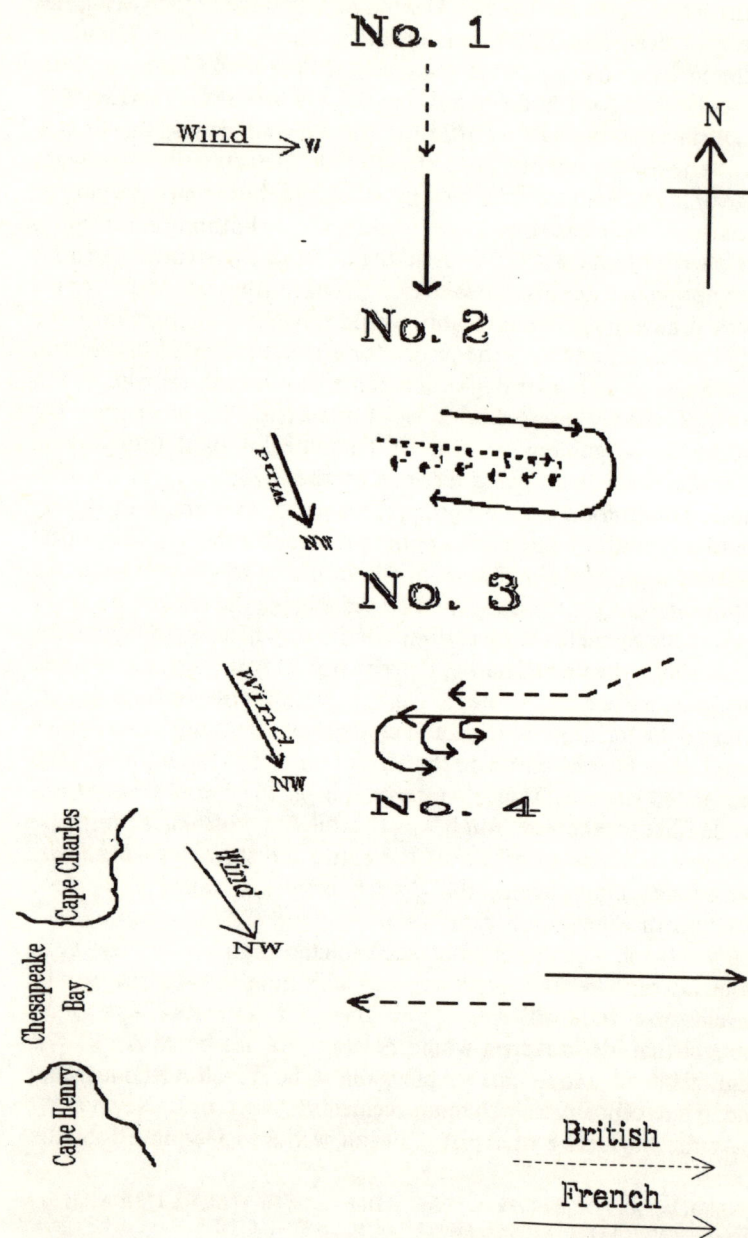

Figure 5.1
Arbuthnot and Destouches, 16 March 1781

success and 'even the safety' of the British forces in the Chesapeake depended 'upon our having a decided naval superiority in these seas.' The general then went on to state that all military operations in America depended on the co-operation of the navy and that he had 'great satisfaction to be informed . . . that Vice-Admiral Arbuthnot was appointed to releave Sir Peter Parker on the Jamaica station', for Arbuthnot was impossible to work with and, as a result, all operations were at a standstill.[165]

Nevertheless, on 12 April, Clinton again attempted to gain Arbuthnot's co-operation, but according to a memorandum drawn up by Clinton, the admiral said that he was sick, 'his fleet was in a most wretched condition', he was determined to renew the blockade of Rhode Island and he had not received any letters from England since October. If Clinton's memorandum is any kind of an accurate account of Arbuthnot's mental condition, then co-operation between the army and navy at New York was impossible.[166] On 23 April, Clinton once again approached Arbuthnot to seek his co-operation and to find out if the admiral were going to give up the command of the squadron in America. All Arbuthnot indicated, however, was that he had received a private letter saying he could have command of the Jamaica squadron if he desired, but he would not leave America until he had been officially ordered to do so.[167] At this point, all meaningful activity ground to a halt.[168]

While Clinton's and Arbuthnot's forces lay locked in inactivity at New York, plans were being made and battles were being fought that were paving the road to Yorktown for the Americans, the British and the French. On 15 March, the day before the action off Cape Henry between Arbuthnot and Destouches, Cornwallis made a 12-mile approach march and attacked Major-General Nathanael Greene's army at Guilford Court House, North Carolina. The resulting battle was one of the bloodiest and hardest fought actions of the war. Technically, Cornwallis won the battle, for what was left of his army gained control of the battlefield at the end of the action. Greene, the master *Fabian* strategist, had retreated after inflicting some 500 casualties on a British force of about 1,900 rank and file. Three days later, on 18 March, Cornwallis's footsore, provisionless and shot-up army retreated from Guilford Court House to Wilmington, North Carolina, to be refitted and resupplied.

[165] PRO, CO 5/102, ff. 15-9.
[166] CL, Clinton Papers, memorandum, 12 April 1781.
[167] Ibid., memorandum, 23 April 1781.
[168] E.g. ibid., Arbuthnot to Clinton, 29 April and 12 May 1781, and Clinton to Arbuthnot, 2 May 1781.

The rationale behind British strategy in the South was, in many respects, nothing more than a mindless series of invasions conducted in quest of meaningless or impossible goals. Georgia was invaded because it was believed that there were a large number of Loyalists in the province who, if given the opportunity, would support King George's forces. South Carolina was invaded to protect the British position in Georgia and because of its supposedly large Loyalist population. In the South, the British found a very difficult country in which to conduct military operations where they were confronted with a rising tide of savage guerrilla warfare and they found that winning such battles as Camden and Guilford House was meaningless. Cornwallis's army, as it marched through the Carolinas in 1780 and 1781, resembled in many respects *Groupement Mobile* No. 100 in the French-Indochinese War: *Groupement Mobile* No. 100 was an élite, heavily armed taskforce put together in 1954 to operate in the Vietnamese Highlands against the Vietminh. As *Groupement Mobile* No. 100 marched through the Highlands along Route 14, the Vietminh destroyed the French force piecemeal with landmines, booby-traps and large and small ambushes.[169] Like *Groupement Mobile* No. 100, then – 173 years later – Cornwallis's army, by the time it entered Wilmington, had marched and fought through the backcountry of the Carolinas almost to the point of self-destruction.

The big question confronting Cornwallis at Wilmington in the spring of 1781 was what to do next. The campaigns in the backcountry of the Carolinas clearly had been failures. Few Loyalists had appeared, the rebel forces were hard to locate and, when found, difficult to beat in battle. Cornwallis had won empty victories at Camden and Guildford Court House while the Americans had destroyed two large bodies of the king's troops at King's Mountain and Cowpens. After Guildford Court House, Greene's army began to move south to attack the British in South Carolina. Should Cornwallis move south, either by land or sea, to counter this move? Cornwallis's orders from Clinton were months out of date, but they cited the defence of South Carolina as the main objective of Cornwallis's army. Cornwallis ordered transports to be sent to Wilmington from Charleston in order to move south by sea, but he never used them. Cornwallis had come to the conclusion that the war in the South could be won only if the British invaded and conquered Virginia; he believed that as long as that province remained unconquered, men and arms would continue to be sent into the Carolinas

---

[169] Bernard B. Fall, *Street Without Joy* (New York, 1972 reprint), pp. 185–250.

and there would never be an end to the fighting. Cornwallis knew that there was a large British force conducting a campaign of raids against the Americans in Chesapeake Bay. If his army were combined with British forces, then in the Chesapeake Bay, Cornwallis thought that Virginia could be turned into a major theatre of operations and that its conquest would perhaps end the fighting in the Carolinas. On 25 April, without Clinton's knowledge or orders, Cornwallis left Wilmington with some 1,400 rank and file and marched north towards Virginia and, ultimately, Yorktown.[170] To carry Cornwallis's strategic thinking to its logical end, the war in America could be brought to a victorious conclusion only by marching a British army from Georgia northward to Canada.

While Cornwallis's army was marching north to Virginia, the British troops under the command of Phillips and Arnold in the Chesapeake were conducting a series of fast-moving, hard-hitting amphibious raids against Virginia with the objective of destroying American shipping, tobacco and stores of provisions. Lafayette's force of Continentals tried to stop these British raids, but Phillips's and Arnold's forces moved too quickly to be caught by the Americans. On 2 May, Phillips became ill with a fever; ten days later he died, leaving Arnold in command of the British forces in the Chesapeake. But on 19 May when Cornwallis's army at Petersburg, Virginia, joined forces with Arnold's troops, the command of the whole force passed to Cornwallis.[171]

With the junction of Cornwallis's and Arnold's armies in Virginia, the British forces in America were now divided into three major groups that could not support one another if the British lost naval superiority in American coastal waters. On 1 June 1781 there were 7,272 rank and file in South Carolina, 9,997 in and around New York City, and another 4,665 in Virginia.[172] One American historian has called the British moves leading up to Yorktown 'a Study in Divided Command'.[173] This dispersal came about because of bad communications, the inability of Germain, Clinton and Cornwallis to work together, and their failure correctly to perceive the military situation. When he marched to Virginia, Cornwallis was acting against Clinton's orders; he did not even bother to write a dispatch

---

[170] Franklin and Mary Wickwire, *Cornwallis and the War of Independence* (London, 1871), pp. 316–21.
[171] *American Rebellion*, p. 279; CL, Clinton Papers, Arnold to Clinton, 12 May 1781.
[172] PRO, CO 5/102, f. 150.
[173] William B. Willcox, 'The British road to Yorktown: a study in divided command', *American Historical Review* (October 1946), vol. 52, pp. 1–35.

informing his commander, Clinton, of his destination. Clinton only learned of his intentions when he received a copy of a dispatch the earl sent to Phillips, written on the day before he left Wilmington.[174] In London, Germain did not see or understand the dangers of Cornwallis's undertaking operations in Virginia.[175] It must have appeared to many in England that Cornwallis, because of his victories at Camden and Guilford Court House and the great number of miles that his army had marched, was conquering huge areas in the South when in fact the British only controlled the ground they stood on.

As Cornwallis's troops were fighting and marching northward through the Carolinas towards Virginia and defeat at Yorktown, Spanish and French forces were destroying the last vestiges of British power on the shores of the Gulf of Mexico. In 1779 and 1780, Spanish forces captured British military posts at Manchac, Baton Rouge, Natchez and Mobile. The only remaining British base in West Florida was Pensacola, which was garrisoned without any naval support by about 1,200 British, German and Loyalist troops under the command of Major-General John Campbell. With the fall of all the other British posts in West Florida, Pensacola in 1781 was totally isolated from the rest of the British forces in North America and the West Indies. The nearest British base to Pensacola in 1781 was St Augustine, scores of miles distant across the wilds of northern Florida. Moreover, Pensacola depended on supplies and military and naval support from the island of Jamaica. At the beginning of 1781, Pensacola was at the mercy of an enemy who appeared with a naval force and enough troops to besiege successfully the British post.

The Spanish, aided by the French, began operations with the objective of capturing Pensacola on 9 March 1781 when a small number of Spanish troops under the command of the governor of Cuba landed near the port. Galvez's first landing was quickly reinforced by several thousand Spanish troops from Havana supported by a naval force of more than twenty warships, including four French ships of the line.[176] The Spanish quickly drove the British defenders
within the fortifications of Pensacola and then settled in for a long siege. The battle or siege of Pensacola did not amount to much when compared to other operations or battles during the American war, but it is a perfect example of what could happen to a British force in

[174] *American Rebellion*, pp. 512–13.
[175] PRO, CO 5/101, ff. 311–15.
[176] *Le Palmir, Le Destin, L'Intrepide* and *Le Triton*.

America when an enemy gained naval control of adjacent coastal waters. The British at Pensacola were caught, for their enemies controlled the seaward approach to the post and the British could not break out and retreat across the wilds of Florida to St Augustine or to the British forces in Georgia. On 9 May after a prolonged but not very hard-pressed siege in which the British lost only ninety-one men killed, Campbell surrendered to the Spanish. The British force at Pensacola was doomed from the moment that the Spanish and French arrived with overpowering military and naval forces. Isolated completely from other British forces, the only hope that the defenders of Pensacola had was that their enemies would make a colossal blunder, but Galvez was too good a commander for that to happen.[177]

During 1779 and 1780, and the first months of 1781, British forces had fought battle after battle in America with no result. Huge areas of the South were overrun by the king's troops, but it was found impossible to control these regions even after the Continental troops had been pushed out. The British fought and won major battles, such as the siege of Charleston, Camden, and Guilford Court House, only to discover that the mere winning of a battle did not result in political or military victory over the American rebels. Large-scale amphibious raids had been undertaken in Chesapeake Bay and along the coast of Connecticut in which invaluable property was destroyed; yet these actions scarcely appeared to affect the rebels' war effort. But of much greater importance than battles and raids was that the emerging pattern of defeat or near-disaster was not perceived by British commanders in America or officials in London. British forces operating in isolation in the American interior sooner or later suffered the same fate as Burgoyne at Saratoga; they were cut off, overpowered and destroyed. This is what happened at Cowpens, King's Mountain and Stony Point. And there was another recurring pattern: the king's forces in American coastal waters were left wide open to attack by an enemy who gained local naval superiority. All the British bases on the Gulf of Mexico were forced to surrender to an enemy with superior naval strength. The British at Rhode Island in 1778, and at Castine and Savannah in 1779, were only saved from the fate that befell Pensacola in 1781 by the almost total ineptitude of the Americans and the French. The strategic milestones on the road to Yorktown were already laid out for all to see even before Cornwallis's army left Wilmington, North Carolina, for Virginia. The Americans and the French perceived,

---

[177] N. Darwin Rush, *Spain's Final Triumph over Great Britain in the Gulf of Mexico: The Battle of Pensacola, March 9 to May 8, 1781* (Tallahassee, Fla, 1966).

America when an enemy gained naval control of adjacent coastal waters. The British at Pensacola were caught, for their enemies although somewhat dimly, that victory could be gained by trapping a British army between a fleet and a superior army. The British did not, until it came to pass.

6
YORKTOWN AND BEYOND, 1781-83

The battle of Yorktown was the decisive battle of the American Revolution because it broke the will of the British to continue the war. The most complex battle of the war, it actually encompassed two distinct contests: a British and French naval engagement off the entrance of Chesapeake Bay, and the ensuing successful attack on the British forces at Yorktown by the American and French troops under the command of Washington. To understand these battles, however, one must look at far more than the fighting itself. The Battle of Yorktown was preceded by, and born of, a number of very complex military and naval command decisions and movements involving thousands of American, British and French soldiers and seamen in such widely separated places as Europe, North America and the West Indies. Furthermore, transcending the importance of the Battle itself the effects of the campaign spread like ripples around a stone thrown into a calm pond. The Battle of Yorktown influenced events in America, the West Indies and Europe and took many long months after the gunfire ended before its repercussions ceased to shape the fates of men and nations.

The French and American forces took the first tentative steps towards Yorktown on 8 May 1781, when a courier arrived at Newport, Rhode Island, with information from the French consul at Boston that the frigate *Concorde* had arrived in Massachusetts after a 42-day passage from France. Aboard the *Concorde* were about one million livres in specie, secret orders for the French forces in America and Admiral Comte de Barras, who was to take command of the French squadron at Newport. The orders from Paris to Comte de Rochambeau, the commander of the French army at Rhode Island, stated that the main French effort in the summer of 1781 would be in the West Indies; however, a large French squadron, under the command of Admiral Comte de Grasse, would be able to undertake operations on the American coast in 'July or August'. Although Halifax and Hudson Bay were mentioned as possible objectives, the orders from Paris did not outline or suggest a set plan of the campaign. It was left to Rochambeau to work out a plan in conjunction with de Barras, de Grasse and Washington. The French general was ordered, however, not to tell anyone, even Washington, of the impending arrival of de Grasse's squadron lest the British learn the secret. The next day Rochambeau wrote to Washington requesting a meeting, but when they conferred at Wethersfield, Connecticut, on 21-23 May, both Rochambeau and Washington acted out a charade; for although both generals knew that de Grasse's squadron was under orders to come to America, each had to pretend he did not. So Rochambeau and Washington talked only in general and speculative terms about what form the 1781 campaign should take. One of the few decisions made at Wethersfield was that as soon as possible Rochambeau's army at Rhode Island would join Washington's army before New York City.[1]

As early as 25 January 1781, Clinton had heard rumours that the French were going to reinforce their fleet and army in New England,[2] and intelligence from Brussels arriving at Whitehall on 5 February 1781 confirmed that the French were fitting out ships at Brest for overseas service: successive reports named the East Indies, the West Indies and North America as possible objectives.[3] Clinton learned about the Wethersfield meeting when a British patrol between New Windsor and Morrisania intercepted a number of letters from Washington's headquarters. From these documents the British at New York deduced the following: the French army at Newport was to join Washington's army north of New York City, the French fleet was going to appear on the American Coast and the Americans and French were going to attack either New York City or Cornwallis's army in Virginia. In a long dispatch, dated 9 June, Clinton told Germain of the contents of the intercepted American documents, of the great threat posed to the British forces by the impending arrival of an overpowering French fleet and of his intention to write Rodney in the West Indies to send reinforcements

---

[1] Lee Kennett, *The French Forces in America, 1780-1783* (Westport, Conn., 1977), pp. 104-6.
[2] E.g. PRO, CO 5/104, ff. 238, 240.
[3] PRO, ADM 1/4144, ff. 69, 82; CO 5/101, 170-1; CO 5/144, ff. 1, 3.

to New York if the French sent a fleet to America.[4]

On 17 June at his headquarters in New York City, Clinton discussed with Arbuthnot and several other army and navy officers the military situation in America. Everybody agreed that the French and Americans would attack New York City if they could raise an army and keep it together. It was also thought that 'de Grasse would come . . . in the hurricane season with ships and troops'. When Arbuthnot and Commodore Edmund Affleck suggested that de Grasse's objective might not be New York but rather Cornwallis's army in Virginia, Clinton bluntly stated, 'I had, I hoped, provided against that by advising Lord Cornwallis to take post at Yorktown . . . I had left his Lordship at Liberty with respect to operations'.[5] Clinton clearly wanted things both ways: to have Cornwallis defend Yorktown and yet be authorized to conduct any other operations he saw fit. It is also clear that Clinton did not yet perceive the danger the French and the Americans posed to Cornwallis's army in Virginia and that he thought that Washington and the French had firmly decided to attack New York City. Arbuthnot saw the danger of a French fleet in Chesapeake Bay but was prepared to concede the loss of Cornwallis, for the admiral wrote to Clinton on 27 June that in July he was going to move his squadron over the bar at Sandy Hook into New York Harbor, 'the only place of security for them and order the Ships in the Chesapeake to make the best of their way within the bar of Charlestown South Carolina for should they be left in Virginia I think they must be inevitably lost'.[6] On 28 June, Clinton did the only logical thing he could, other than removing Cornwallis's army from Virginia, by writing to Rodney in the West Indies to explain the seriousness of de Grasse's impending arrival and to request that the admiral and his squadron reinforce the ships of the Royal Navy in American waters.[7]

During the summer of 1781, the Cabinet in London knew what the French planned to do in North America during the West Indian hurricane season. But it perceived neither the grave dangers that would confront the British forces in North America if a large French fleet arrived in American coastal waters, nor the strategic perils inherent in dividing the British army in America into three groups –

---

[4] CL, Clinton Papers, Clinton to Arbuthnot, 6 June 1781; PRO, CO 5/102, ff. 154–8.
[5] CL, Clinton Papers, Minutes of a conversation . . . at Headquarters, 17 June 1781.
[6] Ibid., Arbuthnot to Clinton, 27 June 1781.
[7] Sir Henry Clinton, *The American Rebellion: Sir Henry Clinton's Narrative of his Campaigns, 1775–1782, with an appendix of original documents* (ed. William B. Willcox) (New Haven, Conn., 1954), pp. 532–3.

based in New York, Virginia and South Carolina – that could not support each other in the face of enemy naval superiority. As early as 14 April 1781, Germain wrote to Clinton that a powerful French squadron under the command of de Grasse was being sent to the West Indies with orders to conduct operations in North American coastal waters during the hurricane season. Germain, it seems, simply assumed that Rodney's squadron in the West Indies would rush after the French to North America and arrive there in time and with enough strength to check any French naval operations along the coast. In his 14 April dispatch to Clinton, Germain approved of operations in Virginia and expressed the hope that this effort would be successful in the future. At no point in this communication did the American secretary mention the possibility of a British army in America being trapped by a hostile fleet and army. It is clear from this dispatch that although Germain knew the general outline of French naval thinking for the 1781 campaign in the West Indies and North America, he did not think that it posed any danger to the British army in America because he assumed that the Royal Navy would always have naval superiority in American waters.[8]

At the Admiralty insight into operations in North America was not any more lucid than Germain's; for Sandwich believed, as did Germain, that naval superiority in North American coastal waters would be maintained by the timely arrival of Rodney's squadron from the West Indies to support the British position from French naval attack. Sandwich assumed, as did Germain, that the Royal Navy would have a superiority of force in America, no matter what the enemy did.[9] In fact the Admiralty tended to see the main problem in North America as one of command. Clinton and Arbuthnot obviously could not work together and the general had demanded the admiral's recall. Rodney and Arbuthnot had disagreed with each other in the winter of 1780 when the West Indies squadron was at New York. Arbuthnot himself wanted to return to England, but it was thought in London that Graves was not the proper person to command the squadron in America. On 1 May, Sandwich wrote to Arbuthnot that the admiral could return to England, but that a new commander of the North American squadron would not be named until the Channel Fleet had returned to England from Gibraltar.[10]

On 2 June the Cabinet met at Sandwich's house and decided to

[8] PRO, CO 5/101, ff. 171–96.
[9] NMM, SAN/T/6, Précis of Instructions to Vice-Admiral Arbuthnot, 14 July 1781.
[10] NRS, *Sandwich Papers*, vol. 4, pp. 172.

send Rear-Admiral Robert Digby, with three ships of the line, to take Arbuthnot's command.[11] Digby's departure was delayed because of operations of the Channel Fleet,[12] but on 22 July he finally sailed from Torbay for New York.[13] By permitting Digby's departure from England to be delayed for so long, the British government ensured that Graves, or perhaps Rodney, would be in command in North America to counter the expected French naval operations in that theatre.

In the summer of 1781 both Germain and Sandwich appeared to view the British position in America with varying degrees of complacency. On 7 July, for example, Germain wrote to Clinton that a French squadron was going to appear in American waters, while stating that Cornwallis's operations in Virginia 'promise more towards bringing the Southern Colonies to obedience, than any offensive operations which have been undertaken in the course of the war'.[14] Obviously, Germain did not see the danger to the British posed by the imminent arrival of a French fleet in North American coastal waters. King George III, however, saw that the British position not only in North America, but also in the West Indies, depended on naval superiority. His Majesty believed, 'if we could demolish either a considerable French or Spanish squadron, we should then be in a situation to gain our wanted superiority at sea, without which an honourable end to the war is not to be effected'.[15] However, the king was in the minority of officials in London. Although most of them thought that the war in America probably would not be won in 1781, they did not perceive the strategic dangers confronting Britain. It was not until September, when Rodney appeared at Plymouth when he was thought to be in New York, that a number of people, including Germain, began to think that events in America might not be unfolding as expected.[16]

At the beginning of June a number of French supply ships began arriving at Boston. In addition to supplies for the French forces at Newport, one of these ships carried 1.8 million *livres* and letters for Rochambeau and de Barras written at sea by de Grasse on 29 March. In these letters the French admiral said that his squadron would arrive off the coast in the middle of July and requested that pilots

---

[11] G, no. 3348.
[12] Ibid., no. 3370.
[13] PRO, ADM 1/490, f. 25: *Prince George, Canada, Lion* and *Perseverance*.
[14] PRO, CO 5/102, ff. 141–4.
[15] NRS, *Sandwich Papers*, vol. 4, p. 162.
[16] HMC, *Various Collections*, vol. 6, p. 179.

familiar with the coast be sent to Cape François. De Grasse also wanted to know where his fleet was to be employed in America and what type of operations he was expected to undertake. No longer able to keep the imminent arrival of de Grasse's squadron from Washington, on 10 June, Rochambeau wrote Washington from Newport telling him that de Grasse's squadron would be off the coast in the middle of July. He also enclosed a copy of de Grasse's letter and stated that he had advised de Grasse to steer for Chesapeake Bay instead of directly to Sandy Hook.

A number of people, especially French historians, think that Rochambeau's advice that de Grasse's squadron make its first landfall in the Chesapeake was an attempt by the French general to move the entire weight of the campaign away from New York to Virginia; however, this is a misreading of Rochambeau's letter. Rochambeau and Washington had not yet agreed upon a plan for the 1781 campaign. Generalities were all that had been discussed at the meeting at Wethersfield. Rochambeau knew that Washington considered an attack on New York City to be the objective. What Rochambeau suggested to de Grasse was that, with his forces from the West Indies, he first attack and destroy the British forces in Virginia before sailing on to Sandy Hook. On 20 June the French frigate *Concorde* sailed from Boston for Cape François with seven American pilots and Rochambeau's encoded dispatches to de Grasse.

On 10 June the French army consisting of some 3,000 men left Newport by boat for Providence, Rhode Island, to join Washington's army before New York. The army's siege train and the French squadron under de Barras would remain at Newport to wait for the arrival of de Grasse. Rochambeau also left behind 700 troops to help man the French squadron and an additional 400 men to form, with American militia, part of the garrison of Newport. Rochambeau's troops marched westward across Connecticut in slow stages and joined the Continental Army on 6 July at Phillipsburg, New York. Although Rochambeau and Washington had not yet settled on an objective for the campaign, during the next few weeks American and French troops, in preparation for an attack on New York City, drove British outposts in Westchester and the Bronx southward towards Kingsbridge. In the course of these minor operations north of New York City, the French saw for the first time what war in America was like. What the French noticed at once was that the American revolutionary war was in marked contrast to wars of the *ancien régime* in Europe. The Americans and British fought each other with a cruelty and bitterness that the French officers neither liked nor understood. A French army chaplain, on first seeing looting, burned-out houses and the cruelty to prisoners that were common in America, thought that the American troops had been 'transformed into monsters, implacable, bloody and ravenous'.[17] What the French did not understand was that they were now participating in an ideologically motivated civil war that was tearing apart a country and an empire.

During June, July and August 1781, British armies in New York and Virginia did nothing while Clinton and Cornwallis exchanged unrealistic letters about strategy. Clinton knew that Rochambeau's army had joined Washington's troops north of New York City. Clinton also knew that there was an extremely good possibility that a large French fleet from the West Indies would arrive soon in American coastal waters. In hindsight, the only proper course of action for the British was to remove immediately Cornwallis's army from Virginia to New York by sea and prepare to repel a Franco-American attack. Instead, Clinton wanted to attack Pennsylvania in the hope that large amounts of American military supplies would be destroyed and that Loyalist support could be found in that region.[18] But Clinton really did not know if this strategy would work, for he wrote to Germain that he did not know why the British effort in the Carolinas had failed, 'nor dare I say it will not likewise fail in Pennsylvania. But that is now the only place on this continent untried.'[19] Some days later, Clinton seemed to turn his attention to setting up a post in Virginia to be used by the navy and engaged in a correspondence with Cornwallis over the question of whether the earl should set up his base at Portsmouth or Yorktown, Virginia. On 27 July, Cornwallis wrote Clinton that he was going to occupy and fortify Yorktown and Gloucester, Virginia. And on 22 August the earl reported that the fortifications at Yorktown would require six weeks to complete.[20]

One of the reasons why the British occupied and fortified Yorktown was that Admiral Graves, when he took command of the squadron in America, thought that both Gardiner's Island at the east end of Long Island and New York City were not suitable as winter base for the squadron in America. Graves also was under the impression that he could obtain provisions for his ships' crews in

---

[17] Kennett, *French Forces*, pp. 106, 107-9, 112-21; the quotation is from page 121.
[18] Clinton, *American Rebellion*, pp. 528-9.
[19] PRO, CO 5/102, f. 155.
[20] Clinton, *American Rebellion*, pp. 552-7, 560-1.

Virginia.[21] Ever since Lord Dunmore and Captain Andrew Snape Hamond, RN, had been driven out of Chesapeake Bay in 1776, various British officers had toyed with the idea of setting up a naval base in the Chesapeake, but the only reason they gave for such a base was that it would be of help in raiding Virginia and Maryland and in maintaining the blockade of America. This reasoning made little sense because Collier's raid on Virginia had shown that this type of operation could be carried out from New York, and the attempt to blockade America had failed years ago. Nevertheless, in August 1781 a British army under Cornwallis was fortifying Yorktown in order that the British could have a naval base in Virginia.

For a long time it had been common knowledge that Arbuthnot wanted to give up command of the squadron in America and return to England.[22] But the admiral would not give up his command until he received official orders from the Admiralty. Finally, on 29 June, Arbuthnot informed Clinton, much to the general's relief, that he was turning the command of the squadron at New York over to Graves and returning to England.[23] On 4 July, Graves officially assumed command of the squadron in America, and Arbuthnot departed from New York the next day.[24] Graves was an officer with at best average abilities who by default became commander of the British navy in America just in time to fight and lose one of the decisive battles in history. On 21 July, Graves's squadron sailed from Sandy Hook for Boston Bay. The admiral intended to intercept ships carrying military supplies from France to America; however, he encountered nothing but fog and, after making a landfall at Cape Ann, decided to return to New York. When Graves's ships anchored at Sandy Hook on 18 August, the admiral learned that HM Sloop *Swallow* had just arrived at New York from the West Indies with dispatches from Rodney saying that a large enemy squadron was about to leave the West Indies for American waters and that Rodney was sending a force to America that would make its first landfall at the Virginia capes and then proceed north along the coast to New York.[25]

This dispatch apparently did not force Clinton and Graves to see the danger that a large enemy squadron in American waters would

[21] NRS, *Sandwich Papers*, vol. 4, p. 176.
[22] CL, Clinton Papers, Arbuthnot to Clinton, 30 May 1781.
[23] Ibid., 29 June 1781.
[24] French Ensor Chadwick (ed.), *The Graves Papers and Other Documents (Relating to the Naval Operations of the Yorktown Campaign, July to October, 1781* (New York, 1968 reprint), pp. 52–3.
[25] Ibid., pp. 32–3, 39.

pose. On 17 August, Clinton wrote to Graves proposing that a joint expedition consisting of Graves's ships and several thousand troops be sent to Rhode Island to attack the French squadron at Newport. Clinton and Graves gave this idea serious consideration in an exchange of letters that at first belittled and then forgot the possibility that a large enemy squadron was sailing for America.[26] Their scheme was finally dropped when they learned that the French had sailed from Newport for an unknown destination. Perhaps one of the reasons why Clinton and Graves did not see the dangers facing them was that both the general and the admiral assumed that they would be reinforced by ships from Rodney's squadron in the West Indies if the French squadron there came to America. Further, Graves thought that the British could barricade themselves in New York City and that the British forces were 'strong at Charlestown and in the Chesapeake, Virginia'.[27] On 25 August a frigate arrived at Sandy Hook that had been sent ahead by Admiral Sir Samuel Hood, who was proceeding to New York from the West Indies with a large squadron. Hood's dispatches informed Graves that de Grasse's squadron was coming to America. Not even this information, nor the sailing of the French squadron from Newport, galvanized Clinton and Graves into action, for five days later Graves still did not have his ships over the bar at Sandy Hook.[28] A huge Franco-American trap was about to close on the British in America, but Clinton and Graves, despite mountains of information about enemy movements, did not appear to see what was happening.

Rodney, in the West Indies, saw the dangers to the British if de Grasse's squadron went to America during the West Indian hurricane season. However, he did not know who was in command of the British squadron at New York: Arbuthnot might still be in command, but either Graves or Digby might have taken over. As a combat commander, Digby was an unknown quantity, but Rodney must have known that Arbuthnot and Graves were not capable of fighting de Grasse. For several weeks Rodney could not decide what to do. Hood wrote at the time, 'It is quite impossible from the unsteadiness of the commander-in-chief [Rodney] to know what he means three days together; one hour he says his complaints are of such a nature that he cannot possibly remain in this country, and is determined to leave the command with me; next he says he has not

---

[26] Clinton, *American Rebellion*, pp. 559–61.
[27] NMM, MID, Graves to Middleton, 2 July 1781.
[28] Chadwick, *Graves Papers*, pp. 52–3.

thought of going home'.[29] In the end, Rodney decided that he was too sick to go to America and must return to England to regain his health. Whether or not this was his real reason, it is now impossible to tell. By not going to America himself, Rodney made it almost certain that the squadron there would not be led by Hood, his second in command, who was junior in rank to Arbuthnot, Graves and Digby and who were at best inferior leaders. On 24 July at Antigua, Rodney issued orders for Hood to proceed with the bulk of the West Indies squadron to America to counter the expected arrival there of the French West Indian squadron;[30] Rodney himself would go to England escorting the homeward-bound trade with six warships.[31]

On 10 August, Hood sailed for America from Antigua with ten ships of the line[32] and four smaller warships. Hood's squadron of copper-bottomed ships had a fast passage to America and easily beat de Grasse's squadron, which had sailed from Cape Francois on 5 August. Hood's squadron made a landfall at Cape Henry. The frigate *La Nymphe* was then sent ahead to New York to tell Clinton and Graves of the arrival of the squadron from the West Indies. Seeking the French, Hood looked into Chesapeake and Delaware bays with his main force as he made his way northward to New York. The squadron anchored off Sandy Hook on the morning of 28 August.[33]

Washington was one of the few commanders on either side whose generalship and understanding of the nature of the war in America improved during the course of the conflict. By the summer of 1781, Washington and the Continental Army had come a long way since he took command of an armed mob outside Boston in 1775. In 1781, Washington wanted, in conjunction with Rochambeau's army and de Grasse's fleet, to attack and destroy the British forces at New York City; but in case the assault on New York City could not be undertaken, Washington also prepared the Franco-American forces for an assault on the British in Virginia.[34] He had learned, at great cost, that successful military operations required detailed planning and preparations in addition to great flexibility. Although Wash-

[29] NRS, *Hood Letters*, p. 18.
[30] PRO, 30 20/22/5, Rodney to Hood, 24 July 1781.
[31] *Gibraltar, Triumph, Panther, Boreas* and two bomb vessels: NRS, *Hood Letters*, p. 24.
[32] *Alfred, Belligeux, Invincible, Barfleur, Monarch, Resolution, Montagu, Terrible, Alcide, Shrewsbury, Princessa, Centaur, Ajax* and *Intrepid*.
[33] NMM, HOO, Hood to Stephens, 30 August 1781.
[34] John C. Fitzpatrick (ed.), *The Writings of George Washington* (Washington, DC, 1937), vol. 22, pp. 401–2.

ington did not know if de Grasse's squadron would appear first off Sandy Hook or Virginia, on 21 July he ordered Brigadier-General David Forman to position lookouts at Sandy Hook and set up a relay of mounted messengers to carry information to Washington as quickly as possible about the movement of warships off Sandy Hook. Ten days later he ordered that pilots with a knowledge of the Hudson River and the approaches to New York be assembled near Sandy Hook to be ready to assist de Grasse's squadron. But Washington was not thinking solely in terms of attacking New York. On 2 August he wrote to Robert Morris, the superintendent of finance, to assemble provisions and boats in the Philadelphia area and the upper reaches of Chesapeake Bay to be used in an operation against the British in Virginia.[35]

On 14 August, Washington's strategy for the 1781 campaign was settled when he learned that de Grasse was proceeding to Chesapeake Bay with between twenty-five to twenty-nine ships of the line and a large number of troops. The next day Washington wrote to Lafayette, the commander of the Continental forces in Virginia, that de Grasse would arrive soon in Chesapeake Bay. He ordered Lafayette to use every means in his power to prevent Cornwallis's army from breaking out of Yorktown and retreating into North Carolina. Washington also told Lafayette that reinforcements from the army before New York would soon be marching to Virginia, and that Yorktown not New York City, was going to be the main target for the Americans and French in 1781.[36] But Washington still kept his strategy flexible; for he wrote to de Grasse on 17 August that Cornwallis's army might possibly be moved to New York before the French and the Americans could trap it in Virginia. If this was indeed the case, then de Grasse ought to think in terms of attacking either New York City or Charleston, South Carolina, but in any event Washington was going to attempt to trap Cornwallis in Virginia.[37]

Washington's strategy for the campaign of 1781 was simple in concept: trap Cornwallis's army at Yorktown between de Grasse's squadron and a Franco-American army. Putting this strategy into effect, however, was going to be extremely difficult, for it called for the junction of de Barras's and de Grasse's squadrons in Chesapeake Bay and the movement of a large part of the army from before New York City to Virginia, a distance of 450 miles. Moreover, these

[35] Ibid., vol. 22, pp. 407-8, 440-1, 450-1.
[36] Ibid., pp. 501-2.
[37] Ibid., vol. 23, pp. 7-11.

movements had to be conducted discreetly in order to mask their objective for as long as possible. Another problem, and one over which Washington had no control, was the possibility that a large squadron under Rodney might appear off Virginia and attempt to destroy or drive away de Grasse's squadron. Washington had no control over the movements of the British navy, but the American commander-in-chief could control the movements of armies, and he had been planning the move to Virginia even before he had learned that de Grasse was bound for Chesapeake Bay.

Washington was one of the few commanders-in-chief during the American war who learned the lesson that to mount a successful campaign required co-ordination of various forces, hiding one's objectives and, most important, moving with great speed and striking with cold fury. The first problem to be solved was getting de Barras's squadron at Rhode Island to sail for Virginia. de Barras did not want to serve under de Grasse, who had just been promoted; de Barras was putting forth an incredible scheme to take his squadron, carrying the French army's siege train and reserves of provisions, to Newfoundland. In an exchange of letters Rochambeau and Washington persuaded de Barras to go to Virginia instead of Newfoundland, and the French squadron sailed from Newport on 25 August. In order to avoid the British naval forces, de Barras steered southeast out into the Atlantic and then turned south-west and arrived at Chesapeake Bay on 10 September without meeting any British ships of war.[38] On 19 August orders were issued by Washington to General William Heath, who was to command the troops that would remain before New York City, and the next day units of the Continental Army began crossing the Hudson River en route for Virginia. In the next few days Washington wrote again to Robert Morris and other officials requesting boats and provisions to assist his and Rochambeau's troops on their march to Yorktown. Washington knew that he could not hide a large-scale troop movement from the British, but they could be misled for as long as possible before learning the real American and French objective. The route followed by Washington's and Rochambeau's troops after crossing the Hudson River was designed to make the British think that the Americans and French were mounting an attack on Staten Island. Both armies marched south from Stony Point to Springfield and Chatham, New Jersey. Then to increase the deception and to close up various columns and units, on 29 August, the French and

---

[38] Kennett, *French Forces*, pp. 130-1, 136.

American forces moved in a direction that would indicate that they were now heading for Sandy Hook to meet de Grasse. The next day Washington abandoned deception and began marching towards Princeton, New Jersey and Philadelphia.[39]

Washington knew that as soon as the British learned that Washington's and Rochambeau's armies were moving directly towards Philadelphia, Clinton would realize that their objective was Cornwallis's army at Yorktown, not New York City. But at this point, the rapid movement of his forces was of the utmost importance. The march of Washington's and Rochambeau's forces towards Yorktown was extremely fast, but the move created administrative and logistic confusion because American officials at Philadelphia and in the Chesapeake Bay region did not have the time or the resources to collect the boats, money and provisions to support a troop movement of this size. Washington, and to a lesser extent Rochambeau, pushed problems of logistics aside and made the best of a bad situation. The American army passed through Philadelphia on 2 September, and the French followed in two units on the third and fourth. At Chester, Pennsylvania, Washington learned that de Grasse had arrived in Chesapeake Bay. Washington and Rochambeau arrived at the Yorktown Peninsula on 14 September, and learned on the following day both that de Grasse's squadron had fought an action with the British, who had since returned to New York, and that de Barras also had arrived safely in Chesapeake Bay. Owing to a shortage of boats in the Delaware River and Chesapeake Bay, it was not until 26 September that all the French and American troops from New York arrived in Yorktown. With considerable skill and a lot of luck, Washington, Rochambeau, de Grasse and de Barras had achieved a huge strategic success: Cornwallis and his army were now trapped between a fleet that had control of Chesapeake Bay and a powerful army. Now all that remained was to crush the British at Yorktown by siege warfare. For French army engineers, who had been trained in the school of Vauban, this was almost a minor operation.

Clinton at New York City was supplied with very good intelligence about American and French troop movements. On 19 August the British learned that American and French troops were going to cross to the west side of the Hudson River. The next day Captain George Beckwith, a British intelligence officer, concluded that the enemy's 'whole plan of operation has undergone a material change'. On 21

---

[39] Fitzpatrick, *Writings of Washington*, vol. 23, pp. 6–12, 20–8, 33–7, 39–43, 50–61.

August, Beckwith still could not figure out whether the objective of the Americans and French was Staten Island or Virginia. It was reported on 23 August that Washington's and Rochambeau's armies were marching towards Philadelphia; but as late as 27 August the British at New York were sent a conflicting report that Washington was at Chatham, New Jersey, and that his objective was Staten Island. Two days later a report maintained that the 'Chesapeake is the object of all the motion'.[40] By the time that Hood anchored at Sandy Hook on the morning of 28 August, both Clinton and Graves must have known that the forces under Washington were preparing some kind of operation against either Staten Island or Cornwallis's army in Virginia and that this action most likely would be in conjunction with de Grasse's squadron. The questions that the British admiral and general should have been asking, but apparently did not, were the following: why had Washington removed more than half his army from Westchester County, New York? Why was he now marching south through northern New Jersey? And what connection, if any, did these movements have with the impending arrival of de Grasse's squadron from the West Indies?

In the best of circumstances, the value of intelligence reports is very difficult to judge. After the war Clinton wrote that he knew 'the moment' that Washington's troops crossed the Hudson River that New York City was not the objective, yet he did not think that Washington would move against Cornwallis with as large a force as was actually sent to Virginia.[41] Neither Clinton nor Graves explained how the expected arrival of de Grasse's squadron in America and large enemy troop movements in New Jersey produced the complacency among the British at New York City that greeted Hood when he arrived at Sandy Hook.

When Hood's squadron anchored at Sandy Hook on the morning of 28 August, the admiral received a letter from Graves requesting that the ships from the West Indies not remain at Sandy Hook, but cross the bar into New York Harbor. Graves's letter also stated that his ships were not ready to put to sea and that he was with Clinton at Denis, on Long Island, planning an attack on Rhode Island.[42] Hood did not move his squadron over the bar at Sandy Hook and anchor in

---

[40] CL, Clinton Papers, Marquard to Delancy, 19 August 1781; Beckwith to Delancy, 20 and 21 August 1781; Intelligence Report by William Sproule, 23 August 1781; Intelligence from New Jersey, 27 August 1781; Isaac Ogden to Delancy, 29 August 1781.
[41] Clinton, *American Rebellion*, p. 328.
[42] NMM, MID, Graves to Hood, 28 August 1781.

New York Harbor; instead he went to Clinton and Graves by ships' boat. Hood was a fighter and a realist, so when he met Clinton and Graves, he must have been surprised at what he discovered. All Graves's ships were in New York Harbor and a number of them were unfit for service. A large French squadron was expected to arrive in American waters at any moment, and Washington was moving south in New Jersey with a large number of troops. Clinton and Graves, however, were endlessly discussing schemes to attack Rhode Island. Hood must have wondered what possible connection there was between the British at New York mounting an attack on Rhode Island and the expected arrival of de Grasse and Washington's troop movements in New Jersey. In a letter dated 30 September, Hood reported to the Admiralty that he had 'humbly' informed Clinton and Graves of 'the necessity which struck [him] very forcibly', was for those of Graves's ships that were fit for sea to join the West Indian squadron off Sandy Hook in order to hunt down and fight the enemy. What Hood told Clinton and Graves politely but firmly was that they were, strategically speaking, living in a Mad Hatter's world. At this meeting Graves agreed to move his ships out of New York Harbor to Sandy Hook.[43] That same evening any remaining reason for attacking Rhode Island disappeared when it was learned at New York that the French squadron at Newport had sailed on 25 August. On 31 August, Graves's five ships of the line[44] crossed the bar at Sandy Hook to join Hood's ships, and the combined force of 19 ships of the line, under the command of Graves, who was senior to Hood, sailed for Chesapeake Bay in search of de Grasse.[45]

On 29 August, de Grasse's squadron of 26 ships of the line, one 50-gun ship, and seven frigates anchored off the entrance to Chesapeake Bay.[46] On 1 September, 3,000 French troops under the command of the Marquis de Saint-Simon were landed by ships' boats on the banks of the James River to join Lafayette's army of Continentals and militia. Cornwallis had managed to get a letter out of Yorktown on 31 August, which reached Clinton on 4 September, saying that a large French squadron was anchored in the entrance of

---

[43] Chadwick, *Graves Papers*, p. 58.
[44] NRS, *Barham Papers*, vol. 1, p. 121: *London, Royal Oak, Bedford, America* and *Europe*.
[45] Chadwick, *Graves Papers*, p. 61.
[46] *Glorieux, Triton, Pluton, Marseillais, Bourgogne, Diadème, Réfléchi, Auguste, Saint-Esprit, Caton, Destin, Ville de Paris, Victoire, Sceptre, Northumberland, Palmier, Solitaire, Citoyen, Scipion, Maganime, Hercule, Languedoc, Zelé, Hector, Souverain*, the 50-gun ship *Experiment*, and the frigates *Amdromaque, Rallieuse, Surveillance, Concorde, Gentille, Diligente* and *Aigrette*.

Chesapeake Bay and that he was trapped at Yorktown.[47] With the arrival of de Grasse's squadron in Chesapeake Bay, the landing of French troops in Virginia, and the headlong march towards Virginia of Washington, there were only three ways that Cornwallis's army could be saved from destruction: Cornwallis could fight his way through Lafayette's and Saint-Simon's troops and then retreat into North Carolina, which was an action that the British general never attempted; the squadron under Graves could fight and either destroy or drive de Grasse's squadron away from Chesapeake Bay; or Clinton could take some action that would induce Washington and Rochambeau to return to New York, or figure out some way to reinforce Cornwallis. However, the only thing Clinton could think of was to send Benedict Arnold with about 1,500 troops to attack New London, Connecticut, in an attempt to draw American attention away from Virginia. On 6 September, Arnold attacked and burned to the ground his hometown, and during the assault on New London, Arnold's name was further blackened by a number of atrocities committed by Loyalist troops under his command. The raid on New London had no effect on the American and French operations against Yorktown.[48] Because Cornwallis either could not or would not attempt to break out from Yorktown and Clinton could only think of the raid on New London to assist Cornwallis, the fate of the British forces in Virginia then depended solely on the squadron under Graves.

More words have been written about the mismanaged action on 5 September between de Grasse's and Graves's squadrons off the entrance to Chesapeake Bay than the total number of shot and bullets expended by both sides during the battle. In terms of ships engaged, damage inflicted or men killed, this action really did not amount to much when compared to other eighteenth-century naval battles. To add to the irony, some have argued that it was an unnecessary battle since naval control of Chesapeake Bay not, as others maintain, a battle between de Grasse's and Graves's squadrons off Virginia, was what was critical to the success of the French and the Americans at Yorktown. The American naval historian French E. Chadwick, among others, maintains that de Grasse should have barricaded himself in the Chesapeake[49] since Graves would have found it very difficult to enter the bay with only 19 ships of the line and defeat de Grasse's squadron anchored in a defensive

---

[47] CL, Clinton Papers, Cornwallis, to Clinton, 31 August 1781.
[48] Clinton, *American Rebellion*, pp. 331, 565–6.
[49] Chadwick, *Graves Papers*, p. lxxxiv.

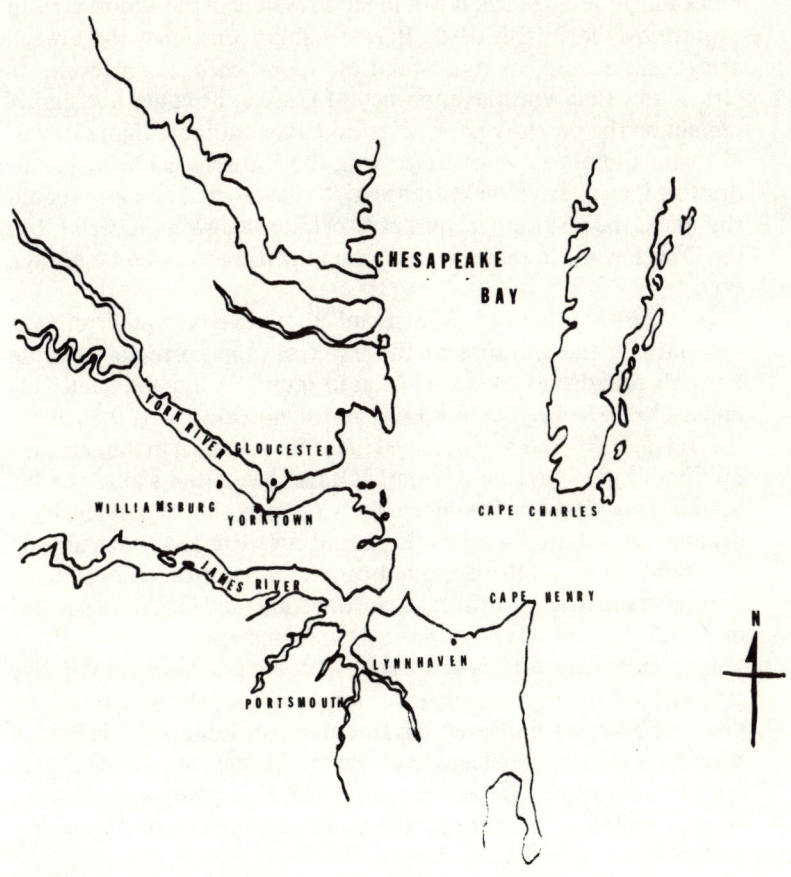

Map 8
Yorktown and Chesapeake Bay

formation. Barrington employed a barricade at St Lucia in 1778 against d'Estaing, and Hood turned to the same tactic at St Kitts against de Grasse in January 1782. There were, however, a number of compelling reasons, beyond his desire for a victory over the British, for why de Grasse had to fight Graves. For example, Graves possibly could have entered Chesapeake Bay without defeating de Grasse first, which undoubtedly would have caused problems for the French and American armies before Yorktown, although Graves might have found himself in the same fix as Cornwallis – trapped in Chesapeake Bay by a superior French naval force. More important, if de Grasse had remained in the bay with Graves's squadron blockading the entrance, it would have resulted in the almost certain capture by the British of de Barras's ships, including the French army's siege train, as that squadron approached. As a result, de Grasse saw that with the approach of Graves, he could not simply remain on the defensive in Chesapeake Bay but must fight Graves, not with the objective of destroying the British squadron, but of drawing it away from the entrance to the bay, so that de Barras could slip in. In the resulting naval battle neither side won tactically, but the French won strategically and maintained control of Chesapeake Bay.

On the morning of 5 September, Graves's squadron was approaching the entrance of the bay from the north-east and de Grasse's squadron was at anchor at its mouth in Lynnhaven Roads under Cape Henry. The wind was north-north-east. At 9.30 a.m., the frigate HMS *Solebay* signalled that she saw a fleet in the entrance of Chesapeake Bay. At 11 a.m., Graves made the signal for his squadron to form a line of battle with each ship separated by a distance of two cable lengths. Becoming aware at about this time of the approach of the British squadron, de Grasse ordered 24 ships of the line to slip their moorings, clear for action, and proceed eastward out of Chesapeake Bay in a line-astern formation.

It is extremely difficult to make a comparison of the relative strengths of the two squadrons. Graves had nineteen ships of the line, one 50-gun ship, seven frigates and one fireship.[50] The British ships were fully manned and had copper bottoms, but some of them were in need of repairs and refitting. HMS *Terrible*, for example, was in no condition to take part in a battle and went into action with

---

[50] *Alfred, Belligueux, Invincible, Barfluer, Monarch, Centaur, America, Resolution, Bedford, London, Royal Oak, Montagu, Europe, Terrible, Ajax, Princessa, Alcide, Intrepid, Shrewsbury, Adamant*; 50-guns, *Santa Monica, Richmond, Solebay, La Nymphe, Sybil, La Forutnée*, frigates; and *Salamander*, fireship.

her pumps working. De Grasse had to leave two ships of the line and a 50-gun ship to blockade Yorktown,[51] but he still had five more ships of the line than his opponent. Nevertheless, his 24 ships of the line[52] were slower than the British ones because they were not copper-bottomed and were undermanned because 1,500 crew members had been left in Chesapeake Bay to man small craft, but the French ships were in a better state of repair than the British ones.

At 2 p.m., Graves saw the number of ships in the French squadron and that they were steering east about 3 miles south of his squadron. In the rush to get out of Chesapeake Bay, the French squadron was in a disordered line-astern formation, with the van of the French squadron separated from the centre and rear of the French line. Hood, who was one of Graves's harshest critics, maintained that the whole British squadron should have fallen on the van of the French line and destroyed it before the centre and rear of the French force could come into action. Hood thought that if Rodney were in command instead of Graves, this course of action would have been followed and 'the 5th of September would I think have been a most glorious day for Great Britain'.[53] Perhaps in that situation Rodney might have made the signal for a general chase and led the British squadron in a headlong assault against the van of the French line, but the world will never know. After a defeat, it is easy to maintain that different tactics should have been employed. Making headlong assaults on a superior enemy can be dangerous, and there were a number of factors that Graves had to take into account before making such an attack. Graves was outnumbered by the French and a number of his ships were in need of repairs. Strategically, what would have happened if Graves made a hasty attack on de Grasse's squadron and was defeated? This possibly could have resulted in the loss to the enemy of both New York and Cornwallis's army at Yorktown. It can be argued, however, that the British stakes were so high at Yorktown that any risk was justified to save the British army in Virginia. But Graves probably did not see the situation in this light, for he thought that Cornwallis could withstand a siege for a reasonable length of time and was unaware that Washington was marching on Yorktown with a large army. Graves, a conservative

---

[51] *Glorieux, Triton* and *Experiment*, 50-guns.
[52] *Pluton, Marseillais, Bourgogne, Diademe, Réfléchi, Auguste, Saint-Esprit, Canton, Cesar, Destin, Ville de Paris, Victoire, Sceptre, Northumberland, Palmier, Solitaire, Citoyen, Scipion, Hercule, Maganime, Languedoc, Zelé, Hector* and *Souverain*. De Grasse also had the frigates *Andromaque, Rallieuse, Surveillante, Concorde, Gentille, Diligente* and *Aigrette*.
[53] NRS, *Barham Papers*, vol. 1, p. 125.

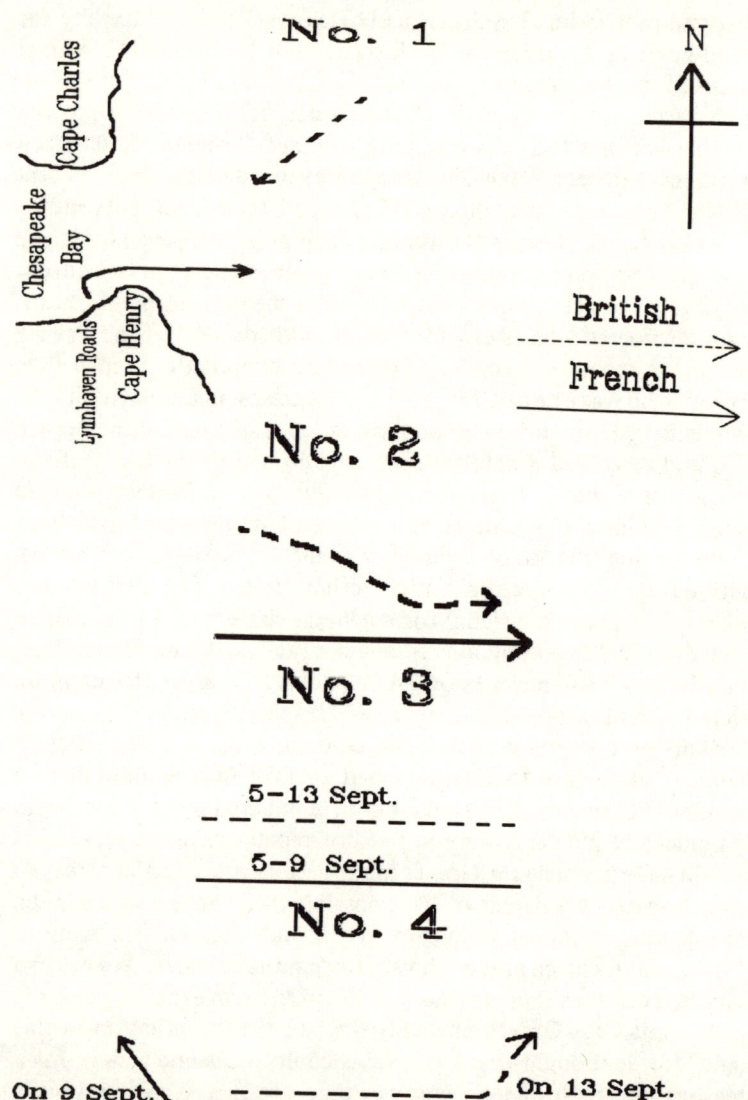

Figure 6.1
Graves and De Grasse, 5 September 1781

admiral, was going to fight the French according to the Fighting Instructions which were the rules and guidelines for fleet actions issued by the Admiralty.

At 2.04 p.m., Graves, seeing that the van of his squadron was approaching a shoal known as the Middle Ground at the entrance to Chesapeake Bay, made the 'preparative signal to wear'. Eleven minutes later the British admiral made the signal for his squadron to turn 'on to a new course'.[54] Each British ship then turned from a course of roughly south-west to east and parallel to the course of de Grasse's squadron. With this movement, Graves's entire squadron reversed its order of sailing. HMS *Alfred*, which was in the van of the British formation when it was on a south-west course, became the stern-most ship in the line, while HMS *Shrewsbury*, which began the action at the end of the squadron's line, was now the leading ship of the van. With this manoeuvre, Graves was upholding the Royal Navy's tradition of attacking an enemy by letting 'the centre of the enemy come abreast' of the centre of the British line, an eighteenth-century naval tactic that would allow each British ship to engage, one on one, the ship opposite her in the enemy's line of battle. According to the log of Graves's flagship, HMS *London*, at 2.30 p.m. the British admiral made the signal for the van of the British squadron to steer more to the starboard, which would result in the leading British ships closing with the French squadron's van before the main bodies of both squadrons went into the action. As the head of the two lines of ships converged, Graves signalled several times for the ships at the rear of the British line to make more sail in order to close up the British formation. The vans of the British and French squadrons were slowly converging in line-ahead formations, and at 3.46 p.m. Graves made the signals both for each British ship to maintain the line-astern formation while keeping one cable length between them, and 'for the ships to bear down and engage their opponents'. At 4.05 p.m., HMS *Intrepid*, the second ship in the British line, began to engage the second ship in the French line; and within ten minutes the entire British van and part of the centre were firing into French ships. The great weight of the fighting fell on the ships of the British van and to a lesser extent on the centre of the British line because Graves's and de Grasse's squadrons were not on parallel courses, but rather on converging ones. The battle lasted for about two hours with the vans and centres of the British and French lines engaging each other at various ranges. After the battle, Hood would maintain that

[54] PRO, ADM 51/552, 6 September 1781.

one of Graves's tactical mistakes was not having his rear properly engage de Grasse's line. But Graves was afraid that the French ships, because they outnumbered the British, would attempt to slip through gaps in the British line and thus enable two French ships simultaneously to engage one British ship. Therefore, instead of ordering that the rear of the British line close with the enemy, Graves ordered that the ships of his squadron maintain a tight line-astern formation. At about 6.15 or 6.30, depending on the position of a particular ship, the fighting ended when both sides drew apart.[55]

When the gunfire stopped, both the British and the French squadrons were still in sight of each other. At 6.15 p.m., Graves sent the frigates *Solebay* and *Fortune* to the van and rear divisions of his squadron to tell the commanders to keep 'parallel line with the enemy and well abreast of them during the night'.[56] If winning a battle is decided by damage inflicted on enemy ships or the number of men killed and wounded, then neither Graves nor de Grasse won. Both sides suffered about the same casualties in the action. The British lost 90 men killed and 246 wounded, sixteen guns were dismounted and a number of ships had been badly shot up. Most of the casualties had been suffered in the van division, which was the part of the British line that engaged the enemy the longest time and at the shortest range and that suffered the most damage from enemy fire – HMS *Shrewsbury*, *Intrepid* and *Terrible*.[57] The type of damage inflicted on the British ships was the result of Graves's attacking from the windward side, which depressed the British guns and aided the French tactic that called for disabling enemy ships by firing high in order to cut their standing rigging to pieces and to bring down masts and yards.

The French did not get off lightly in the action off Virginia. One uninformed French observer in de Grasse's squadron put French casualties at 412 officers and men.[58] Most likely, the French lost about 200 men killed and wounded, and the ships in the French van, like those of the British van, were badly shot up. Even with a number of ships damaged, however, the French still outnumbered the British

---

[55] PRO, ADM 51/37, 88, 137, 475, 552, 905, 6 September 1781; NMM, MS70/132, Graves and De Grasse: the Battle off the Chesapeake, 5 September 1781; NRS, *Hood Letters*, pp. 28–9; NRS, *Sandwich Papers*, vol. 4, pp. 181–7; Chadwick, *Graves Papers, op. cit.*, pp. 61–2; John Dawson Gilmary Shea (ed.), *The Operations of the French Fleet under the Count de Grasse in 1781-1782, as Described in Two Contemporaneous Journals* (New York, 1971 reprint), pp. 69–73, 155–6.
[56] NRS, *Sandwich Papers*, vol. 4, p. 188.
[57] Chadwick, *Graves Papers*, pp. 201–3.
[58] Shea, *Operations*, p. 73.

and had the strategic advantage. In order to gain their strategic objective of destroying Cornwallis's army at Yorktown, the French had only to hold their ground and prevent Graves from assisting or evacuating the British troops in Virginia. de Grasse understood this. Graves, on the other hand, did not understand the strategic situation at the end of the battle because he did not yet know that Washington's and Rochambeau's armies were marching on Yorktown. Graves did know that evening, however, that his task still remained one of either driving the French squadron away from American waters or destroying it in battle. But Graves had only nineteen ships of the line, of which five were badly damaged.[59] The problem facing Graves was how to go on the offensive against the superior French squadron.

At first light on the morning of 6 September, the officer of the watch on Graves's flagship noted in the ship's log that most of the ships of the British van were 'much disabled' and 'the French fleet [was] to leeward about 5 miles ye king's ships in a parallel line with them.'[60] Graves, observing the French squadron, thought that the enemy 'had not the appearance of near so much damage as we had sustained.[61] There was almost no wind and the crews of the British and French squadrons spent the day carrying out repairs. The main problem confronting the British was to make a number of their ships, whose standing rigging had been shattered, capable of being sailed. Little more than one per cent of the total number of guns in the squadron had been dismounted, but the damage to the standing rigging of the British ships in most cases had made them very slow sailers and unable to manoeuvre. Even if Graves could repair his ships such that they could operate as a formation, what was he to do next? Attack de Grasse's squadron or return to New York or attempt to enter Chesapeake Bay? Graves did not know.

Hood was enraged at Graves for botching the battle. He spent the morning of the 6th writing up an account of the battle and pointing out what he thought were Grave's mistakes. While Hood was working on his account of the battle, Captain Charles Holmes Everitt came on board Hood's flagship, HMS *Barfleur*, with an inquiry from Graves about whether Hood thought the battle should be renewed. Hood coldly replied 'I dare say Mr. Graves will do what is right; I can *send* no opinion, but whenever he, Mr. Graves, wishes

---

[59] Chadwick, *Graves Papers*, p. 255; Harold Atkins Larrabee, *Decision at the Chesapeake* (New York, 1964), pp. 201-3.
[60] PRO, ADM 51/552, 6 September 1781.
[61] Chadwick, *Graves Papers*, p. 63.

to see me, I will wait upon him with great pleasure.'⁶² This was the first shot in a conflict between Graves and Hood over the conduct of the previous day's battle. Being the best strategist and tactician in the British squadron, Hood should have responded to Graves's inquiry with advice on a strategy for the squadron. Aside from repairing ships, the only positive action taken by the British on 6 September was to send two frigates, the *Medea* and *Iris*, to look into Chesapeake Bay. The two frigates entered the bay the next morning and saw a number of French warships. While the *Iris* remained in the entrance of Chesapeake Bay cutting the mooring buoys of de Grasse's squadron in Lynnhaven Road, the *Medea* returned to Graves's squadron and her captain reported to Graves on 8 September.⁶³

Graves, Hood and Rear-Admiral Sir Francis S. Drake, the commander of the British Van, met on board the *London* to discuss the problems confronting the British squadron off Virginia. It is difficult to date this meeting or to tell if there were in fact two meetings. In a letter to George Jackson, Hood says that the meeting took place on 6 September; yet he says that intelligence about Chesapeake Bay obtained by the *Medea* was discussed, when that ship did not return from Chesapeake Bay until the morning of 8 September. It does not really matter if the meeting was on 6 September or 8 September, or if there were two meetings. What is important is that the meeting, or meetings, were stormy and resolved nothing. A London magazine later reported that Hood told Graves to his face that it was Graves's fault that the British rear division did not engage the enemy more closely during the battle; when Graves asked Hood why he had not engaged the enemy closer, Hood purportedly replied: 'You had up the signal for the line.' Graves then asked Drake why the van bore down on the enemy and engaged them at short range. Drake answered, 'On account of the signal for action'. When Graves asked, 'What say you to this Admiral Hood?' Hood replied, 'The signal for the line was enough for me'.⁶⁴ Although the magazine story may not be entirely accurate, such an exchange between Hood, Graves and Drake is quite possible; for during the battle Graves had hoisted two contradictory signals: one to close up the line, and another to engage the enemy more closely. There was further

---

⁶² NRS, *Hood Letters*, p. 33; Kenneth Breen, 'Graves and Hood at the Chesapeake', *Mariner's Mirror* (February 1980), vol. 66, pp. 53–61; J.A. Sulivan, 'Graves and Hood', *Mariner's Mirror* (May 1983), vol. 69, pp. 175–94.
⁶³ NRS, *Naval Miscellany*, vol. I, pp. 202–4.
⁶⁴ Larrabee, *Decision*, p. 213.

confusion over signals because Graves and Hood had never worked together and were using two different sets of signal books and employing different doctrine. The ships that came to America from the West Indies under Hood used signals issued by Rodney, while Graves employed a modified version of a system of signals issued by Lord Howe.[65] Apparently no major effort was used to co-ordinate signals, for weeks later on 6 November Graves issued a memorandum to Hood in an attempt to clarify the confusion and misunderstanding caused by the differences in the sets of signals. Hood sent a copy of Graves's memorandum to Sir Charles Middleton, Comptroller of the Navy, along with a note stating that Graves's memorandum only added to the confusion.[66] Arguments and misunderstandings among the three senior British admirals about signals on 6 or 8 September were somewhat academic; for they did not in any way resolve the strategic issue of what Graves's squadron should do next.

A note of reality penetrated the meeting aboard the *London* when Graves showed Hood and Drake a copy of a letter to Cornwallis written by Clinton on 2 September, stating that Washington was marching to Virginia with 6,000 American and French troops,[67] and the intelligence just received from the *Medea* that there appeared to be four French ships of the line, a 40-gun ship and a frigate in Chesapeake Bay. According to his account of the conference, Hood immediately saw the strategic implications of Washington's movement towards Virginia: he believed that Graves should forget de Grasse's squadron and proceed at once to Chesapeake Bay with the objective of destroying the French ships there and saving Cornwallis's army. Hood's strategic thinking was absolutely correct, although perhaps impossible to carry out and certainly too bold a move for Graves.[68]

During 7 and 8 September, Graves's squadron remained in sight of the French squadron under de Grasse, and the French admiral was content to let the British ships sit out in the Atlantic. But with every hour that passed, the British admiral must have realized more and more clearly that his squadron was in no condition to fight a fleet action or even manoeuvre as a squadron. Several of the ships that Hood had brought from the West Indies were running out of water

[65] Richard W. Hale, 'New light on the naval side of Yorktown', *Proceedings of the Massachusetts Historical Society*, vol. 71, pp. 124–32.
[66] NMM, MID, Graves memorandum, 6 November 1781; Hood to Middleton, n.d.
[67] Clinton, *American Rebellion*, p. 563.
[68] NRS, *Hood Letters*, p. 29.

and provisions; the masts and rigging of the *Montagu, Intrepid* and *Shrewsbury* were so badly damaged that they could barely keep up with the rest of the squadron; the *Ajax* was leaking badly, and the *Terrible* was scarcely able to stay afloat.[69] Apparently neither Graves nor de Grasse intended to do anything except watch each other, for while Graves's squadron was in no state to attack the French, de Grasse had several opportunities to attack the British but did not take advantage of them.

On the evening of 9 September, de Grasse decided that the time had come to return to Chesapeake Bay. The wind was fair and the French squadron, under 'a press of sail', turned north-west. At times, de Grasse has been criticized by navalists for breaking off the action with Graves and leaving the 'field of battle' to the enemy. But de Grasse's strategic objective was the destruction of Cornwallis's army, and not a tactical victory over Graves, which it can be argued the French admiral had already achieved. The reason for fighting Graves on 5 September had been to prevent the British from entering or blockading Chesapeake Bay in order that de Barras's squadron from Rhode Island could enter that body of water. By the evening of the 9th, de Grasse must have concluded that Graves's squadron was in no condition to hinder American and French operations in Virginia, and that if de Barras's squadron had not yet reached Chesapeake Bay, there was little chance it ever would. On the morning of 11 September, de Grasse arrived off the entrance of Chesapeake Bay to find de Barras's squadron at anchor just inside its entrance.[70]

When Hood saw the French squadron setting sail and steering north-west, he knew that it was heading for Chesapeake Bay. According to Hood's account of events, the more he thought about the strategic situation, the more worried he became. On the morning of 10 September, with the French nowhere to be seen, Hood sent a note to Graves saying that he thought that de Grasse was returning to Chesapeake Bay and hinting that perhaps Graves's squadron should attempt, if it was not too late, to get into the bay before de Grasse. When he received Hood's note, Graves requested that both Hood and Drake meet with him on board his flagship. At this meeting, according to Hood, he discovered that Graves did not know where de Grasse's squadron was, and Graves requested Hood's advice about the further conduct of operations. Hood responded that he

---

[69] Chadwick, *Graves Papers*, p. 63.
[70] Shea, *Operations* p. 158.

had already said what should have been done, but he was now 'afraid the opportunity for doing it was passed by, as doubtless de Grasse ... had most effectually barred the entrance against us, which was what we *ought* to have done against him'.[71] It was not much help, at this late hour, for Hood to tell Graves what he thought should have done several days earlier.

When the fighting ended on the night of 5 September, Graves had several courses of action open to him. He could patch up his ships as best he could and then attack de Grasse. This would have been dangerous because after the battle on 5 September the British squadron was much weaker than that of the French. Graves could have adopted Hood's rash suggestion and sailed at once to Chesapeake Bay, getting there if possible before de Grasse and barricading the entrance against the French squadron. Or Graves could have returned to New York at once, quickly repaired his ships, perhaps even have been reinforced by Digby who was momentarily expected to arrive from England, and then with a repaired or even larger squadron returned to Chesapeake Bay to engage de Grasse once again with the objective either of decisively defeating the French or at least breaking open the trap Cornwallis was in by forcing the French squadron to leave American waters. The problem was that Graves did not re-engage de Grasse, he did not attempt to gain control of Chesapeake Bay and he did not sail at once for New York. What Graves did do was to sit out in the Atlantic for three days watching de Grasse, and even when the French squadron had left for Chesapeake Bay, he remained paralysed by indecision.

On 10 September, Graves decided that the *Terrible* was so badly damaged that it would be impossible to keep the ship from sinking, so after all that could be salvaged from the ship had been removed, it was burned at sea off Virginia.[72] Two days later Graves sent the frigate *Medea* again to look into Chesapeake Bay.[73] The next morning her captain, Henry Duncan, reported that a large number of French ships of the line were anchored there, and that this French force was much larger than the one the British had fought on 5 September.[74] At 6 a.m. on 13 September, Graves informed Hood of the intelligence he had received from Duncan and requested Hood's opinion on what to do next. At 7 a.m., Hood wrote to Graves saying that the French were doing just what he had expected they would do

[71] NRS, *Hood Letters*, pp. 29–30, 33–4.
[72] Chadwick, *Graves Papers*, pp. 76–80.
[73] NRS, *Naval Miscellany*, vol. I, p. 205.
[74] Chadwick, *Graves Papers*, p. 83.

and reassuring Graves that he 'would be very glad to send an opinion but . . . really knows not what to say in the truly lamentable state we have brought ourselves'.[75] Later in the day, Graves summoned Drake and Hood to his flagship for a formal council of war. At this meeting, they concluded that the British squadron should return to New York City to be repaired before any further offensive operations were undertaken against the French squadron in Virginia. This decision was based upon the fact that Graves's squadron was in such a state of disrepair that it was now impossible to take any effective action against the French ships in Chesapeake Bay. The British army in Virginia would have to hold out until Graves's squadron had been repaired and was made into an effective fighting force. At this meeting, all three admirals signed a minute stating 'the impracticability of giving any effectual succour to General Earl Cornwallis in the Chesapeake'. On 20 September, Graves's battered squadron arrived off Sandy Hook to begin refitting for the operation of rescuing Cornwallis's army.[76]

On 2 September, Clinton had received intelligence at New York City that Washington was marching south with 6,000 troops to undertake operations against Cornwallis's army at Yorktown.[77] Several days later, when Clinton learned that de Grasse's squadron was in Chesapeake Bay, he decided that Cornwallis must be reinforced by troops from New York City and ordered 4,000 troops embarked on transports in New York Harbor, but these transports could not sail for Virginia until Clinton was sure they would be intercepted by French naval forces.[78] By 6 September, Clinton had deduced that between 7,000 and 8,000 French troops, 4,000 American Continentals and numerous American militia were moving against Cornwallis at Yorktown; but without naval control of American coastal waters, Clinton could do little to help the king's troops in Virginia.[79] On 8 September, Clinton sent Graves copies of letters from himself and Cornwallis that explained the strategic situation, along with a covering note stating that 4,000 troops were on board transports at New York and ready to sail to Virginia to reinforce Cornwallis as soon as Graves thought it safe to send them.[80] Graves received this letter on 9 September, and wrote at

[75] NRS, *Hood Letters*, pp. 34–5.
[76] Chadwick, *Graves Papers*, pp. 83–4, 96.
[77] PRO, CO 5/103, f. 134.
[78] Ibid., f. 138.
[79] Ibid, ff. 124–7, 138; CL, Clinton Papers, Clinton to Cornwallis, 6 September 1781.
[80] Ibid., f. 158.

once to Clinton telling the general of the engagement between his and de Grasse's squadrons. Graves also told Clinton that because of the naval strength of the French, it was impossible to move anything by water to Yorktown. At this time, Graves could say only 'that every resistance the Fleet can make, shall not be wanting, for we must either stand or fall together'.[81] Both Graves and Clinton were at strategic dead-ends. Both knew that a trap was closing around Cornwallis's army. Graves did not have the naval strength or a plan to be able either to withdraw or reinforce Cornwallis; and Clinton could think of nothing more effective to help Cornwallis than sending Arnold to burn New London, Connecticut, to the ground and embarking 4,000 troops on transports in New York Harbor in the hope that Graves could figure out how to get this reinforcement to Cornwallis by sea in the face of a superior French naval force.

The lack of naval superiority in American coastal waters due to the strategy of dispersal was the root cause of the British defeat at Yorktown. In a dispatch to Germain on 12 September, Clinton pointed this out to the American secretary: 'For (as I have often had the Honour of suggesting to Your Lordship) if the Enemy retain only a few Weeks of Superiority at Sea, we shall certainly be beat in detail'. Clinton also told Germain that unless Graves could defeat the French squadron in Chesapeake Bay, 'I shall despair of being able by any means to relieve the Army there as long as circumstances continue in that situation'.[82]

In a series of meetings and exchanges of letters on 13 and 14 September the British at New York attempted to formulate a scheme to save the British army in Virginia from destruction. At a 13 September meeting at New York attended by Clinton, a number of ranking army officers and Commodore Edmund Affleck, the senior navy officer at New York, Affleck suggested that 5,000 troops be sent to Yorktown escorted by the ship of the line HMS *Robust*, which was just completing a refit. The *Robust* was 'to force the way for their being thrown ashore on York Island'. This suggestion was obviously unrealistic because de Grasse's squadron was in Chesapeake Bay. Moreover, as Clinton pointed out, 5,000 additional troops, without supplies, would hinder more than help Cornwallis's defence of Yorktown. Next a scheme for landing a number of troops in New Jersey and marching on Philadelphia was discussed. Then General James Robertson suggested that nothing be done until the

---

[81] Ibid. ff. 168–9.
[82] Ibid., ff. 140–3.

arrival of Digby, who 'was hourly expected' with several ships of the line, which might give the British the naval strength to act against the French and the Americans in Virginia.[83] The meeting ended without reaching any firm decisions.

That night Clinton requested that Robertson think over the whole question of Yorktown and give his opinion of what course of action should be taken. The next morning Robertson wrote three different drafts of a letter to Clinton, laying out various schemes, ideas and conclusions about the problem. In the first draft Robertson pointed out that if the army at Yorktown were lost, the British would lose not only the war in America, but also America itself. This could only be prevented by taking bold offensive action that would directly affect the operations of the Americans and French at Yorktown for 'No diversion we can make will recall the enemy's force from pursuing the great object of their concerted design'. Robertson's second draft suggested that 6,000 troops be sent from New York to Virginia to attack the French and Americans. This plan, Robertson told Clinton, had risks, but they had to be run, for 'all the ills that may be foreseen are at most probabilities; possibly they may not happen. But the destruction of the whole is certain if the army in Virginia be destroyed'. Robertson's third draft pointed out a number of different situations revolving around British naval strength in America, such as the arrival of Digby with reinforcements, but stated that the plan for sending 6,000 troops by sea to Virginia to fight the American and French armies should be undertaken, no matter what the naval situation was or what various admirals thought because the stakes were so high.[84] Robertson gave all three drafts to Clinton.

At his headquarters Clinton assembled a number of ranking army officers and Affleck for a second council of war. At this meeting Clinton had all the correspondence between himself, Cornwallis and Graves read to the assembled officers. Clinton reported that Graves thought 'there is little Probability of anything getting into York River.' Clinton also told those assembled that Cornwallis's army, counting seamen and marines, was about 8,000 men and had enough provisions to last until the end of October and that it was the opinion of officers who had recently left Yorktown that Cornwallis could defend the place for three weeks against 20,000 attackers. Clinton then asked the council of war whether 5,000 or 6,000 troops should be sent to Virginia immediately regardless of the naval situation or if

---

[83] CL, Clinton Papers, Report of a Council of War, 13 September 1781.
[84] Ibid., Robertson to Clinton, 14 September 1781.

sending this force should be put off until either Graves defeated de Grasse or Digby arrived at New York. The council was 'unanimous' in wanting to wait for 'more favourable Accounts from rear Admiral Graves or the arrival of Rear Admiral Digby'. The meeting ended with Affleck stating that if they changed their minds and wanted to send troops to Virginia under escort of only the *Robust* and a few frigates, he would not comply without 'their unanimous Voice to the Necessity of the Measures'.[85] Affleck's statement reflects the attitude of all those who attended this council of war and others that followed: they were pessimistic and anxious to protect their individual reputations in a blanket of apparent unanimity.

After the council of war, Clinton wrote to Graves saying that the only way to assist Cornwallis's army would be to land a force from New York on the shores of Chesapeake Bay. The General requested Graves, after he had been reinforced by Digby and two other ships of the line, to force de Grasse's squadron further up into Chesapeake Bay in order that Clinton could land troops either at Yorktown or Gloucester Neck. Clinton then offered to meet with Graves at any time in order to formulate a joint plan for operations in Virginia but that Cornwallis must be assisted before the end of October.[86] The following day Graves responded that the French had firm control of Chesapeake Bay and that his force was so damaged that he thought it 'should not be exposed to a storm', much less attack a superior enemy in a strong defensive position. He further informed Clinton that the British squadron was proceeding to New York and that 'I fear that nothing by Sea can be got up to Lord Cornwallis'.[87]

Clinton believed that Cornwallis could hold out until the end of October, but troops and provisions had to be sent to Yorktown from New York City. He also believed that the British army then would have brought the American and French armies in Virginia to battle and defeated them, but that this could not be done without naval support. Even if Clinton could figure out how to get a reinforcement of troops and provisions to Yorktown, the British still could not win in Virginia as long as the French navy had control of Chesapeake Bay and the major rivers that empty into it, so the Royal Navy first would have to gain control of the bay. The question, which Clinton could not answer, was whether Graves's squadron, even when patched up and reinforced by Digby, could gain control of it in time

[85] Ibid., Minutes of a Council of War, 14 September 1781.
[86] PRO, CO 5/103, ff. 170-1.
[87] Ibid., f. 172.

to save Cornwallis.[88]

Graves's badly damaged squadron arrived off Sandy Hook on 20 September, and on the same day the admiral received a letter from Clinton requesting a meeting to formulate a joint strategy to rescue Cornwallis.[89] The next day Graves wrote to Clinton that his ships were in great need of repairs, and that as soon as the wind would permit he was going to move the squadron into New York Harbor. Graves also informed Clinton that he was prepared, when his ships were fit for sea 'to undertake any service in conjunction with the Army that shall be thought advisable' and that as soon as he got his ships into New York Harbor he would meet with Clinton.[90]

The British at New York City thought that Cornwallis's army in Virginia could hold out until the end of October, when their provisions would be gone, and that Washington's troops coming from the north would not be in a position to begin siege operations until about 26 September. But on 23 September Clinton received two notes from Cornwallis dated 16 and 17 September reporting that he had provisions for six weeks, that the French squadron in Chesapeake Bay consisted of 36 ships of the line and that 'This place is in no state of Defense. If you cannot relieve me very soon, you must be prepared to hear the Worst'.[91] These two notes painted such a black picture that Clinton thought that Cornwallis might attempt to break out of Yorktown in an effort to reach North Carolina before the arrival of Washington's troops. Moreover, Clinton now doubted if the British naval forces in America were strong enough to force an entry into Chesapeake Bay in the face of 36 French ships of the line.[92]

When Cornwallis's notes arrived, Clinton called a council of war that was attended by the four ranking army officers at New York. After reading Clinton's correspondence with Cornwallis and Graves, the council unanimously agreed that the only way Cornwallis could be rescued was by landing troops from New York near Yorktown and that this operation had to be mounted and carried out quickly or Cornwallis would be forced to surrender. They further agreed that the loss of Cornwallis's army in Virginia would 'have most fatal Consequences; and that an attempt to relieve him should be made by both the Fleet and army even at great Risk'. The general

[88] Ibid., ff. 176-7.
[89] Ibid., f. 178.
[90] Ibid., ff. 180-1.
[91] Ibid., f. 182.
[92] CL, Clinton Papers, Clinton Memorandum, 23 September, 1781.

requested that a meeting with Graves and his flag officers be held as soon as possible.[93]

At 2 p.m. on 24 September, Clinton convened another council of war with the ranking army and navy officers at New York present.[94] After a re-reading of Clinton's correspondence with Cornwallis, they explained to the navy officers the decisions made the previous day and the catastrophic consequences that would probably attend the loss of Cornwallis's army. A proposal was then made that, as soon as Graves's squadron was refitted, troops be embarked on the warships and that the whole force proceed to Chesapeake Bay and attempt 'to form a Junction with Lord Cornwallis's Army at Yorktown'. This proposal was unanimously accepted. It was also agreed that the following letter be sent to Cornwallis:

> At a meeting of the Flag and General Officers held this day, in Consequence of Your Lordship's Letters of the 16th and 17th Instant, it was unanimously determined that above 5,000 Men shall be embarked on board the King's Ships; and the joint Exertions of Fleet and Army shall be made in a few days to relieve You. There is every Reason to hope, we shall start from hence the 5th of October.

The council of war decided to convert, as quickly as possible, three ships into fireships.[95]

If the plan to rescue Cornwallis's army agreed upon by that council of war was to have any chance of success, it would have to be carried out with great speed, skill and daring. Speed was required because Cornwallis possibly could be overpowered by the sheer weight of numbers of the French and American forces at Yorktown before the British expedition to Virginia had departed from New York. The very nature of the plan called for great skill and audacity, and a considerable amount of luck, for the British were going to attempt an amphibious assault in the face of a superior army and navy. Even if Clinton and Graves managed to reach Chesapeake Bay and, against great odds, forced an amphibious lodgement near Yorktown, the overwhelming numbers of Americans and French

---

[93] Ibid., Minutes of a Council of War, 23 September 1781.
[94] Clinton, Lt-General Wilhelm Baron von Knyphausen, Lt General Alexander Leslie, Major-General James Paterson, Graves, S. Hood, Rear-Admiral Francis Drake and Commodore Edmund Affleck.
[95] CL, Clinton Papers, Minutes of a Council of War . . . 24 September 1781; PRO, CO 5/103, ff. 186, 192.

might possibly trap Clinton and Graves along with Cornwallis. Every military operation has an element of risk, but even with the best of luck this plan was a long shot.

On the day that this amphibious expedition was decided upon, the British were reinforced at New York by the arrival of Digby with three ships of the line.[96] Digby had orders from the Admiralty appointing him commander-in-chief of the squadron at New York and directing Graves to proceed to Jamaica in the *London* to become second in command of the squadron there; however, Digby agreed that Graves should remain in command of the squadron at New York until the Yorktown crisis had been resolved. The Admiralty's order that he should become second in command at Jamaica enraged Graves, and on 26 September Graves wrote a bitter letter to Philip Stephens saying that being succeeded in command at New York by an officer junior to himself and his new orders implied 'such a disapprobation of my conduct.'[97]

Graves was not the only enraged admiral at New York; Hood thought that Graves had mismanaged the action off the capes of Virginia but also discovered that Graves was attempting to control the filling of vacancies in the ships that Hood had brought with him to New York from the West Indies. Everybody in the Royal Navy knew that the entire Graves clan would grasp at any patronage opportunity that came its way. Hood, however, would not permit Graves to make appointments in the ships of his squadron, and he sent Graves a blunt letter to that effect.[98] Although Digby did not take *actual* command of the squadron as soon as he arrived at New York, he thought he was legally the squadron's commander and became increasingly angry when he discovered Graves was appointing captains and masters and commanders 'in a clandestine way, without ever consulting me'.[99] As the refitting of the British squadron at New York progressed at a maddeningly slow pace, relations between Graves, the *de facto* commander of the squadron, and his two subordinates, Hood and Digby, became increasingly strained.

A number of officers at New York were worried about the state of Cornwallis's army because they doubted whether Graves's squadron would be refitted by 5 October, as planned at the council of war held on 24 September. Because Clinton himself had doubts, he wrote to

[96] *Prince George, Canada* and *Lion*.
[97] Chadwick, *Graves Papers*, pp. 110–11.
[98] NMM, HOO, Hood to Graves, 24 September 1781.
[99] NRS, *Sandwich Papers*, vol. 4, pp. 193–5.

Cornwallis the day after the council of war asking how long the army at Yorktown could hold out if the expedition from New York could not be mounted on 5 October, as planned.[100] On 26 September the ranking army officers at New York held a council of war at Clinton's headquarters to formulate an alternate plan that did not involve the Royal Navy. They discussed whether or not landing troops in New Jersey and attacking towards Philadelphia might draw some of Washington's army away from Yorktown, but this idea was rejected when the generals concluded that they would not be able to withdraw the force from New Jersey in time to undertake the planned amphibious expedition to rescue Cornwallis.[101]

During a 27 September meeting of Admirals Digby and Hood with Clinton at his headquarters, Digby suggested to Clinton that since the proposed amphibious expedition to rescue Cornwallis was a very difficult naval operation, that another council of war be held 'in order to settle every doubt which could arise'. When in answer to their query Clinton informed them that the army's objective in Chesapeake Bay would be to 'bring about a Junction with Lord Cornwallis', Digby replied that in that case all that was required of the Royal Navy was to put the army ashore in Chesapeake Bay. Clinton protested that if the navy 'did nothing more than put the Troops on shore without cooperating with and feeding them they should be undone' and reminded him that Cornwallis had been promised a joint army-navy rescue operation. But when Digby next asked Clinton if British troops would remain in or be withdrawn from Chesapeake Bay if Cornwallis were rescued, the general admitted that he did not know what would happen at that point. At the meeting's end, the three officers agreed only that every effort should be made to succour the army in Virginia 'and that the sooner the Attempt was made the better'.[102] This visit by Digby and Hood should have upset Clinton, for he had been unable to put to rest their serious doubts concerning the British ability to mount a successful amphibious operation to rescue Cornwallis.

At the 28 September council of war at his headquarters, Clinton informed the five ranking army officers at New York of Digby's and Hood's visit the previous day and stated that if the rescue operation could not be staged by the agreed-upon 5 October deadline, then Cornwallis should be informed at once and ordered to adopt any measures he thought necessary to save his army. When Clinton told

[100] PRO, CO 5/103, f. 194.
[101] CL, Clinton Papers, Minutes of a Council of War, 26 September 1781.
[102] Ibid., 28 September 1781.

the assembled army officers that there was a very strong possibility of major delays in refitting the ships of Graves's squadron, the council agreed that Clinton should write to Graves to ask when his squadron would be ready to mount the operation in Chesapeake Bay.[103] Replying immediately to Clinton's letter of the same day, Graves stated that 'the Fleet will be ready sooner than the 8th of next month'.[104] Even with this assurance, Clinton doubted the navy's ability to begin the operation on or before 8 October.

On 30 September, at yet another council of war, the ranking army and navy officers at New York unanimously agreed that the relief of Cornwallis by an amphibious expedition from New York was the objective of both services and was 'to be uniformly pursued without suffering any circumstances to divert the attention from it'. Graves informed the assemblage that in his opinion the squadron would be ready to sail on 12 October, 'if the winds permit and no unforeseen accident happens'. But Clinton still was not satisfied; and after the navy officers had left his headquarters, he convened a council of war made up of ranking army officers at which it was agreed that Clinton should write to Cornwallis explaining the situation at New York to the earl,[105] which he did. Clinton added that, if there were a delay, he was willing to undertake the operations as late as the middle of November, but if Cornwallis could not hold out that long, Clinton then would attempt to draw American troops away from Yorktown by staging an attack overland through New Jersey towards Philadelphia.[106] Although he did not tell either Cornwallis or the admirals, by the end of September, Clinton was beginning to believe that he might have to attempt to rescue Cornwallis's army, without the aid of the navy, by an overland attack against Philadelphia.[107]

Clinton's suspicions that Graves really did not want to undertake the planned amphibious assault were further confirmed when on 6 October Graves sent him a letter asking, in the event that nothing could be done to assist the British forces at Yorktown, what would happen if the warships of Hood's squadron with Clinton's troops on board received orders to sail directly to the West Indies.[108] Graves was attempting to weaken Clinton's resolve by suggesting the possibility that a large part of Clinton's army would be carried to the

[103] Ibid.
[104] PRO, CO 5/103, ff. 224, 226.
[105] CL, Clinton Papers, Minutes of a Council of War, 30 September 1781.
[106] PRO, CO 5/103, f. 205.
[107] CL, Clinton Papers, Clinton Memorandum, [30 September] 1781.
[108] PRO, CO 5/103, f. 218.

West Indies, but in his reply the next day Clinton reasserted that the objective of the expedition was 'by our joint exertions' to rescue Cornwallis at Yorktown; however, if the expedition were to be a failure, 'I should hope, Sir, the whole Fleet would return to this Port. For should any misfortune happen to the Army in Virginia, and a considerable part of this Army should be carried to the West Indies, these posts would be exposed to great danger'. After suggesting that one possible solution was for Graves to arrange for enough transports to follow his squadron to Chesapeake Bay to carry all the troops embarked on warships back to New York if the men-of-war were ordered directly to the West Indies from Virginia, Clinton offered to discuss the problem with Graves and his flag officers at the meeting the admiral had scheduled for the next day.[109] Clinton's underlying message to Graves was twofold: if he backed out of an attempt to rescue Cornwallis on a technicality such as uncertainty about where the troops would end up after the operation, then the loss of Cornwallis's army would be the navy's fault; and if after the army in Virginia were destroyed, New York were attacked and captured because Graves had sent a large part of the army based at New York to the West Indies, then that loss would be on Graves's head.

Before drafting this response, Clinton had called his ranking officers to a council of war to consider Graves's letter of 6 October; the army officers resolved that Clinton seek a conference with the flag officers of Graves's squadron.[110] Clinton did not tell the admiral in his letter that he was acting with the support of the ranking officers of the army. However, Graves no doubt quickly learned of the council of war held at Clinton's headquarters, for the next day in his response to Clinton, he tried to put off the general with assurances that his letter of 6 October had been based on mere speculation and that he had rejected the idea of taking transports to Virginia because they would slow up the operation. Therefore, he concluded, Clinton need not attend the meeting of the squadron's flag officers because 'the subject of our debate tomorrow is intended to be confined to naval matters'.[111]

Although he had backed down after Clinton called his bluff, Graves was not finished with his attempt to withdraw his squadron from the planned expedition to Yorktown. Clinton, however, knew his man, and the first thing the general did on 8 October was to write

[109] Ibid., ff. 214-15.
[110] CL, Clinton Papers, Minutes of a Council of War, 7 October 1781.
[111] PRO, CO 5/103, f. 216.

Graves another letter to apologize for interfering in naval matters, but, after all, his suggestion that transports accompany the expedition to Yorktown had been made off the top of his head. He insisted, however, that on a close reading of the letter, Graves would realize that Clinton had not departed 'from the Resolution of the First Consultation (on 24 September) or any other since held', and he again offered to meet with Graves and his flag officers at a time and place of the admiral's choosing.[112] After writing to Graves, Clinton assembled yet another council of war attended by the ranking army officers at which he submitted for their consideration all of his and Graves's correspondence of the last two days. After reading the letters, the officers expressed their approval of Clinton's letters and then moved on to discuss what action the army should take once it arrived at Yorktown.[113]

While the generals were discussing strategy and tactics at Clinton's headquarters, the admirals were having a knock-down-drag-out fight on board Graves's flagship over policy and strategy. Graves had got nowhere with Clinton and the generals in his attempts to revise or modify the agreed-upon scheme to mount an amphibious expedition. According to Hood, at this meeting of the squadron's flag officers and several senior captains Graves attempted to have this question resolved, 'Whether it was practicable to relieve Lord Cornwallis in the Chesapeake?' As soon as Graves posed this question, Hood exploded in anger because he saw it as an attempt to undercut the policy that both 'the generals and the admirals had *most unanimously* agreed to' at the meeting on 24 September. Hood declared that he 'was ready to give in writing with my name on it', a statement to the effect that almost any risk should be run to rescue Cornwallis's army at Yorktown and that the proper course of action was to follow the policy laid down at the meeting on the 24th. Further, after the army had been landed at Yorktown, 'the first favourable opportunity should be embraced of attacking the French fleet'.[114] When confronted with Hood's opposition, Graves apparently dropped the subject. That night the admiral again wrote to Clinton that the question posed in his letter of 6 September was mere speculation and that Hood thought the stakes so high that he was prepared to embark troops on his ships even if he had to return to New York City before sailing for the West Indies.[115]

[112] CL, Clinton Papers, Clinton to Graves, 8 October 1781.
[113] Ibid., Minutes of a Council of War, 8 October 1781.
[114] Chadwick, *Graves Papers*, pp. 117–18.
[115] CL, Clinton Papers, Graves to Clinton, 8 October 1781.

Graves's strategic question 'Whether it was practicable to relieve Lord Cornwallis in the Chesapeake?' was the correct one for the British to ask at New York. Their planned strategy was extremely risky. Clinton, Graves, Hood and the other British flag and general officers at New York knew that there were more than thirty French ships of the line in Chesapeake Bay and that there were at least 6,000 or 7,000 French troops, 4,000–5,000 Continental troops and a large number of American militia confronting Cornwallis's force, which consisted of about 8,000 men. The British at New York were planning to force their way into Chesapeake Bay and then to land a force of 5,000 men near Yorktown, Gloucester or Newport News and then join forces with Cornwallis.[116] This scheme was intended to be carried out in the face of a superior French naval force in Chesapeake Bay; and the troops from New York, if they could be combined with the British forces at Yorktown, would at best equal the strength of the French and Continental troops there. Obviously victory does not always go to the side that has the biggest battalions, but what Clinton, Hood and the others were committing themselves to was a headlong rush to Chesapeake Bay, trusting more to boldness and luck than to planning and preparation.

There were a number of ways that the combined American and French forces in the Chesapeake Bay region could have defeated the intended British rescue of Cornwallis. The easiest way would be for de Grasse's squadron simply to block the entrance to Chesapeake Bay. A much more risky plan would be for de Grasse to permit Graves's squadron with the 5,000 troops on board to enter Chesapeake Bay and then trap the British squadron, the troops on board and Cornwallis's army by blocking the exit from the bay with French warships. But among the British at New York only Graves appears to have seriously considered, or wished to consider, the great strategic risks involved in any attempt to relieve Cornwallis. This may have been more the result of timidity or conservatism than strategic insight on Graves's part, but whatever the basis for his reasoning, he apparently never stated his fears at any of the councils of war held by the flag and general officers at New York. Instead, long after a plan had been agreed upon by both services, Graves attempted to reverse the decision at a meeting of only navy officers. Graves should have put on paper his answer to the question of whether or not it was practicable to relieve Lord Cornwallis in the Chesapeake and sent it to Clinton for the general's response. Although this probably would

[116] Ibid., Clinton Memorandum for Questions for a Council of War, 9 October 1781; Minutes of a Council of War, 10 October 1781.

not have forced a rethinking of the plan to rescue Cornwallis — Clinton, Hood and most other British officers at New York were prepared to run almost any strategic risk to relieve him — at least they would have Graves's fears on the table before them.

On 11 October, Clinton at New York received a letter from Cornwallis, dated Yorktown, 3 October. The earl informed Clinton that on the night of 30 September American and French troops had begun siege operations by constructing two redoubts about 1,000 yards from the British fortifications. Fortunately, the Yorktown fortifications were stronger than he had expected them to be. The earl, however, could 'see no means of forming a Junction with me, but by York River, and I do not think that any diversion would be of use to us'.[117] There was in this letter some indication that Cornwallis's army was not at the point of being destroyed or forced to surrender. However, the next letter to arrive at New York from Cornwallis, which was considered by a council of war attended by the ranking army officers on 12 October, painted a much darker picture. In this letter, dated 11 October, Cornwallis flatly stated, that 'nothing but a direct move to York River, which includes a successful Naval Action can save me'. The earl also reported that on the night of 6 October the enemy had dug their first parallels and three nights later had begun bombarding the British positions with some 40 heavy cannon and 16 large mortars at a range of 600 yards. Cornwallis warned that 'With such Works on disadvantageous Ground against so powerful an attack we cannot hope to make a long Resistance'.[118] Clearly, the British at New York had to move fast.

The ships of Graves's squadron had to be repaired before any action to rescue Cornwallis could be mounted. From the minute Graves's squadron had arrived off New York on 20 September, efforts were undertaken to repair the ships, but 'immense repairs wanted for a crazy and shatter'd squadron' were very difficult to carry out because New York lacked a dockyard and was short of naval stores. Re-provisioning Graves's ships also proved difficult owing to a shortage of provisions at New York. The refitting of the squadron was further retarded by a series of accidents involving broken anchors, parted cables and three ships running aground. As late as 16 October, Graves saw 'no end to disappointments';[119] but by 17 October, Graves's squadron had been refitted and the ships dropped down to Sandy Hook. The next day, 7,149 troops were

---

[117] PRO, CO 5/103, f. 207.
[118] Ibid., f. 248.
[119] Chadwick, *Graves Papers*, p. 121.

embarked on the warships from transports; and on 19 October, Graves's squadron – 25 ships of the line, three 50-gun ships, and eight frigates – sailed from Sandy Hook for Chesapeake Bay.[120]

When the squadron sailed, two questions hung in the minds of everyone. Could the expedition from New York arrive in Chesapeake Bay in time to save Cornwallis? And if the earl were still holding out at Yorktown, could Graves with an inferior number of ships of the line force his way into the York or James River in the face of de Grasse's superior squadron?

On 24 October the expedition from New York picked up three men in a small boat off the Virginia capes. One of these men was the pilot of HMS *Charon*, who informed Clinton and Graves that they had escaped from Yorktown just before Cornwallis's army surrendered on 19 October, the day the relief expedition had sailed from Sandy Hook. The next day HMS *La Nymphe*, from New York, joined Graves's squadron with a letter from Cornwallis dated 15 October, in which he explained that on the night of 14 October the enemy stormed the two advanced British redoubts and were preparing to destroy what remained of the British fortifications with artillery fire. The earl acknowledged that the British position at Yorktown was 'So precarious that I cannot recommend that the Fleet and Army should run great Risque in endeavouring to save us'. In the days that followed, Clinton and Graves received more than enough intelligence to support the first reports of Cornwallis's surrender. After reconnoitring Chesapeake Bay and confirming that de Grasse's squadron was much stronger than their own, they could do nothing but return to Sandy Hook, where they arrived on 2 November.[121] The British effort to rescue Cornwallis had ended in absolute failure.

Why Yorktown? It is easy to understand what happened at Yorktown: the French navy gained control of Chesapeake Bay and then American and French siege operations reduced the British position at Yorktown before Graves and Clinton could mount a relief expedition from New York. Why it happened is a much more complex question, or rather set of questions. Why were the British so fascinated with the Chesapeake region? Why did they blindly assume that they would always have naval superiority in American coastal waters? Why did Cornwallis go to Virginia and then let himself be trapped on a peninsula? Why did the British commanders

[120] Ibid., p. 136.
[121] Ibid., pp. 137–46.

at New York refuse to accept that Cornwallis was trapped by forces so overpowering that they could not be matched or countered by the British forces in America? These are only a few of the major historical questions posed by the Yorktown campaign.

The British defeat at Yorktown was the logical outcome of a strategy of scattering troops in the entire length of the American coast without adequate naval forces to protect these outposts from attack by an enemy who gained local naval and military superiority. The American and French conduct of the Yorktown campaign is one of the few so-called 'grand designs' that actually worked during the American war. Dr Jonathan R. Dull, in his history of the French navy, lists ten American, French and Spanish officers and officials who made the American and French victory possible.[122] Dr Dull's list, however, can be greatly improved by the inclusion of a number of British names; it was the British, just as much as their enemies, who made Yorktown possible. A major part of the responsibility for the defeat at Yorktown rests with the British government and especially the two members of the Cabinet who, for the most part, were responsible for the conduct of the war: Germain, the American secretary, and Sandwich, the first lord of the Admiralty. Germain and Sandwich permitted – and at times ordered – British commanders to follow a strategy of dispersal in America, although the Royal Navy's ability to protect British enclaves on the American coast was reduced each year that the war continued. Clinton and Cornwallis, whose strategy in America, or lack of it, sooner or later would have produced a major defeat, must also bear a large share of the responsibility. Arbuthnot, although he was in England during the campaign, was in part responsible for the British defeat because on numerous occasions he had refused to join Clinton in undertaking an attack against the French at Newport, Rhode Island. Rodney is also to blame because he sent Hood to North America, knowing that the squadron at New York would be commanded by a second-rate admiral who would outrank Hood. Further, Hood's detachment from the West Indies would have been stronger if Rodney had not weakened the force by sending to Jamaica or returning to England a number of ships that should have been sent to North America. Hood, who was one of the few British officers who actually understood the situation, usually has been let off lightly, even at times praised by naval historians, when during the Yorktown campaign he was not good or helpful as second in command to

[122] Jonathan R. Dull, *The French Navy and American Independence: A Study of Arms and Diplomacy*, 1774–1781 (Princeton, NJ, 1975), pp. 247–8.

Graves. Among the admirals, Graves is assigned the lion's share of the blame for Yorktown. In many respects, this is unfair, for when he was sent to New York, Graves was known to be a second-rate flag officer who never should have been appointed or permitted to command the squadron at New York. Graves's role during the Yorktown campaign was one of a man of limited ability having to put right the strategic mistakes of others. Although Graves's name will forever be linked to the British defeat at Yorktown, the admiral later served with distinction as Howe's second in command on the Glorious First of June.

The defeat at Yorktown was not a direct result of only the sins of omission and commission made by various British commanders. The British had had ample warnings of the dangers inherent in its policy of dispersal: d'Estaing's operations, first at Rhode Island and later at Savannah, the loss of West Florida, and the abortive attack by the Americans on Castine, Maine. But none of the British perceived these events as a weakness in British strategy. As a result, four years to the day after the surrender at Saratoga, Cornwallis was forced to ask for terms at Yorktown.

The surrender of Cornwallis at Yorktown did not end the American war. Cornwallis was granted the usual parole and left America for England.[123] The defeated British army was marched off as prisoners of war either to be exchanged or to await the end of hostilities. The French army, under Rochambeau, went into winter quarters in Virginia, while part of the Continental troops went south to join Greene's army in its bloody assault on the British in South Carolina and Georgia. Other Continental units went north with Washington to join the American army before New York. De Grasse sailed on 4 November with his whole squadron from Chesapeake Bay for Martinique. On 10 November, Graves sailed in HMS *London* from New York to Jamaica to become, as his orders demanded, second in command at that island,[124] and Digby then became commander of the squadron at New York. On 11 November, Hood sailed from Sandy Hook for Barbados with 17 ships of the line and three smaller warships.[125] Clinton tendered his resignation, which was accepted on 6 February 1782, and

---

[123] Franklin B. Wickwire and Mary Wickwire, *Cornwallis and the War of Independence* (London, 1971), p. 387.
[124] NRS, *Sandwich Papers*, vol. 4, p. 203.
[125] Chadwick, *Graves Papers*, p. 156: ships of the line, *Barfleur, Princessa, Royal Oak, Alfred, America, Invincible, Monarch, Canada, Torbay, Alcide, Intrepid, Montagu, Resolution, Centaur, Prince George, Ajax* and *Shrewsbury*; and the *Pegasus, Sybille* and *Salamander*.

returned to England; and General Sir Guy Carleton was named the new commander-in-chief of King George's troops in America.[126] The men and ships who fought at Yorktown were scattered to the winds almost as quickly as they had been assembled for the campaign.

Seventeen days before the news of the surrender of Cornwallis reached London, John Robinson, the first secretary to the lords of the Treasury and North's chief political technician, was warned by the Tory boss of Leicester, the earl of Denbigh, that if the army in Virginia were lost, the government would be forced to resign because it would lose the support of the country gentlemen in the House of Commons.[127] Denbigh's prediction proved to be correct, for although the North government was under attack from many quarters, the ministry, before news of the defeat at Yorktown reached England, could command with ease a majority in both Houses of Parliament. But with the arrival of the news of Yorktown in London on 27 November, support for the North government and for continuing the war against the Americans slowly began to collapse in the House of Commons.

At first, the government did not see that Yorktown would bring about a major parliamentary crisis, for it took time for the full meaning of the event to be translated into votes in the House of Commons. In December 1781, for example, Germain drew up a long and detailed scheme for the future conduct of the war. It is clear from the contents of this document that the American secretary did not understand the profound importance of Yorktown, for he viewed the defeat as a setback that called for only a momentary change in strategy, not as an event that would result in a total change of British policy towards America.[128]

When Parliament met after the Christmas recess on 21 January 1782, the North ministry was confronted with mounting opposition over the American war, opposition that ultimately would force the downfall of the government. Henry Dundas, the Lord Advocate and a leader of a group of Scottish members of the House of Commons, demanded that Germain and Sandwich be removed from the government. Dundas's will prevailed, and Germain resigned as secretary of state for America on 10 February 1782. Dundas himself was content with 'one human sacrifice', but his victory set off a broad-based

---

[126] Clinton, *American Rebellion*, p. 362.
[127] Warwick Record Office, Denbigh Papers, Denbigh to Robinson, 10 November 1781.
[128] NMM, SAN/T/6, Lord George Germain's Plan for Carrying on the American War, December 1781.

attack on the government's conduct of the war and of the war itself. On 7 February the House of Commons began an inquiry into the conduct 'of His Majesty's naval forces during the war, and more particularly in the year 1781'. A motion to censure the government during this debate was beaten back by a vote of 205 to 183. On 20 February the same motion was again debated in the House of Commons and defeated by a vote of 236 and 217. On 6 March a motion in the House of Lords stating that the defeat at Yorktown was owing to 'the want of a sufficient naval force' was defeated by a vote of 72 to 32.[129] Not only the conduct of the Royal Navy, but the government's entire American policy, was under attack in Parliament. On 22 February, and again five days later, there were widely supported attacks on the government's American policy; and on 27 February the government lost a vote. These attacks were followed on 8 and 15 March by two motions of no confidence being made by the opposition. During the parliamentary battles of February and March 1782 the government generally managed to assemble the votes required to avoid an outright defeat in the Commons, but with each passing vote its majority grew a little smaller.

Defeat at Yorktown and the parliamentary fights in February and March 1782 over the government's conduct of the war were forcing not only ordinary rank-and-file members of Parliament, but also members of the government and even King George III himself, to take a long, hard look at the war in America. Ever so slowly, Members of Parliament and others began to see that in seven long and bloody years of fighting in America Britain had gained nothing, but it had lost two field armies and become ensnared in a worldwide naval war with France, Spain and Holland in which the Royal Navy was at a serious strategic disadvantage. After Yorktown, the British still had the resources to continue the war against the Americans, but the defeat of Cornwallis and the ensuing parliamentary crisis led more and more people within and without the Houses of Parliament to believe that to continue the war with the Americans was futile. As a result, North's government resigned late in March and was replaced by a government that was headed by the Marquis of Rockingham and the earl of Shelburne and that pledged to end the war with the Americans.[130]

---

[129] For the papers about the inquiry into the state of the navy in 1781 see NRS, *Sandwich Papers*, vol. 4, pp. 217–364.
[130] All the many turns and twists of parliamentary politics leading up to the fall of the North government are delineated in I.R. Christie, *The End of North's Ministry, 1780–1782* (London, 1958).

When the Rockingham-Shelburne government came to power, the new ministers had no real understanding of the day-to-day conduct of the war and no fixed objectives other than to end the fighting. The new ministry did not realize that the entire British war effort was confronting a crisis owing to a shortage of transport, victualler and storeship tonnage, nor was it aware of either the strategic situation in America or the sheer size and scope of the effort required to evacuate the British enclaves in America, given the shortage of shipping.

At best, the strategic situation in America was vague. The king's troops were pinned down in New York, Charleston, Savannah and St Augustine – four enclaves that could only be supported from the sea. But the squadron in America was weak. On 29 March 1782, for example, it consisted of one ship of the line, four 50-gun ships, 20 frigates and 43 smaller warships.[131] American and, to a lesser extent, French strategic intentions and capabilities were unknown. For instance, were the Americans and French, perhaps even the Spanish, planning to stage another Yorktown-type campaign against one of the remaining British enclaves in America? When the Rockingham-Shelburne government came to power, nobody in London could answer such questions.

As early as 14 January 1782, the Navy Board had warned the Admiralty about the shortage of transports and victuallers and had also requested that the lords commissioners of the Admiralty state the transport and victualler tonnage that would be required during 1782 for operations in the West Indies and North America.[132] On 22 February 1782 the Navy Board further informed the Admiralty that, because of the great shortage of transport tonnage, it would be impossible in less than three months' time to find the ships required to carry 2,700 British recruits from England to America.[133] One of the first things that the Earl of Shelburne did upon taking office was to direct the Admiralty to furnish him with an 'Account of the State of the Transports in the Service of Government now in North America and West Indies distinguishing their present stations'.[134] It is not known how the Admiralty responded to this request, but clearly the importance of transports to British military operations in America was not fully understood.

[131] PRO, SP 42/57, f. 360: *Lion*, 64-gun ship of the line, and the 50-gun ships *Adamant, Chatham, Warwick, Centurion* and *Rotterdam*.
[132] Ibid., f. 41.
[133] PRO, ADM 106/2607, 22 February 1782.
[134] PRO, ADM 1/4147, f. 89.

General Sir Guy Carleton was sent to America to replace Clinton, who had resigned, with orders to evacuate New York, Charleston, Savannah and, perhaps, St Augustine. Carleton was ordered also to send as many troops as possible to the West Indies in order to shore up the British position in that theatre.[135] Sir Charles Middleton, Comtroller of the Navy and head of the Navy Board, the agency which controlled most of the shipping used by the government for military purposes, only learned of the ministry's intention to evacuate America from the newspapers. Upon learning of Carleton's orders, Middleton immediately drew up a detailed memorandum outlining a plan for the evacuation of New York and Charleston. According to Middleton, it would require 85,000 tons of shipping, which was not available, to remove these two garrisons, but it could be done with existing transports and victuallers if the government acted quickly and with skill in deploying them. Middleton gave this memorandum to Keppel several days after the admiral had become first lord of the Admiralty, but no action was taken to put Middleton's scheme into effect.[136]

It is easy to understand why the government did not act on Middleton's memorandum. When the Rockingham-Shelburne government came to power, Britain, with many strategic disadvantages, was engaged in a worldwide naval war against America, France, Spain and Holland. In a situation such as this, when victory or defeat, war or peace, hung in the balance, a memorandum on transports, victuallers, and the like, does not at first sight appear to be of much importance when compared with the larger issues of policy and grand strategy involving the movements of fleets and armies. The Rockingham-Shelburne government failed to see that transports, victuallers and storeships were an absolute necessity in order to put into effect almost any policy or strategy during the American war, but its blindness is easy to understand. The new ministry simply did not have the knowledge or experience to solve such a problem. In fact, Middleton himself, even though he had been struggling with problems of military sea transport since 1778, did not understand the size of the problem; for his estate of 85,000 tons of shipping for the evacuation of New York and Charleston was far too low.

In the spring of 1782, Shelburne attempted, with little success, to gain a measure of control over the transport crisis and the evacuation

[135] PRO, CO 5/106, ff. 2-4.
[136] NRS, *Barham Papers*, vol. 2, pp. 47-8, 77.

of America. On 3 April 1782 he ordered that Digby at New York report directly to him on matters of policy and not through the Admiralty.[137] Seven days later Shelburne issued orders to the Admiralty for speeding up the dispatch of army provisions to North America and the West Indies.[138] Although Shelburne did not know it at the time, this order would reduce the number of ships available to evacuate America. On 19 April, in order to stop the flow of provisions into New York, where they were not needed, Shelburne ordered that victuallers carrying provisions to America drop off their cargoes at Halifax before proceeding to New York.[139] Then in the middle of May the government decided to send to New York all the American prisoners of war being held in Britain to be exchanged. This measure would get American prisoners out of England and, at the same time, send some transports to America to be used in the evacuation.[140] And on 5 June, Shelburne wrote to Carleton that twenty transports and victuallers en route for the West Indies would, after their cargoes had been discharged, be ordered to Charleston to assist in the evacuation there;[141] the re-routing of transports, however, was a minor detail. The problem was that as late as August 1782, the government in London still did not understand the huge problem of evacuating America. On 7 August at a Cabinet meeting the government scaled new heights of strategic unreality. Blinded by Rodney's smashing victory against the French and Spanish fleets at the Battle of the Saints, the ministry decided that Carleton should undertake an expedition to the West Indies with troops from America. The objective of this expedition was to enable the ministry to enter into peace talks with the French and Spanish with a West Indian prize, such as Puerto Rico, to be used as a bargaining chip. At the time he was ordered to undertake the West Indian expedition, Carleton also was directed to withdraw all German troops and Loyalists with their familiies from America to Nova Scotia.[142] What the government in London did not realize was that Digby and Carleton did not have the transport and victualler tonnage to carry either one of these orders into effect.

When Carleton arrived at New York City on 5 May 1782, he was confronted not only with a huge logistical problem of evacuating

[137] PRO, ADM 1/4147, f. 96.
[138] Ibid., f. 109.
[139] HMC, *American MSS*, vol. 2, p. 460.
[140] PRO, ADM 106/2608, 14, 18 and 20 March 1782.
[141] PRO, CO 5/106, ff. 44–5.
[142] Bedford Record Office, Grantham MSS, L. 29/660, Cabinet meeting, 7 August 1782; transcript of the original document made by Professor I.R. Christie.

America, but also political and military difficulties. In all the British enclaves in America, there were hundreds of embittered Loyalists whose hatred of the American rebels knew no bounds. These Loyalists were totally and absolutely opposed to the government's policy of ending the war with the American rebels and would go to almost any lengths to prevent the end of fighting in America and the withdrawal of the King George's forces. The Associated Loyalists at New York, in an attempt to discredit the British and to prevent the end of the war, murdered an American militia officer, Captain Joshua Huddy, and enraged Washington. The American commander threatened to hang a British captain if justice were not done. After Huddy's murder, Clinton had clipped the wings of the Associated Loyalists; but if the British were going to be able to withdraw from America without having to fight as they embarked, then the Huddy problem must be solved. After weeks of negotiation and with the intervention of the French Crown, the Americans and the British agreed to end the Huddy affair. Shortly afterwards, the British withdrew from America after the diplomatic arrangements for peace had been worked out.[143]

The military words 'evacuate' or 'withdraw' really do not describe the British departure from America at the end of the war. Perhaps the word 'migration' is more accurate because not only the king's troops and ton upon ton of stores and equipment, but also thousands of American Loyalists, left America. The rate at which the British and Loyalists left for Canada, Europe or the West Indies were governed totally by the ability of Carleton and Digby to amass the necessary shipping. On 11 July 1782, Savannah was evacuated. Every ship that could be obtained was used, amounting to 11,014 tons of transports, in addition to a number of other ships hired by the royal Lieutenant-Governor of Georgia, but even this was not enough and a number of Loyalists had to make their way to St Augustine either overland or in small craft. It took until the last month of 1782 for the British to assemble the 129 transports, victuallers and storeships required to evacuate Charleston, but on 18 December 1782, 6,300 rank and file, tons of military stores and thousands of Loyalists finally set sail.

The British withdrawal from New York City was an enormous operation involving hundreds of ships. On 10 January 1783, at New York, there had to be removed 20,010 effectives, tons of equipment and stores, and the troops that had surrendered at Yorktown.

[143] See Katherine Mayo, *General Washington's Dilemma* (New York, 1938).

Thousands of Loyalists were also at New York; an estimated 10,000 Loyalists left the city before the evacuation began, and the Commissary-General's office reported that 29,278 Loyalists were removed from New York in military shipping. In the course of evacuation, warships, transports, victuallers and any other type of ship that could be obtained were used to lift Loyalists, troops and stores out of New York, but the rate at which the British withdrew depended wholly on the speed with which the necessary ships could be obtained. Finally, almost a year after the terms of the peace treaty had been agreed to by American and British diplomats, the last British troops left New York.

On 28 November 1783, Carleton, on HMS *Ceres* off Staten Island, reported that 'His Majesty's troops, and such of the loyalists as chose to emigrate, were on the 25th instant, withdrawn from the City of New York, in good order, and embarked without the smallest circumstances of irregularity or misbehaviour of any kind'.[144] Immediately after the British left, units of the Continental Army marched into New York City. When the American troops came to attention at the Battery on the southern tip of Manhattan before the flagpole from which the Union Jack still hung, they found that the halyard had been cut and the pole greased. After some confusion the flagpole was climbed, the British colours torn down and the American flag raised as a thirteen-gun salute was fired. More than eight years after the first fighting at Lexington, the British war to conquer America was at last over.

[144] For an account of the evacuation of America, see David Syrett, *Shipping and the American War, 1775–83* (London, 1970), pp. 231–41.

BIBLIOGRAPHY

Manuscripts

Bedford Record Office

Grantham MSS, L. 29/660, Transcripts of the original documents made by Professor I. R. Christie.

British Library

Add. MSS., 21680, 34187, 38343.

National Maritime Museum

ADM/L/A/66, ADM/L/B/115, ADM/L/C/24, ADM/L/G/1, ADM/L/G/192, ADM/L/N/137, ADM/L/R/25, ADM/L/V/83, Ships' logs.
HIS/7, An account of the Services performed by Commodore Sir George Collier in America, 1776-1779.
HOO, The Hood Papers.
MID, the Middleton Papers.
MOS 70/132, Uncatalogued Document.
SAN/1-7, Transcripts of the papers of the Fourth Earl of Sandwich made by the Navy Records Society.

Public Archives of Nova Scotia

MacLean to Germain, 29 August 1779; Collier to Stephens, 20 August 1779.

Public Record Office

ADM 1/240, 309, 310, Admirals' dispatches from the West Indies.
ADM 1/386, Admirals' dispatches from Gibraltar.
ADM 1/484, 485, 486, 487, 488, 489, 490, Admirals' dispatches from North America.
ADM 1/4129, 4130, 4131, 4134, 4142, 4144, 4147, 4168, Secretary of State to the Admiralty.
ADM 2/100, 101, 102, 103, 104, 373, 1332, 1333, Admiralty instructions.
ADM 3/81, 82, 83, 86, Admiralty Minutes.
ADM 51/37, 41, 48, 88, 137, 238, 475, 552, 905, Ships' logs.
ADM 106/2607, 2608, Navy Board Minutes.
CO 5/92, 93, 94, 95, 96, 97, 98, 99, 100, 101, 102, 103, 104, 106, 235, 236, Military Dispatches from America.
CO 5/130, 144, Secretary of State to the American Secretary's office.
Index of High Court of Admiralty Prize Papers, 1776-1786.
SP 42/57, State Papers, Naval.
WO 17/1154, Monthly Returns.
PRO 30/ 20/9, 10, 12, Rodney Papers.
PRO 30/ 20/22/5, Rodney Papers.

University of Virginia Libraries

The Hamond Papers.

Warwick Record Office

The Denbigh Papers.

The William L. Clements Library, University of Michigan

The Douglas Papers; The Clinton Papers; The Sackville-German Papers; The Shelburne Papers.

Printed primary sources

Brown, Gerald Saxon (ed.), *Reflections on a Pamphlet entitled 'a Letter to the Right Honble Lord Vict. H—e'* (Ann Arbor, Mich., 1959).

Burgoyne, John, *A State of the Expedition from Canada as Laid before the House of Commons by Lieutenant-General Burgoyne* (London, 1780).
Calef, John (ed.), *The Siege of Penobosot* (New York, 1971 reprint).
Carter, Clarence Edwin (ed.), *The Correspondence of General Thomas Gage* (New Haven, 1933).
Chadwick, French Ensor (ed.), *The Graves Papers and Other Documents Relating to the Naval Operations of the Yorktown Campaign July to October 1781* (New York, 1968 reprint).
Clark, William Bell and Morgan, William James (eds.), *Naval Documents of the American Revolution* (Washington, DC, 1964).
Cutter, Richard (ed.), 'A Yankee privateersman in prison in England, 1777–1779', *New England Historical and Genealogical Register* (April and July 1876), Vol. XXX, pp. 75–7.
Dobrée, Bonamy (ed.), *The Letters of King George III* (London, 1935).
Doniol, Henri (ed.), *Histoire de la Participation de la France à L'Éstablissement Des États-Unis D'Amerique* (Paris, 1886–92).
Fitzpatrick, John C. (ed.), *The Writings of George Washington* (Washington, DC, 1931–44).
Fortescue, Sir John W., *The Correspondence of King George the Third from 1760 to December 1783* (London, 1927–8).
[Galloway, Joseph], *A Letter to the Right Honorable Lord Viscount H—e* (London, 1779).
Hammond, Otis, G. (ed.), *Letters and Papers of Major-General John Sullivan, Continental Army* (Concord, NH, 1931).
Historical Manuscript Commission, *Report on the Manuscripts in Various Collections* (London, Dublin and Hereford, 1901–14).
Historical Manuscript Commission, *Report on American Manuscripts in the Royal Institution of Great Britain* (London, Dublin and Hereford, 1904–09).
Historical Manuscript Commission, *Report on the Manuscripts of Mrs. Stopford-Sackville, of Drayton House, Northamptonshire* (London and Hereford, 1904–10).
Historical Manuscript Commission, *Report on Manuscripts of the Late Reginald Hastings, Esq., of the Manor House, Ashby de la Zouche* (London, 1928–47).
Jones, Charles C., Jr. (ed.), *The Siege of Savannah by the Fleet of Count D'Estaing in 1779* (New York, 1968).
Lincoln, Charles Henry (comp.), *Naval Records of the American Revolution* (Washington, DC, 1906).

Lodge, Henry Cabot (ed.), *Major André's Journal* (New York, 1930).
Lydenberg, Harry Miller (ed.), *Archibald Robertson, Lieutenant-General Royal Engineers, His Diaries and Sketches in America, 1762-1780* (New York, 1930).
Mackenzie, Frederick, *Diary of Frederick Mackenzie: Giving a Daily Narrative of His Military Service as an Officer of the Regiment of Royal Welch Fusiliers during the Years 1775-1781 in Massachusetts, Rhode Island and New York* (Cambridge, Mass., 1930).
[Mauduit, Israel], *Strictures on the Philadelphia Mischianza or Triumph Upon leaving America Unconquered . . .* (London, 1779).
Morgan, William James, *see* Clark, William Bell.
Navy Records Society, *Letters Written by Sir Samuel Hood in 1781-2-3* (London, 1895).
Navy Records Society, *Journal of Rear-Admiral Bartholomew James, 1752-1828* (London, 1896).
Navy Records Society, *The Naval Miscellany* (London, 1902).
Navy Records Society, *Fighting Instructions, 1530-1816* (London, 1905).
Navy Records Society, *Letters and Papers of Charles, Lord Barham* (London, 1907-11).
Navy Records Society, *Signals and Instructions, 1776-1794* (London, 1908).
Navy Records Society, *The Keith Papers* (London, 1927-45).
Navy Records Society, *The Private Papers of John, Earl of Sandwich* (London, 1932-38).
Navy Records Society, *Letters and Papers of Admiral the Hon. Samuel Barrington* (London, 1937-41).
Neeser, Robert Wilden, (ed.), *The Dispatches of Molyneux Shuldham* (New York, 1913).
Neeser, Robert Wilden (ed.), *Letters and Papers Relating to the Cruises of Gustavus Conyngham: A Captain of the Continental Navy, 1777-1779* (New York, 1915).
New York Historical Society, *The Montressor Journals* (New York, 1881).
New York Historical Society, *The Kemble Papers* (New York, 1884-85).
New York Historical Society, *Letter-Books and Order Book of George, Lord Rodney, Admiral of the White Squadron, 1780-1782* (New York, 1932).

[O'Beirne, Thomas] (ed.), *A Candid and Impartial Narrative of the Transactions of the Fleet under the Command of Lord Howe . . .* (London, 2nd edn, n.d.).

Parsons, H. S. (ed.), 'Contemporary English accounts of the destruction of Norfolk in 1776'. *William and Mary Quarterly* (October 1933), 2nd ser., vol. XIII, pp. 219-24.

Robson, Eric (ed.), *Letters from America, 1773-1780.* (New York, 1950).

Scull, G. D. (ed.), *Memoir and Letters of Captain W. Glanville Evelyn of the 4th Regiment ('King's Own') from North America, 1775-1776* (Oxford, 1879).

Shea, John Dawson Gilmay (ed.), *The Operations of the French Fleet under the Count de Grasse in 1781-1782, as Described in two Contemporaneous Journals* (New York, 1971 reprint).

Tatum, Edward H. Jr., (ed.), *The American Journal of Ambrose Serle* (San Mario, Calif., 1940).

Uhlendorf, Bernard Alexander (ed. and tr.), *The Siege of Charleston with an Account of the Province of South Carolina: Diaries and Letters of Hessian Officers from the von Jungkenn Papers in the William L. Clements Library* (Ann Arbor, Mich., 1938).

Wharton, Francis (ed.), *The Revolutionary Diplomatic Correspondence of the United States* (Washington, DC, 1898).

Willcox, William B. (ed.), *The American Rebellion: Sir Henry Clinton's Narrative of His Campaigns, 1775-1782, with an appendix of original documents* (New Haven, Conn., 1954).

Wortley, E. Stuart (ed.), *A Prime Minister and His Son* (London, 1925).

Secondary works

Albion, Robert Greenhalgh, *Forests and Seapower: The Timber Problem of the Royal Navy* (Cambridge, Mass., 1926).

Allen, Gardener, W., *A Naval History of the American Revolution* (New York, 1962 reprint).

Anderson, T. S., *The Command of the Howe Brothers during the American Revolution* (New York, 1933).

Baker, Norman, *Government and Contractors* (London, 1971).

Barrington, Shute, *The Political Life of William Wildman, Viscount Barrington* (London, 1814).

Barrow, Sir John, *The Life of Richard, Earl Howe* (London, 1838).

Bemis, Samuel F., *The Diplomacy of the American Revolution* (New York, 1935).
Billias, George Athan (ed.), *George Washington's Opponents* (New York, 1969).
Bonner-Smith, D., 'The capture of the *Washington*', *Mariner's Mirror* (October 1934), vol. 20, pp. 420-5.
Breen, Kenneth, 'Graves and Hood at the Chesapeake', *Mariner's Mirror* (February 1980), vol. 66, pp. 53-61.
Brown, Gerald Saxon, *The American Secretary: The Colonial Policy of Lord George Germain, 1775-1778* (Ann Arbor, Mich., 1963).
Bryant, Arthur, *The Turn of the Tide, 1939-1943* (London, 1957).
Christie, I. R., *The End of North's Ministry, 1780-1782* (London, 1958).
Clark, William Bell, *George Washington's Navy* (Baton Rouge, La, 1960).
Cornwallis-West, G., *The Life and Letters of Admiral Cornwallis* (London, 1927).
Davis, Ralph, *The Rise of the English Shipping Industry in the Seventeenth and Eighteenth Centuries* (London, 1962).
Donoughue, Bernard, *British Politics and the American Revolution: The Path to War, 1773-75* (London, 1964).
Dull, Jonathan R., *The French Navy and American Independence: A Study of Arms and Diplomacy, 1774-1781* (Princeton, NJ, 1975).
Fall, Bernard B., *Street without Joy* (New York, 1972 reprint).
Fayle, C. Ernest, *see* Wright, Charles.
Ford, Worthington C., 'Parliament and the Howes', *Proceedings of the Massachusetts Historical Society* (Boston, October 1910-June 1911), vol. XLIV, pp. 120-43.
Fortescue, J. W. *A History of the British Army* (London, 1910-35).
Fowler, William M., Jr., *Rebels under Sail: The American Navy during the Revolution* (New York, 1976).
Freeman, D. S., *George Washington* (New York, 1951-52).
Gottschalk, Louis Reichenthal, *Lafayette and the Close of the American Revolution* (Chicago, 1942).
Gruber, Ira D., *The Howe Brothers and the American Revolution* (New York, 1972).
Hale, Richard W., 'New light on the naval side of Yorktown', *Proceedings of the Massachusetts Historical Society* (Boston, October 1953-57), vol. LXXI, pp. 124-32.
Hamilton, Peter Joseph, *Colonial Mobile* (Boston, Mass., 1943).

Harte, C. R. 'The river obstructions of the Revolutionary War', *Annual Report of the Connecticut Society of Civil Engineers* (1946), vol. 62, pp. 135-186a.
Higginbotham, Don, *Daniel Morgan, Revolutionary Rifleman* (Chapel Hill, NC, 1961).
Higginbotham, Don, *The War of American Independence: Military Attitudes, Politicies and Practice 1753-1783* (New York, 1971).
Jenkins, E. H., *A History of the French Navy* (London, 1973).
Johnston, Henry Philps, *The Storming of Stony Point on the Hudson, Midnight July 15, 1779: Its Importance in the Light of Unpublished Documents* (New York, 1900).
Johnston, Ruth Y., 'American privateers in French ports', *Pennsylvania Magazine of History and Biography* (October, 1929), vol. LIII, pp. 352-74.
Kennett, Lee, *The French Forces in America, 1780-1783* (Westport, Conn., 1977).
Larrabee, Harold Atkins, *Decision at the Chesapeake* (New York, 1964).
Lawrence, Alexander A., *Storm over Savannah: The Story of Count d'Estaing and the Siege of the Town in 1779* (Athens, Ga., 1951).
Lowell, Edward L., *The Hessians and other German Auxiliaries of Great Britain in the Revolutionary War* (New York, 1884).
Mackesy, *The War for America, 1775-1783* (London, 1964).
McCusker, John, Jr., 'The American invasion of Nassau in the Bahamas', *American Neptune* (July 1965), vol. 25, pp. 189-217.
Mahan, A. T. *The Major Operations of the Navies in the War of American Independence* (New York, 1969 reprint).
Mayo, Katherine, *General Washington's Dilemma* (New York, 1938).
Middleton, C. R., 'A reinforcement for America, 1757', *Bulletin of the Institute of Historical Research* (May 1968), vol. XLI, pp. 57-72.
Moomaw, W. Hugh, 'The British leave colonial Virginia', *Virginia Magazine of History and Biography* (April 1958), vol. LXVI, pp. 147-60.
Moomaw, W. Hugh, 'The Naval Career of Captain Hamond, 1775-1779' (unpublished PhD dissertation, University of Virginia, 1955).
Moomaw, W. Hugh, 'The denouement of General Howe's campaign of 1777', *English Historical Review* (July 1964), vol. 79, pp. 498-512.
Owen, J. H. and Sir George Barnes, 'Lieutenant Edward Sneyd,

Royal Navy, of Keele Hall, Staffordshire', *Mariner's Mirror* (November 1958), vol. 44, pp. 240-4.
Partidge, Bellamy, *Sir Billy Howe* (London, 1932).
Robson, Eric, 'The expedition to the southern colonies, 1775-1776', *English Historical Review* (October 1951), vol. LXVI, pp. 538-9.
Robson, Eric, *The American Revolution* (London, 1955).
Rush, N. Darwin, *Spain's Final Triumph over Great Britain in the Gulf of Mexico: The Battle of Pensacola, March 9 to May 8, 1781* (Tallahassee, Fla., 1966).
Spinney, David, *Rodney* (London, 1969).
Stephenson, Orland W., 'The supply of gunpower in 1776', *American Historical Review* (January 1925), vol. 30, pp. 277-81.
Stout, Neil R., *The Royal Navy in America, 1760-1775* (Annapolis, Md, 1973).
Stryker, William S., *The Battles of Trenton and Princeton* (Cambridge, Mass., 1898).
Sullivan, J. A. 'Graves and Hood', *Mariner's Mirror* (May 1983), vol. 69, pp. 175-94.
Syrett, David, *Shipping and the American War, 1775-83* (London, 1970a).
Syrett, David, 'The disruption of HMS *Flora's* convoy, 1776', *Mariner's Mirror* (November 1970b), vol. 56, pp. 423-27.
Syrett, David, 'Methodology of British amphibious operations during the Seven Years War and the American War', *Mariner's Mirror* (August 1972), vol. 58, pp. 269-80.
Syrett, David, 'Lord George Germain and the protection of military storeships, 1775-1778', *Mariner's Mirror* (November 1974), vol. 60, pp. 395-404.
Syrett, David, 'HM Armed Ship *Vigilant*, 1777-1780', *Mariner's Mirror* (February 1978), vol. 64, pp. 57-62.
Syrett, David, 'A checklist of Admiral Lord Howe manuscripts in United States archives and libraries', *Mariner's Mirror* (August 1982), vol. 67, pp. 273-84.
Wallace, Willard M., *Appeal to Arms* (New York, 1951).
Wallace, Willard M., *Traitorous Hero: The Life and Fortunes of Benedict Arnold* (New York, 1954).
Wickwire, Franklin and Wickwire, Mary, *Cornwallis and the War of Independence* (London, 1971).
Willcox, William B., 'The British road to Yorktown: a study in divided commands', *American Historical Review* (October 1946), vol. 52, pp. 1-35.
Willcox, William B., 'Too many cooks: British planning before

Saratoga', *Journal of British Studies* (November 1962), vol. II, pp. 56–90.

Willcox, William B., *Portrait of a General: Sir Henry Clinton in the War of Independence* (New York, 1964).

Willson, Beckles, *The Life and Letters of James Wolfe* (New York, 1909).

Wright, Charles and Fayle, C. Ernest, *A History of Lloyd's* (London, 1928).

Yerxa, Donald A., 'Vice-Admiral Graves and the North American squadron, 1774–1776', *Mariner's Mirror* (November 1976), vol. 62, pp. 371–84.

Zapatero, Juan Manuel, *La Guerra del Carribe en el Siglo XVII* (San Juan, Puerto Rico, 1964 reprint).

INDEX

Actaeon, 35, 38, 39
Active, 38, 127
Adamant, 169, 194
Aderney, 67
Adventure, 23, 47, 78
Aeolus, 140
Affleck, Commodore Edmund, 179, 205, 206, 207
Aigrette, 191, 195
Aimable, 98
Ajax, 186, 194, 202, 219
Albany, NY, 59, 73, 75
Albany, 127
Albion, 101, 114
Alcide, 152, 160, 186, 194
Alcmene, 98
Alfred, 186, 194, 197, 219
Ambuscade, 54
America, 144, 145, 164, 169, 191, 194, 219
American Revolution, 177
Amherst, Lord, 33
Amphirite, 145
André, Major John, 152, 153, 155
Andromaque, 191, 195
Andromeda, 93, 95
Anglo-French Treaty of 1763, 65
Ann, 135
Ann, Cape, Mass., 6, 7, 8, 9, 184
Antigua, 59, 115, 186

Apollo, 78, 104, 107
Appalachian Mountains, 158
Arbuthnot, Admiral Marriot, 11, 86, 121, 122, 129, 130, 131, 135, 136, 138, 139, 140, 142, 143, 145, 146, 147, 148, 149, 150, 151, 153, 154, 155–7, 159–60, 161, 162, 163, 164, 165, 166, 167, 168, 169, 170, 172, 179, 180, 181, 185, 186, 218
Ardent, 84, 96, 104, 196
Arethusa, 67
Argo, 20
Arhusa, 32
Ariel, 115, 132
Arnold, Major General Benedict, 142, 153, 154;
 a brigadier in British service 162, 163, 164, 165, 166, 167, 168, 170, 174, 192, 205
Ascension Island, 32
Ashley River, SC, 138, 139
Asia, 14, 15, 16, 29, 47, 54
Associated Loyalists, 225
Astoria, Queens Co., NY, 50
Atlanta, 30
Atlantic, 32
Augusta, 70, 78, 83
 blows up, 84

238   INDEX

Auguste, 191, 195

Bahama Islands, 133
Baltic, 86
Banks, Captain Francis, 25
Barfleur, 186, 194, 199, 219
Barkley, Captain Andrew, 20
Barrington, Admiral Samuel, 104, 127, 194
Barrington, Lord, Secretary at War, 35
Barras, Admiral de, 177, 178, 181, 182, 187, 188, 189, 194, 202
Bataan, 141
Baton Rouge, La., 133, 175
Battery, The, New York City, 15
Beckwith, Captain George, 152, 189, 190
Bedford, 111, 115, 145, 164, 169, 191, 194
Bedlows Island, NY, 16
Belle Isle, 67
Belligeux, 186, 194
Bergen, Norway, 66
Betsy, 18
Beverly, Mass, 6
Bienfaisant, 72
Billingsport, NJ, 81
Biscay, Bay of, 67
Black Prince, 127
Block Island, RI, 26, 108, 148, 149
Blonde, 42, 128, 140
Bloomingdale Road, New York City, 51
Boer Republics, 44
Bolton, 14, 25, 26
Bonetta, 168
Bordentown, NJ, 95
Boreas, 152, 186
Boston, 1, 2
  supplying of 3-4, 5, 6, 8, 9, 10, 11, 14, 16, 17, 20, 23, 24, 25, 27, 28, 32, 35, 36, 37, 62, 71, 110, 111, 112, 115, 131, 177, 181, 182, 186
Boston, 18, 71, 72

Boston Bay, 5, 110, 114, 115, 184
Boston Harbor, 5, 6, 24, 110
Boston Light House, 5
Boston Port Act, 3
Bourgogne, 191, 195
Boyne, 29
Brandywine Creek, Battle of, 80-81
Brest, 67
Bricole, 138
Brisbane, Captain John, 102
Bristol, RI, 74
Bristol, 35, 38, 47
Bristol Ferry, RI, 110
Bristol Neck, RI, 110, 147
British trade protection measures, 66-8
British strategy in America, 94, 143, 144
Bronx, NY, 52, 54, 182
Brooklyn, NY, 47, 50, 54, 98
Brooklyn Heights, NY, 47, 48, 50, 54
Brune, 42, 47, 54
Brunswick troops, 42
Brussels, 178
Bunker Hill, Mass, 10, 55
Burgoyne, General John, 72, 73, 74, 75, 77, 86, 90, 92, 117, 176
Bute, Lord, 113
Buzzard's Bay, RI, 110
Byng, Vice Admiral John, 10
Byron, Vice Admiral John, 96, 97, 100, 101, 109, 111, 112, 114, 115, 120, 121, 143

Caicos Islands, 21
Camden, Battle of, 151, 173, 175, 176
Cameleon, 67
Campell, Major General John, 175, 176
Canada, 11, 34, 39, 40, 41, 42, 43, 57, 58, 73, 75, 76, 119, 174
Canada, 219
Canceaux, 7

INDEX

Canso, 93
Canton, 195
Capture Act, 30, 56
Carcass, 42, 47, 104
Caribbean, 23, 88
Carleton, General Sir Guy, 76, 220, 223, 224, 225, 226
Carlisle Commission, 94, 117
Carpenter's Island, Pa, 83, 84
Carysfort, 42, 51, 54, 115
Castine, Me, 120, 122, 176, 219
Caton, 191
Cecil Court House, 80
Centurion, 23, 54, 96, 107, 108, 115, 152, 186, 219
Ceres, 225
Cesar, 98, 108, 109, 195
Chadwick, French E., 192
Channel Fleet, 64, 65, 67, 144, 180
Charles, Cape, 17, 168
Charleston, SC, 36–9, 135, 138, 139, 140, 146, 159, 176, 179, 187, 223, 225, 227
Charlottetown, P.E.I., 6
Charon, 219
Chatham, NJ, 188, 199
Chatham, 23, 54, 168
Chesapeake Bay, 16, 17–20, 29, 58, 78–80, 87, 93, 98, 100, 112, 123, 124, 125, 134, 135, 142, 146, 152, 153, 154, 158, 159, 162, 164, 165, 166, 167, 168, 170, 173, 174, 176, 177, 179, 182, 184, 185, 186, 187, 188, 189, 191, 192–204, 208, 209, 211, 212, 213, 214, 215, 217, 219
Chester, Pa, 189
Chesterfield, Va., 163
Chevaux-de-frise, 81, 83, 84
Chimère, 98
Chocta Indians, 133
Citoyen, 191, 195
Clear, Cape, 67
Clinton, General Sir Henry, 15, 36, 47, 48, 50, 51, 52, 54, 75, 95, 96, 97, 100, 108, 110, 113, 114, 115, 119, 121, 122, 123, 124, 125, 126, 130, 131, 135, 136, 138, 139, 140, 141, 142, 145, 146, 147, 148, 149, 150, 151, 152, 153, 154, 155, 158, 159, 161, 164, 165, 166, 167, 168, 170, 172, 173, 174, 178, 179, 180, 181, 183, 184, 185, 186, 189, 190, 191, 192, 201, 204, 205, 206, 207, 208, 209, 210, 211, 212, 213, 214, 215, 216, 217, 218, 219, 223, 225
Clinton-Parker expedition to the Southern Colonies, 8, 18–20, 35–9
Clyde, 43
Cod, Cape, 9, 109, 110, 115
Colden, Lt Gov. of New York, 14
Collier, Commodore Sir George, 86, 122, 123, 124, 125, 126, 127, 128, 129, 184
Collier-Mathew raid in Virginia, 1779, 123–4
Commons, House of, 66, 92
Conanicut Island, RI, 102
Concord, Mass, 1, 11
Concorde, 177, 182, 191, 195
Confederacy, 44
Connecticut, 125, 134, 147, 176, 182
Conquéirant, 168
Conqueror, 111, 115
Continental Army, 55, 69, 77, 79, 97, 98, 142, 156, 164, 166, 182, 186, 188, 226
Continental Congress, 53, 76
Continental Navy, 60
Conyngham, Captain Gustavus, 65, 66
Cooper River, SC, 138, 139, 140
Cork, 35, 36, 41, 43
Cornwall, 101, 104, 113
Cornwallis, General Lord, 53, 78,

86, 102, 122, 123, 124, 139, 141, 157, 158, 159, 161, 162, 165, 167, 172, 173, 174, 175, 176, 178, 179, 181, 184, 187, 189, 190, 191, 192, 194, 195, 199, 216, 217, 218, 219, 220, 221
Cowpens, SC, Battle of, 164, 173, 176
Croton River, NY, 52
Cruiser, 20
Cuba, 120, 133, 175
Culloden, 101, 115, 152, 164
Curcass, 115
Custon Service, 41
Cyclops, 160
Cygnet, 32

Dalrymple, General Wiliam, 149, 150, 151
Daphne, 129
Dartmouth, 67
Declaration of Independence, 25, 43, 47
Defence, 127, 128
Delaware Bay, 16, 17-18, 19, 20, 27, 58, 78, 79, 80, 96, 99, 100, 112, 142, 145, 152, 186
Delaware River, 17, 18, 53, 54, 61, 62, 74, 78, 79, 81, 83, 84, 85, 86, 87, 94, 95, 189
Denbigh, Earl of 220
Denis, Long Island, NY, 190
Deptford, 41
Destin, 191
Destouches, Captain, 168, 169, 170, 172
Diadéme, 191, 195
Diamond, 54, 115
Digby, Rear Admiral Robert, 181, 185, 186, 203, 206, 207, 210, 219, 224, 225
Diligence, 127
Diligent, 23, 115, 124
Diligente, 191, 195
Dispatch, 23, 25, 78

Donop, Colonel Carl Emil Kurt von, 83
Dorchester Heights, Mass, 24
Dove, 66
Downs, The, 30
Drake, Rear Admiral Sir Francis S., 200, 201, 202, 204
Drake, 67
Drayton Hall, SC, 139
Duc de Bourgogne, 169
Dull, Jonathan R., 218
Duncan, Captain Henry, 98, 203
Dundus, Henry, 220
Dunkirk, 65, 66, 67
Dunmore, Earl of, 16, 17, 18, 19, 184

Eagle, 47, 78, 79, 96, 97, 104, 111
East Florida, 93, 115, 134
East Hampton, NY, 149
East Indies, 144, 178
East River, NY, 15, 16, 47, 48, 50, 52, 54, 55, 125
Effingham, 95
Egmont schooner, 32
Eisenhower, General, 40
Elbe River, 41
Elizabeth, River, Va., 17, 18, 124, 158, 162, 164
Elk River, 80, 165, 167
Elphinstone, Captain George Keith, 136-8, 139
Emeral, 24, 47, 54, 78
Engageante, 98
England, 11, 29, 32, 36, 57, 59, 60, 70, 72, 94, 101, 114
English Channel, 30, 64, 66, 90, 109, 131
d'Estaing, Admiral, 96, 97, 98, 99, 100, 101, 102, 104, 105, 107, 108, 109, 110, 111, 112, 114, 115, 120, 130, 131, 133, 135, 147, 152, 194, 219
Europe, 142, 148, 169, 191, 194
Eveille, 164, 169
Everitt, Captain Charles Holmes,

INDEX

199
Experiment, 38, 47, 54, 96, 97, 104, 132, 191, 195

Fairfield, Conn., 126
Falcon, 102
Falmouth, Me, 7-8, 10, 27, 56
Fame, 11, 115
Fantasque, 98, 169
Faro, 63
Fear, Cape, NC, 18, 36, 37, 159
Ferguson, Major Patrick, 139, 140, 157
Finsterre, Cape, 67
Firth of Clyde, 88
Five Fathom Hole, SC, 138
Flora, 47, 72, 102
Florida, 11, 43, 93, 94, 95, 96, 114, 116, 119, 121, 122, 133, 175, 176
Florida, 20
Florida, Straits of, 132
Forman, Brigadier General, 187
Fortescue, Sir John, 55
Fort Island, Pa, 81, 83, 85
Fortune, 152, 198
Fowey, 9, 16, 23, 25, 32, 47
Fox, 32, 72, 86
France, policy towards American cruisers, 63-6
possibility of war with, 93
Franco-Americo Alliance, 94
Francis, Cape, 182, 186
Franklin, 6
French army leaves Newport, IR, 182
French-Indochinese War, 173
French Revolutionary War, 44
Friendship, 35, 38
Fundy, Bay of, 3, 11

Gage, General Thomas, 7, 8, 16
Galatea, 108, 128
Galves, Governor Bernardo, 133, 175, 176
Gambier, Rear Admiral James, 97, 111, 120, 122
Gardiner's Island, NY, 149, 151, 156, 165, 167, 168, 183
Gayton, Rear Admiral, 21, 22
Gentille, 191, 195
George III, 45, 91, 96, 141, 181, 221
Georges Bank, 25, 109
Georgia, 3, 20, 113, 114, 115, 122, 130, 132, 134, 158, 163, 173, 174, 176, 219
Germain, Lord George, 7, 39, 41, 46, 64, 69, 70, 73, 74, 75, 76, 77, 78, 81, 85, 88, 112, 113, 122, 123, 130, 134, 135, 143, 144, 161, 170, 174, 175, 178, 180, 183, 205, 218, 220
Germantown, Battle of, 92
Germany, 41, 42
Gibraltar, 29, 57, 127, 180, 186
Glasgow, 14, 26, 27
Glorieux, 191
Glorious First of June, 44, 219
Gloucester, Mass, 6
Gloucester, Va., 183, 207, 215
Governors Island, NY, 16
Grafton, 111, 115
Grant, US, 44
Grantham, 96
Grasse, Admiral Comte de, 178, 179, 180, 181, 182, 185, 186, 187, 188, 190, 191, 192, 194, 195, 197, 198, 199, 201, 205, 207, 217, 219
Graves, Rear Admiral Samuel, 1, 2, 3, 5, 6, 7, 8, 9, 10, 11, 16, 23, 24, 27, 32, 69
Graves, Rear Admiral Thomas, 143, 144, 145, 150, 159, 161, 164, 180, 181, 183, 184, 185, 186, 189, 190, 191, 192, 194, 195, 197, 198, 199, 200, 201, 202, 203, 204, 205, 206, 207, 208, 209, 210, 212, 213, 214, 215, 216, 217, 219

Gravesend, NY, 43, 48
Great Bridge, Va., 17
Great Inagua, 21
Great Neck, NY, 126
Greene, Major General Nathanael, 172, 219
Green Frams, Conn., 126
Greenland, 68
Grenville, George, 144
Grenville Act, 144
Greyhound, 47, 128, 152
Groupement Mobile No., 100, 173
Guadaloupe, 101
Guerrier, 98n
Guilford Court House, Battle of, 172, 175, 176

Haerlem, 78, 124
Hague, The, 30
Halifax, NS, 11, 17, 23, 24, 25, 27, 42, 59, 60, 93, 94, 97, 100, 101, 111, 112, 119, 131, 132, 143, 144, 146, 178, 224
Halifax, 7, 47, 168
Halifax schooner, 23
Hamond, Captain Andrew Snape, 17, 18, 19, 20, 78, 79, 80, 81, 99, 110, 184
Hampten, 127, 129
Hampton Roads, Va., 163
Hanau troops, 42
Hancock, 6, 71, 72
Harlem, NY, 50
Harlem Heights, NY, 51, 54
Harlem River, NY, 41, 48, 50, 53, 126
Harper's Ferry, Va., 141
Harwich, 66
Havana, 133, 175
Hawke, 26
Hazard, 127
Heath, General William, 188
Hector, 98, 127, 191, 195
Hell Gate, NY, 50, 52, 126
Henlopen, Cape, 18, 26, 78
Henry, Cape, 172, 186, 194

Hercule, 191, 195
Hessians, 40, 42, 84, 88
Hind, 20
Hinrichs, Captain Johann, 134
Hobcaw Point, SC, 140
Hog Island, Pa, 83, 84
Holland, 41
Hood, Admiral Sir Samuel, 120, 185, 186, 190, 191, 194, 195, 197, 199, 200, 201, 202, 203, 204, 210, 211, 212, 214, 215, 216, 218, 219
Hope, 6, 23
Hopkins, Commodore Esek, 18, 26, 27, 53, 60, 71
Hotham, Commodore William, 42, 56, 99, 115
Hound, 67
Hovering Act, 30
Howe, Admiral Lord Richard, 44, 46, 48, 54, 55, 56, 57-60, 69, 70, 71, 79, 81, 84, 86, 87, 92, 93, 94, 95, 96, 97, 98, 99, 100, 101, 104, 105, 107, 108, 109, 110, 111, 112, 113, 114, 120, 122, 131, 201, 219
Howe, George, 45
Howe, General Sir William, 8, 9, 24, 25, 44, 45, 46, 48, 50, 51, 52, 53, 54-5, 57, 69, 70, 72, 73, 76, 77, 78, 79, 80, 81, 85, 87, 90, 92, 93, 95, 134
Huddy, Captain Joshua, 225
Hudson, Captain Charles, 148, 167, 168
Hudson Bay, 68, 178
Hudson Highlands, 47, 74, 75, 123, 125, 132, 134, 152, 153, 154
Hudson River, 15, 34, 47, 48, 50, 51, 52, 53, 59, 73, 74, 75, 76, 78, 123, 124, 125, 126, 134, 165, 187, 188, 189, 190
Hull, 67
Hunter, 127, 128, 129

INDEX

Huntington Bay, NY, 126, 148, 149, 150
Hussar, 104

India, 89, 90
Indian Ocean, 90
Intrepid, 152, 160, 186, 194, 197, 198, 202, 219
Invincible, 101, 144, 186, 194, 219
Inwood, Manhattan, NY, 51
Ipswich, Mass, 7
Ireland, 34, 35, 36
Irish Sea, 66, 67, 88
Isis, 40, 78, 84, 85, 96, 97, 104, 108, 115, 168, 200
Isle of Palms, SC, 37

Jackson, George, 160, 200
Jackson, Stonewall, 141
Jamaica, 32, 59, 88, 130, 133, 161, 172, 175, 210, 218, 219
James Island, SC, 138, 140
James River, V., 159, 162, 191, 217
Jason, 169
Jefferson, Governor Thomas, 163
Jersey, 42, 160
Johns Island, SC, 136, 146
Johnson, Fort, 138
Juno, 42, 102

Kingsbridge, Bronx, NY, 47, 48, 50, 51, 52
King's Ferry, NY, 123, 125
Kingsfisher, 14, 17, 18, 47, 54, 102
King's Mountain, Battle of, 157, 158, 173, 176
Kips Bay, NY, 50, 51, 52
Kitchener, Lord, 44
Knox, William, 113
Knyphausen, General Wilhelm, 152

Lafayette, Major General Marquis de, 165, 167, 174, 187, 191, 192
La Forutnée, 194
L'Aventure, 141

Languedoc, 98, 107, 108, 109, 191, 195
La Nymphe, 186, 194, 217
Lark, 102
Lee, 6
Lee, Fort, NJ, 53
Leeward, Islands, 20, 21, 22, 32
Legge, Governor Francis, 3, 11
Leicester, 220
Leslie, Major General Alexander, 149, 158, 159
Lesser Antilles, 152
Leviathan, 99
Lexington, Mass, 1, 11, 226
Light House Island, SC, 138
Lincoln, Major General Benjamin, 132, 133, 138, 140
Lisbon, 101
Lively, 23, 25
Liverpool, NS, 11, 25
Liverpool, 17, 18, 20, 83, 84, 85
Lizard, 160
London, 3, 8, 9, 11, 17, 28, 30, 31, 34, 35, 39, 43, 55, 73, 76, 77, 87, 88, 92, 117, 119, 120, 121, 123, 141, 142, 143, 151, 161, 176
London, 145, 169, 191, 194, 197, 200, 201, 210, 219
Long Island, Me, 127
Long Island, NY, 3, 14, 25, 47, 48, 54, 97, 109, 126, 148, 149, 150, 151, 164, 183
Long Island, SC, 37, 39, 52
Long Island Sound, 25, 71, 108, 110, 125, 126, 147, 166
Lords, House of, 221
Louisiana, 120, 133
Lovell, Brigadier General Soloman, 127, 128, 129
Lower New York Bay, 98, 99, 100
Loyalists, 34, 35, 36, 39, 46, 47, 62, 76, 96, 148, 152, 173, 183, 192, 225
Lynn, Mass, 6

Lynnhaven, Bay, Va., 170, 194
Lynx, 20

Machias, Me, 3, 94
Maganime, 191, 195
Maidstone, 20, 21
Maine, 3, 25, 122, 127, 128, 129
Manchac, La., 133, 175
Manhattan, NY, 47, 50, 51, 54, 226
Manley, Captain John, 71, 72
Manot Creek, Pa, 85
Marblehead, Mass, 6, 7, 8, 9
Margaretta, 3
Marion, Francis, 158
Marseillais, 98, 107, 108, 109, 191, 195
Martha's Vineyard, Mass, 109, 110
Martin, 32, 40
Martinique, 22, 23, 115, 159, 219
Maryland, 18, 184
Massachusetts, 1, 14, 28, 29, 127, 129, 177
Massachusetts, General Court of, 45
Massachusetts Bay, 5, 6, 8, 9, 23, 24, 110, 114, 115
Mathew, Brigadier Edward, 124, 125, 149, 150
May, Cape, NJ, 108
McGown's Pass, Manhattan, NY, 51
Medea, 200, 201, 203
Mediterranean, 69, 83, 90
Mercer, Fort, NJ, 83, 84, 85
Mercury, 54
Merlin, 84, 83
Mexico, 11, 133
  Gulf of, 120, 133, 175, 176
Middle Channel, RI, 104
Middle Ground, SG, 38
Middleton, Captain Sir Charles, 120, 201, 223
Mifflin, Fort, Pa, 81, 83, 84, 85
Milford, 67
Minorca, 29
Mischianza, 95

Mississippi River, 119, 120, 134
Mobile, Ala, 133, 134, 175
Mobile Bay, Ala, 133
Monarch, 186, 194, 219
Moncrieff, Major James, 140
Monmouth, Battle of, 97
Montagu, 186, 194, 202, 219
Montauk Point, NY, 150
Montreal, 39
Montressor, Captain John, 50
Moore's Bridge, Battle of, 36, 39
Morgan, Major General Daniel, 164
Moriches, NY, 149
Morris, Robert, 187, 188
Morrisania, NY, 178
Moscow, 73
Moultrie, Fort, 136, 140
Moultrie, General William, 38, 138
Mount Pleasant, SC, 140
Mowat, Captain Henry, 7, 8, 56, 128, 129
Murray, Captain Thomas, 147, 148
Murray, General James, 33
Murray Hill, Manhattan, NY, 51
Muskegek Channel, RI, 109

Nancy, 6, 10
Nantasket Roads, Mass, 6, 9, 24
Nantucket, Mass, 109
Nantucket Shoals, 150
Napoleon, 73
Napoleonic Wars, 45
Narragansett Bay, RI, 14, 53, 101, 102, 105, 110
Narragansett Passage, RI, 104
Narrows, The, NY, 16
Natchez, La, 133, 175
Nautilus, 18, 23, 104, 127
Nautilus Island, Me, 128
Navesink, NJ, 97
Nelson, Fort, Va., 123
Neptune, 169
New Bedford, Mass, 110, 113, 114
New Brunswick, NJ, 122
Newburyport, Mass, 7

INDEX

New Castle, Del., 79
New England, 3, 6, 7, 8, 14, 15, 25, 26, 34, 59, 69, 70, 71, 72, 74, 77, 86, 93, 98, 100, 105, 111, 122, 178
Newfoundland, 32, 33, 68, 72, 144, 188
New Hampshire, 113
New Haven, Conn., 126
New Jersey, 53, 54, 62, 71, 73, 74, 78, 79, 83, 85, 90, 96, 117, 163, 191, 205, 211, 212
New London, Conn., 126, 147, 192, 205
New Orleans, La, 133, 134
Newport, RI, 14, 53, 54, 58, 59, 60, 87, 93, 101, 102, 104, 105, 108, 110, 111, 131, 133, 145, 146, 147, 148, 149, 150, 151, 153, 154, 159, 161, 162, 163, 164, 165, 166, 167, 168, 170, 177, 185, 188, 191, 206, 215, 218
New Providence, Bahamas, 26, 27, 120
New Rochelle, NY, 52
Newton Creek, NY, 50
New Windsor, NY, 178
New York, 2, 14, 15, 16, 19, 24, 25, 34, 37, 39, 43, 46, 47, 48, 50, 54, 55, 57, 58, 59, 60, 62, 71, 74, 77, 78, 86, 87, 94, 95, 96, 97, 98, 100, 102, 104, 105, 109, 111–25, 129, 130, 131, 133, 134, 135, 136, 139, 142, 143, 145, 146, 153, 155, 157, 158, 159, 160, 161, 162, 163, 164, 166, 168, 170, 172, 174, 179, 180–7, 190, 191, 192, 195, 199, 203, 204, 207–13, 215–19, 223, 224, 225, 226
New York City, 15, 48, 51, 53, 54, 62, 73, 74, 75, 76, 78, 80, 87, 93, 98, 126, 127, 131, 132, 134, 145, 149, 150, 153, 156, 157, 165, 166, 167, 178, 179, 183, 185, 186, 187, 188, 189, 190, 208, 214, 225
New York Harbor, 15, 16, 179, 191, 204, 205, 208
Niger, 23, 25, 47
Nonsuch, 70, 78, 96, 97, 104, 115
Nore, The, 40
Norfolk, Va., 17, 27, 56
North, 127
North, Lord, 45, 64, 66, 92, 120, 220, 221
North Carolina, 35, 36, 135, 159, 163, 165, 187, 192, 208
North Edisto Inlet, SC, 136
North River, 157, 167
North Sea, 66
Northumberland, 191, 195
Norwalk, Conn., 126
Notre Dame, 138
Nova Scotia, 1, 2, 3, 11, 25, 59, 86, 94, 122, 127, 224

Orpheus, 51, 71, 102, 167
Ortegal, Cape, 67
Otter, 16, 17, 18, 20, 47, 78, 128

Pacahunta, 160
Palisades, The, 53
Pallas, 30, 32, 127
Palliser, Captain Hugh, 39, 40, 45
Palmir, 191, 195
Panther, 186
Paris, 28, 29, 34, 65
Parker, Captain Hyde, 15, 16, 111, 114
Parker, Rear Admiral Sir Peter, 19, 36, 38, 39, 43, 53, 136, 172
Peace of Paris, 28
Pearl, 42, 50, 83, 84, 85, 104, 115, 168
Pegasus, 219
Pelican, 67
Pells Point, NY, 52
Pennsylvania, 54, 61, 73, 74, 75, 77, 78, 79, 81, 83, 84, 85, 86,

90, 163, 183
Penobscot Bay, Me, 122, 127, 128, 129, 131
Penobscot River, Me, 128, 129
Pensacola, Fla, 115, 119, 133, 134, 175, 176
Penzance, 67
Petersburg, Va., 158, 174
Philadelphia, 17, 18, 74, 75, 76, 77, 78, 79, 80, 81, 82, 83, 84, 85, 87, 93, 94, 95, 96, 104, 187, 189, 190, 205, 211, 212
Phillips, Major General William, 168, 174, 175
Phillipsburg, NY, 182
Phoenix, 14, 15, 16, 47, 52, 97, 104, 107
Pitcairn, Major John, 10
Pluton, 191, 195
Plymouth, 41, 145, 181
Point, Judith, RI, 104, 145
Pomona, 20
Poole, 32
Porcupine, 94
Portland, Me, 7
Port Levis, Quebec, 39
Portsmouth, 35, 42, 145
Portsmouth, NH, 7
Portsmouth, Va., 124, 125, 159, 162, 163, 164, 165, 167, 182
Portsmouth Dockyard, 120, 144
Portugal, 67
Post Road, NY, 51
Potomac River, Va., 19
Preston, 1, 42, 47, 54, 96, 97, 107, 115
Prince Edward Island, 6, 58
Prince George, 219
Prince of Orange, 66
Princessa, 186, 194, 219
Princess Royal, 101, 109, 115
Prize Money, division of, 146
Protecteur, 98
Provence, 98
Providence, RI, 53, 60, 182

Province Island, Pa, 83, 84
Prudent, 145, 169
Puerto Rico, 224
Pulaski, Brigadier General Casimir, 132
Putnam, 127
Pye, Admiral Sir Thomas, 145

Quebec, 3, 39, 40, 42, 93, 143, 144
Queen of France, 138
Queens, County, NY, 50, 125

Rainbow, 42, 47, 72, 124
Raisonable, 70, 78, 96, 104, 115, 124, 128, 142
Raleigh, 140
Rallieuse, 191, 195
Randall's Island, NY, 50
Ranger, 141
Rawdon, Lord, 10
Red Bank, NJ, 83
Red Hook Brooklyn, NY, 48
Réfléchi, 191, 195
Regiments, British
  4th Foot, 115
  5th Foot, 115
  9th Foot, 42
  14th Foot, 16
  15th Foot, 35, 99, 115
  17th Foot, 126
  20th Foot, 42
  21st Foot, 41
  24th Foot, 42
  27th Foot, 11, 115
  28th Foot, 115
  29th Foot, 40
  32nd Foot, 35
  34th Foot, 42
  35th Foot, 115
  36th Foot, 35
  37th Foot, 35
  40th Foot, 115
  42nd Foot, 139
  44th Foot, 99
  47th Foot, 42

INDEX

49th Foot, 115
53rd Foot, 35, 42, 115
54th Foot, 35
57th Foot, 35
62nd Foot, 42
16th Light Dragoons, 40, 42
Regiments, Loyalist,
Prince of Wales Volunteers, 39
Queens Rangers, 139
Renown, 23, 25, 47, 50, 96, 104, 107, 115, 138, 142
Repulse, 47, 50
Resistance, 110
Resolution, 144, 145, 160, 186, 194, 219
Revenge, 66, 127
Rhode Island, 11, 14, 53, 54, 59, 60, 87, 94, 97, 98, 100, 101, 102, 104, 105, 109, 111, 115, 116, 119, 121, 132, 142, 145, 147, 148, 149, 151, 153, 155, 158, 159, 164, 165, 170, 176, 178, 185, 188, 190, 191, 202, 219
Richmond, Va., 163, 165
Richmond, 97, 104, 107, 140, 148, 167, 168, 194
Rising States, 67
Robertson, Lieutenant General James, 25, 165, 167, 205, 206, 220
Robinson, John, 220
Robust, 142, 169, 205, 207
Rochambeau, General Comte de, 177, 178, 181, 182, 183, 186, 188, 189, 190, 192, 199, 219
Rockingham, Marquis of, 221
Rockingham-Shelburne government, 222, 223
Rodney, Admiral Sir George, 33, 151, 152, 153, 154, 156, 158, 159, 160, 161, 162, 163, 178, 179, 180, 181, 184, 185, 186, 188, 195, 201, 218, 224
Roebuck, 17, 18, 20, 47, 48, 50, 52, 80, 83, 84, 85, 97, 104, 107, 110, 131, 138, 140, 168
Rommel, General Erwin, 44
Romney, 32
Romulus, 131, 138, 140, 164, 169
Rose, 14, 47, 50
Rover, 63
Royal Oak, 111, 115, 145, 169, 194, 219
Russell, 101, 142, 152

Sable, Cape, NS, 25, 72
Saco, Me, 7
Sagituaries, 98
St Albans, 70, 96, 97, 104, 110, 115
St Augustine, Fla, 58, 59, 93, 94, 112, 115, 119, 122, 133, 175, 176, 222, 223, 225
St Croix, 21
Saint-Esprit, 191, 195
St Georges Channel, 67
St Georges Island, Va., 19, 20
St Helena, 32
St Helens, 111
St Ives, Cornwall, 135
St John, 20, 26
St John, Island, 6
St John's, Newfoundland, 101
St Kitts, 19
St Lawrence, 6, 20, 47
St Lawrence, Gulf of, 22
St Lawrence River, 58, 59, 60, 112
St Lucia, 94, 95, 104, 114, 115, 127, 194
St Lucia, 160
St Malo, 46
St Pierre, 22
Saint-Simon, General Marquis de, 191, 192
Saints, Battle of, 224
St Vincent, Cape, 63
Sakonnet Passage, RI, 104, 147, 148
Salamander, 194, 219
Salem, Mass, 6, 7, 9, 63

Sally, 127
Saltonstall, Commodore Dudley, 127, 128, 129
Sandwich, Lord, 29, 30, 33, 40, 45, 46, 64, 65, 89, 112, 120, 143, 150, 156, 161, 181, 218, 220
Sandwich, 152, 157, 160
Sandwich, armed ship, 140
Sandy Hook, NJ, 16, 25, 26, 42, 93, 97, 98, 99, 100, 102, 104, 107, 108, 109, 111, 115, 124, 131, 135, 145, 148, 150, 153, 157, 160, 163, 167, 179, 182, 184, 185, 186, 187, 189, 190, 204, 208, 217
Santa Monica, 194
Saratoga, Battle of, 72, 73, 86, 87, 90, 92, 117, 176, 219
Savage, Captain Henry, 148, 149
Savage, 14, 115, 167, 168
Savannah, Ga, 20, 120, 132, 133, 135, 152, 176, 219, 222, 232, 225
Savannah River, 20, 136
Scarborough, 20
Sceptre, 20
Scilly Islands, 11
Scipion, 191, 195
Scorpion, 20
Scotland, 34, 42
Senegal, 11, 47, 78
Seven Years War, 28, 33, 34, 133, 146
Shark, 160
Shelburne, Earl of, 221, 222, 223, 224
Sherman, William T., 44
Shetlands Islands, 67
Shields, 67
Shrewsbury, 144, 152, 160, 186, 194, 197, 198, 202, 219
Shuldham, Rear Admiral Molyneux, 23, 24, 25, 26, 27, 46
Shute's Folly, SC, 138
Simmons Island, SC, 136, 138, 146

Sky Rocket, 127
Slave Coast, 30
Solebay, 35, 38, 47, 78, 194, 198
Solitaire, 191, 195
Somerset, 5, 11, 29, 78, 84, 85, 96, 97, 104, 115
South Bronx, NY, 50
South Carolina, 35, 37, 133, 134, 136, 137, 138, 139, 140, 141, 142, 159, 163, 164, 173, 174, 180, 219
Souverain, 191, 195
Spain, 29, 31, 66, 67, 70, 133, 134
Spanish Louisiana, 133
Spanish River, Cape Breton, NS, 3
Sphinx, 35, 38, 54, 78, 104, 105
Spinkes, 23
Spitfire, 7
Spithead, 42, 44, 144
Springfield, NJ, 188
Spring Hill, Ga, 132
Sproat, David, 159, 160
Spuyten Duyvil, NY, 48, 53
Squirrel, 20, 21
Stamp Act, 32
Stanhope, Lieutenant John, 108
Stanley, 78
Star, 115
Staten Island, NY, 16, 25, 26, 42, 48, 54, 98, 188, 190, 226
Stephens, Philip
Stono Inlet, SC, 136
Stony Point, NY, 125, 126, 127, 129, 131, 136, 154, 176, 188
Stormont, Lord, 66
Strawberry Ferry, SC, 139
Stromboli, 42, 47, 78, 104, 115
Stuart, Colonel Charles, 25, 77, 78, 80, 85, 113, 121
Suffolk, Lord, 30
Suffolk, 152
Sullivan's Island, SC, 37, 38, 39, 52, 140
Sulphur, 104
Sulton, 115

Sumter, Fort, 37, 38
Sumter, Thomas, 158
Surprise, 32, 40
Surveillante, 191, 195
Swallow, 184
Swan, 14, 25, 47
Swift, 78
Sybille, 194, 219
Symmetry, 7
Syron, 38, 47

Tamer, 47
Tappen Zee, 47, 52
Tarleton, Colonel Banastre, 139, 164
Tarrytown, NY, 52
Tartar, 11, 52
Ternay d'Arsac, Chevalier de, 142, 144, 149, 158, 167
Terrible, 67, 152, 160, 186, 194, 198, 202, 203
Thames River, 30, 43
Thetis, 32
Throgs Neck, NY, 52, 126
Thunder, 35, 38, 47, 104
Tonken, Captain Thomas, 147
Tonnant, 98
Torbay, 152, 160, 181, 219
Trenton, NJ, 61, 62, 74
Trial, 47, 50
Trident, 160, 191, 195
Triumph, 106, 186
Tryal, 23
Tryon, Major General William, 14, 126
Truile, 138
Tucker's Mill Point, Va., 17, 19
Turkey Point, Md, 80
Turtle Bay, NY, 14
Tybee Island, SC, 136
Tyrannicide, 127

Unity, 6
Ushant, 67
Utrecht, Treaty of, 65

Upper New York Bay, 131

Vaillant, 98
Vanderput, Captain George, 15
Vauban, 189
Veitminth, 173
Vengeance, 127
Venus, 97, 104, 115
Vergennes, Comte de, 28
Verplancts Point, NY, 125, 131
Victor, 72
Victoire, 191, 195
Vienna, 34
Vietnamese Highlands, 173
Vigilant, 78, 83, 85, 99, 104, 107
Ville de Paris, 191, 195
Viper, 14
Virginia, 16, 17, 18, 20, 98, 123, 124, 129, 134, 135, 158, 163, 165, 166, 167, 173, 174, 175, 176, 178, 179, 180, 181, 182, 183, 185, 186, 187, 188, 190, 192, 195, 198, 199, 201, 203, 204, 205, 206, 207, 208, 209, 211, 213, 219
Virginia, 128, 140
Virginia, Capes of, 169, 170, 185, 210, 217
Volcano, 104
Vulcan, 168

Waldeckers, 42
Wallace, Captain James, 14
Wards Island, NY, 50
War of 1812, 56, 57
Warren, 127
Washington, General George, 6, 9, 47, 48, 50, 51, 61, 73, 74, 75, 77, 78, 79, 81, 85, 92, 119, 123, 125, 126, 127, 131, 134, 138, 153, 154, 163, 164, 165, 166, 167, 177, 178, 179, 182, 183, 186, 187, 188, 189, 190, 191, 192, 195, 199, 201, 204, 208, 211, 219, 225

Washington, 95
Washington, Fort, NY, 48, 52, 53
Washington Heights, NY, 51
Waterford, 67
Wayne, Brigadier General 'Mad' Anthony, 126
Weazle, 30, 32
Webster, Colonel James, 139
Weser River, 42
West Africa, 30
Westchester Co., NY, 51, 182, 190
Western Approaches, 57, 67
West Florida, 133, 134, 175, 219
Westhand, Va., 163
West Indies, 3, 9, 23, 41, 46, 57, 59, 60, 66, 86, 88, 89, 90, 109, 111, 114, 115, 116, 119, 121, 130, 143, 144, 145, 152, 159, 160, 161, 162, 163, 175, 178, 181, 183, 190, 210, 212, 213, 214, 218
Westminster Abbey, 45
Westover, Va., 163
West Point, NY, 125, 126, 152, 153, 154

Wethersfield, Conn., 178
Whitehall, 35, 40
White Plains, NY, 52, 53
Williamsburg, Va., 16
Wilmington, Del., 79, 80
Wilmington, NC, 172, 173, 174, 175, 176
Windsor, NS, 11
Wolfe, General James, 33

Yarmouth, 152
York, 78
York Island, Va., 205
York River, Va., 206, 216, 217
Yorktown, Va., 104, 116, 120, 129, 135, 163, 166, 172, 174, 175, 176, 177, 179, 183, 184, 187, 188, 189, 191, 192, 195, 199, 204-21, 225
Young, Vice Admiral James, 20, 21, 22, 23

Zélé, 98, 191, 195